BUDDHA
THE QUEST FOR SERENITY

buddha, the quest for serenity

A BIOGRAPHY

George N. Marshall

Introduction by Huston Smith

Beacon Press: BOSTON

Copyright © 1978 by George N. Marshall
Beacon Press books are published under the auspices of the Unitarian
Universalist Association
Published simultaneously in Canada by Fitzhenry & Whiteside Limited,
Toronto
Published simultaneously in hardcover and paperback editions
Printed in the United States of America

(hardcover) 9 8 7 6 5 4 3 2 1
(paperback) 9 8 7 6 5 4 3 2 1

Library of Congress Cataloging in Publication Data

Marshall, George N.
    Buddha, the quest for serenity.
    Bibliography: p. 237
    1. Gautama Buddha—Biography. 2. Buddhists—
India—Biography. I. Title.
BQ882.M37   294.3'6'3   78-53787
ISBN 0-8070-1346-3
ISBN 0-8070-1347-1

To
Dara Lynn, Nancy, Sally, Marylou, Jennifer and Dara

All that we are is the result of what we have thought:
It is founded on our thoughts,
It is made up of our thoughts.
If one speaks or acts with a pure thought,
Happiness follows
Like a persistent shadow.

The Dhammapada

CONTENTS

Contents

INTRODUCTION

That Arnold Toynbee should have emerged from his twelve-volume *A Study of History* listing Gautama the Buddha as one of the dozen or so "greatest benefactors of the living generation," surprises no one, I suppose. But who was this Buddha, this "Awakened One"—one of a handful of snowflakes that deserve to be singled out from the total human snowfall for attention and gratitude? Of books on the Buddhist religion there are, as the author of the present book acknowledges, many. Odd, then, that there should be so few, and especially so few remaining in print, that focus on the founder himself.

As this book does focus on the founder there is no need for me to dwell here on the facts of his life. Instead I shall pick up on Toynbee's point and speak to its importance. What was there about the Buddha that made him important in the past and important today? Important for Westerners today, we should add, for this book is obviously addressed to readers who are spatially as well as temporally removed from the world in which the Buddha lived.

Begin with the past. The reason usually given for the Buddha's historical importance is that he founded one of the world's great religions. No one doubts that he did this, but our secular and pluralistic age has contracted the word "religion" so far in the direction of individual belief and practice—"what a man does with his own solitariness," was the way Whitehead defined it—that to peg the Buddha as the founder of a religion is to miss the full scale of his achievement. It would be truer to say, with Trevor Ling, that he founded a civilization—one whose soul was indeed religion, but whose body was a body politic. As a civilization, Buddhism was a total view of the world and man's place in it. It created for the community of its adherents an entire universe, one that gathered into a coherent whole levels and aspects of life that the modern world divides into economics, politics, ethics, law, art, philosophy, and the like. E. F. Schumacher reminded us of this by including a chapter on "Buddhist Economics" in his *Small Is Beautiful,* but the view of Budhism as an exclusively spiritual affair persists.

The Buddha that jumps first to mind is the one iconography so effectively presents to us: the solitary Buddha seated motionless beneath the Bo Tree. So strong is the hold of this other-worldly Buddha that we forget his other side. We forget that no sooner had he launched his ministry than he was drawn back into the royal circles he had renounced to seek his enlightenment. For Indian monarchy was in its infancy then, trying to forge a viable alternative to the village-based Brahmanic *panchayat* (rule by five) that was fumbling with population growth and other changes that were occurring.

The Buddha appreciated the problem and responded to it; his message included a strong social component along with its path to personal release. It called for a society founded like a tripod on a three-fold base: monarchy, the *sangha* (monastic community), and the laity. Each of these had obligations to the others while deriving benefits from them. But this is not the place for details. What I suggest is that the reader may find it instructive to notice how often kings, queens, and princes cross the pages of the life this book recounts. A new civilization was in the making, and royalty no less than commoners were drawn into the act.

The greatness of the Buddha in shaping that civilization is attested by the greatness of the civilization itself. Geographically it spread beyond India to bless all of Asia, while temporally it continues residually, in southern Buddhism, right down to today. Southern Buddhism (Theravada) is usually distinguished from its northern, Mahayana counterpart doctrinally, but the difference that underlies their doctrinal disputes is that Theravada Buddhism, standing closer to original Buddhism, continued to cling to the ideal of Buddhism as a civilization, whereas Mahayana Buddhism never did so cling. I recognize that this is not the usual view of the matter, but a return to the Buddhist world last year in a visit divided between Sri Lanka in the south and Japan to the north convinced me that it is accurate. We have yet to see a history of Buddhism that presents the rise of Mahayana as Buddhism revisioning itself to accommodate to civilizations other than its own—first in India when it became clear that the Vedic tradition and its *varnashrama-dharmic* social stipulations were not going to be displaced, and then in China, whose civilization never did admit of an alternative.

This divestment process—the extraction of Buddhism's spiritual essence from the total civilization in which it was originally cast—points directly to the second question I posed for this introduction, the question of Buddhism's continuing importance. For Buddhist civilization is a thing of the past; even in Burma, Thailand, Sri Lanka and Cambodia we see today only its debris. For the continuing importance of the Buddha's achievement we must look to Buddhism as a religion, capable of accommodating itself to civilizations in the plural. We have it on no less authority than that of Edward

Thomas that the religious essence of Buddhism has never been definitely identified, so what follows will be an approximation only.

Consciousness feels like a passive medium through which the world simply flows in to us as it is in itself, but this is far from the case. To begin with, we select from the world, seeing in the main what we choose to see; as the Tibetans say, when a pickpocket meets a saint, what he sees are pockets. And even what we choose to see we structure by our thoughts and feelings: poor children asked to draw a penny will draw it larger than do rich children—it looms larger in their minds' eyes. In so many ways, what we take for the world's "facts" are actually psychological constructs, as the Latin *factum* ("that which is made") suggests. This much Buddhism shares with virtually all contemporary psychology. What it adds is that at a deeper level our thoughts and feelings are themselves vectored by what the Buddha called The Three Poisons: desire (lust, greed and grasping), aversion (fear, hatred and anger), and ignorance. And the greatest of these is ignorance. For it is ignorance—most pointedly, ignorance concerning our true identity, who we really are—that causes us to divide the world into what we like and dislike. Thinking that we are, in the last analysis, individuals, we seek what augments our isolated selves and shun what threatens them. What we call our "self" is the amalgam of desires and aversions that we have wrapped tightly, like the elastic of a golf ball, around the core of separate identity that is its center.

This tight, constricted, golf-ball self is inevitably in for hard knocks, which is why the Buddha prefaced his teachings with "life is suffering." For a long while Western understanding of Buddhism was arrested at this first of the Buddha's Four Noble Truths; it is from this arrested position that the charges of Buddhism as life-denying and world-negating—in a word, pessimistic—have been leveled. The truth, we now almost see, is more nearly the opposite. The startling claim of the Buddha, announced in the third and fourth of his Noble

Truths, is that the suffering of unregenerate life is dispensable; it can be transcended. And we can see *how* to transcend it. There is only one kind of person I oppose, the Buddha once observed: he who says there is no way.

This is not the place to say in detail what the Buddha saw the way to be—the book in hand presents it, at least in outline. It will be enough here to reverse the two preceding paragraphs' "archaeology of consciousness" that exposed the root of life's routine suffering and construct from bottom up a model of the alternative self the Buddha recommended. The foundation of this reconstituted self will be an enlarged self-identification. Ideally the new self will identify with everything, greeting everything that comes its way as a reflection of an aspect of its own self. But we need not be categorical. Every step in the recommended direction will be to the good. For with each step we will find our desires and aversions relaxed; more of what comes our way will feel congruent with what we sense ourselves to be. Closer to the surface of our awareness we will see that the easing of our demands on life reduces the distortions our thoughts and feelings impose upon it. The logical terminus of this line of reasoning is clear. If we could attain the limit of expanded identity—the point where we relinquished partiality toward our finite selves entirely—there would *be* no separate self and the Buddha's key insight, *anatta* (no separate self), would be directly experienced. We should not let the negative form of the Buddhist terms for this eventuality mislead us: *nirvana* is "nothing" only in the sense of "no (demarcated) thing"; *sunyata* is "void" only in being de-void of separating distinctions. The words point toward the limitlessness of the self we would become.

Needless to say, the succinctness of this formulation is no gauge of the difficulties it presents. The practical agenda it sets before us is more than enough for a lifetime—in Buddhist symbolism innumerable lives are required. Still, the discovery of what life's true agenda is can arrive in an instant. And its arrival is decisive; it is hardly too much to say that to identify life's problem and set foot on the path indicated is more important than traversing the path's full length. For to set forth on the path is to turn one's back forever on the stance of victim. To pass from thinking of ourselves as *having* problems to seeing that we *are* the problem is to step from darkness into at least a glimmering light. Tears and labors may await us, but if we have truly effected the "Copernican revolution" in outlook we are already, in germ, ourselves the "Buddha"—from the root *bodhati:* he awakens; he understands. We can echo for ourselves the words with which the historical Buddha concluded his six-year quest: "I have been a fool, [but] I have found a path."

If this way of putting the Buddhist perspective seems contemporary in a way Buddhist civilization does not, I have discharged the second aim of this introduction, which is to suggest why the Buddha not only was important but continues to be important today. In doing so I suspect I have also suggested why his life and teachings are pertinent for the contemporary West and not just Asia. That I could even attempt to summarize the Buddha's message in contemporary psychological idiom is itself proof that the high walls that separated traditions in the human past are down. In part, at least, we emphatically *can* understand what the Buddha was getting at. And because our Western scientific approaches tempt us to try to explain the more in terms of the less, with the danger that in doing so we shall lose sight of the freedom that constitutes our human opportunity, we *need* to understand what the Buddha was saying. If we succeed in understanding him, a curious prediction that has been attributed to the eighth-century Tibetan saint Padmasambhava will have been strikingly confirmed:

When the iron bird flies,
and horses run on wheels. . . .
the Dharma will come to the land of the red man.

Introduction

For abetting this journey through a biography of the Buddha that is winning and faithful, the author of this book deserves the gratitude of both Buddhism and the West.

Huston Smith
Thomas J. Watson Professor of Religion
and Adjunct Professor of Philosophy
Syracuse University

Cap Haitien, Haiti
March 1978

FOREWORD

Siddhartha Gautama, who became the Buddha, is an historical personality of which there is much written and there are many landmarks to his existence though he lived five hundred years before the time of Christ. This was the same era in which Socrates and Plato lived in a different part of the world. Since Buddha's phenomenal success in attracting the masses to him in his own day goes far beyond almost all other religious leaders, we may expect much to be preserved concerning his life and message, and it is. The Buddha probably has been followed by more persons throughout the passing centuries than any other single religious personality.

Dr. Edwin A. Burtt, for many years the Sage Professor of Philosophy at Cornell University, in a widely circulated American work on Buddha referred to "his keen and winsome personality,"[1] and many have echoed this assessment. Arthur Lillie, a British writer, in his volume on Buddha published in Delhi, India, wrote that the Buddhist movement was "led by one of the most searching reformers that ever appeared upon the pages of history."[2] Huston Smith once wrote, "While the rest of the world was wrapped . . . in sleep, one man aroused himself. Buddhism begins . . . with a man who woke up. Hence 'The Awakened One.' . . . It is impossible to read the accounts of Buddha's life without emerging with the impression that one has been in touch with one of the greatest personalities of all time."[3]

I have tried to approach Buddha from a psychological point of view, and to understand his motivations and the social and behavioral stimuli that played upon him. To consider Buddha—and Gautama, the young prince—through his emotional frustrations and drives, helps one understand the dynamic personality who swayed kings and aroused the populace.

Part of my reason for undertaking this study was the discovery that most works on Buddha available in American bookstores today are more on Buddhist thought than on the life of Buddha. It has not been my intention to write an introduction or explanation of Buddhism, but rather a biography of a dynamic personality. What happened after Buddha's death parallels somewhat what happened to Christianity following the death of Jesus of Nazareth. A biography of either Jesus or Buddha is quite different from a theological volume on Christian thinking or Buddhist thought. Therefore, look elsewhere for a volume on Zen or Tibetan mysteries. This book should help you understand the rich personality that stimulated many centuries of metaphysical, ethical and organizational development.

Accordingly, to paraphrase a favorite passage of Buddha, you should understand what this book is and what this book is not.

We will talk about Gautama, the child, the youth, and the religious seeker who became a forest dweller and, as a monk, studied the philosophic and ascetic traditions. He became the Buddha when he became enlightened. From this point on we will talk about him as the Buddha, not as Gautama. During this latter period, only followers of rival leaders who fail to recognize his enlightenment resort to referring to him as the ascetic Gautama or the monk Gautama. To his supporters and followers he is the Buddha, and our story becomes the story of the Buddha.

There are discretionary prerogatives the author must take in works translated from a different language. How many foreign words, phrases, names and titles should be carried over? Our answer was as few as possible without becoming overly simplified. There are certain words in the Indian and oriental traditions which are making their way into the English language. One thinks immediately of Nirvana, dharma, karma and Buddha itself. All these words have come from the Sanscrit tongue of India, but most of the earliest writings concerning Buddha are found not in Sanscrit but in Pali, and have been preserved and nurtured in Ceylon (now Sri Lanka) and southeastern Asia. In Pali, Nirvana is Nibbana; dharma, dhamma; karma, kamma. Although we follow the Pali accounts and sacred books in this study—this being the tradition of the Elders—we have resorted to Nirvana, dharma, and karma on the assumption that these are the anglicized derivatives in our language.

For over a decade now I have been an associate member of the Buddhist Publication Society in Kandy, Sri Lanka, and I am greatly indebted to the Society for its publications, the kindness and thoughtfulness of the Honorable Secretaries and staff, to the theras—teachers—and authors of their journals (*The Wheel* and the *Bodhi Leaves*). When I asked about quotations and copyright permissions to quote from their works, the Honorable Secretary freely granted permission, quoting the Buddha's words from his death scene, "The Buddha has not the closed fist of a teacher." Accordingly we wish to thank Narada Maha Thera for *The Buddha and His Teachings,* John D. Ireland and Bhikkhu Nanananda for *The Anthology from the Samyutta Nikaya,* Piyadassi Thera for *The Book of Protection,* and Nyanatiloka for *The Buddhist Dictionary.* These works of the Buddhist Publication Society, Kandy, Sri Lanka, are a helpful source of original materials on the life of Buddha and the Buddhist thought of the southern and older schools. As is well known, Buddhist thought

Foreword

has thrived better outside of India than in it, and Sri Lanka is an important center.

Works available through the Pali Text Society in London and books published in the United States will be identified and mentioned in the notes when they are quoted or used as source materials.

The effort to reconstruct the life of the Buddha, on the basis of materials that have come down to us, requires literary license in personal conversations not related to his teachings or drawn directly from the suttras. The process of creating the canon of Buddhist writings is set forth in the epilogue to this volume. In evaluating the author's work, the senior Buddhist scholar in this country, Dr. E. A. Burtt, wrote: "It is a sensitive and understanding reconstruction; I would reconstruct in much the same way."

Finally, I am indebted to many people—far more than can be credited here. The teachers and writers from whom one has gained, and the colleagues who have assisted, are far more than even I am aware. In this endeavor there has not been "the closed fist of a Teacher." The late Professor Clarence Russell Skinner at Tufts University introduced me to the study of comparative religions. His enthusiasm for the teachings of Buddha and his life made a strong impact. Throughout this study I have constantly thought of him and his teachings. I am indebted further to Ray Bentley, former editor of Beacon Press, who first proposed to me that I seriously consider writing a biography of Buddha. My associates at the Church of the Larger Fellowship have given tremendous help, not only those in office, but specifically Mrs. Stephanie Amann, for over 20 years the Director of Religious Education at CLF, who has read each chapter and commented on it; Miss Helen M. Gresty, currently the Director of Religious Education, who has assisted in securing materials; and Janet Robertson, whose assistance in secretarial work and in the preparation of the glossary has been immensely helpful.

—G. N. M.

BUDDHA
THE QUEST FOR SERENITY

A PRINCE IS BORN

The birth of the young prince brought great excitement and joy to the capital and all the people. At last the beloved king had a son, and it was reported that never had such a beautiful and amazing infant entered this world. After all, his mother was the loveliest of queens, and his father a great king under whose rule the kingdom has prospered and expanded while he became famous for his justice and kindness. This was the birth of the infant whom the world recognizes as the Buddha. His story follows.

On the great plains of ancient India, five hundred years before the Christian era, in approximately the same time as that of Socrates in Greece, and of Lao Tze and Confucius in China, there was born a prince among the Sakyas. Where the plains stretch to meet the lofty Himalayas to the east, and in the north reaches the boundaries of Nepal, while Banares, the holy city, guarded its western borders, lay the realm of the Sakya kings. The capital city of Kapilavastu stood on the banks of the Rohini River, and here ruled Suddhodana.

Of him much has been written. He has been called the greatest of the Sakya kings. His city was prosperous and at peace. When it had been at war it had been victorious and an air of optimism and high expectation filled its homes, its streets, its markets and its courts.

In this era only the great kingdom southeast of its borders, that of Magadha, rivalled the Sakya kingdom for control of the vast sub-continent of India. But now all was peaceful.

Prosperity, learning, culture and religion were prominent in the reign of King Suddhodana. Teachers, swamis and wise men from all the Indian realms swarmed to this enlightened land. This was a progressive era when the old traditions were in flux and many persons, freed from the chains of poverty and ignorance were re-examining the traditional religious heritage of the Brahmans. Much experimentation, examination and discussion were underway. The old fearsome gods that held men in bondage were being challenged. An enlightened era called for a reevaluation. Hence many monks and holy men were withdrawing to seek the path of salvation and find the road of fulfillment. Most notable was the great prophet, or teacher, Vardhamana (or Mahavira), who rejected the ancient dogma of the Vedas, and withdrawing from the world proclaimed emancipation from worldly desires through renunciation of all material concerns. Bodily sensation, physical pampering, appeasing the senses, including satisfying the appetite, were rejected. Inner peace was to be found only through freedom from all earthly attachments.

This path of asceticism became the great outreaching, popular movement of the Jains as the followers of Vardhamana were called. It attracted some of the noblest and most idealistic, some of the most thoughtful and spiritually motivated to its cause, and vast numbers of people, in groups, colonies, or schools of wandering vagrant monks were separating themselves from society.

Such was the spirit of freedom and respect for the religious way, that all men gave respect to these movements. Yet this denial of materialism brought great concern to those in power, who feared for the loss of too many of the populace to the non-productive vocations of the spiritual.

A Prince is Born

Yet in spite of such fears the Sakya kingdoms flourished.

We are told by comparative historians that India at the time of the Sakyas was in a similar state of development to that of Greece at the time of Socrates. There were many city-states, and many Sakya kings, forerunners of the Rajahs or Maharajahs that continued down into the present century. Kapilavastu was one such city-state.

Here Suddhodana ruled in peace and tranquility. His city was at its zenith and he hoped, after the manner of kings, for a long reign and a great dynasty. Hence he longed for a first born son who would carry on the traditions and culture, and like his father, extend his lands and holdings over other city-states.

Following the customs of his times the king had many wives, but one was favorite and she was known as the queen. Her name was Maya, and next to her in the king's favor stood her sister, Mahaprajapati, usually called simply Prajapati.

Of Maya it was said that her beauty was as dazzling as the sun. Her hair black and glistening like tar pitch, her eyes were luminous as the deep waters of a mysterious well, her body was slender and swayed like the tall flax, her presence as poised and lovely as the holy lotus, and yet her outward beauty was as nothing when compared to her virtues and character. Sweetest of humans was she, great in compassion, outgoing in love, honest in dealings and tender in relationships. She was the highest jewel in the king's diadem, adding majesty and joyousness to the court and the ways of the city.

Thus did she complement Suddhodana the great king and together they ruled in equanimity. Great therefore was the king's happiness when she sent couriers to ask him to visit her. She confided that an exotic dream, like a great fantasy of the gods, had moved her. Now the time had come for her seclusion and in due course the king would have an heir.

Great was his rejoicing. And though no man was present to hear the queen's words to Suddhodana the soothsayers and lyricists of the palace were soon extolling in thrilling song the wondrous news that an heir was to be born to the beloved king and this son would be a wondrous person. It was sung that he would be in a final and perfected incarnation, reflecting the pleasures of the gods with the reign of the king and the loveliness of Maya.

The songs and tales reached the king's ears; he summoned the wise men and readers of dreams and signs to come forward to forecast the event.

There was no word they dared or wished to give but that he would have a son, one who would be the glory of the world. Yet it is the essence of saga and legend that extravagant expectation must be tempered with reasonable doubt. Before this son would lie two paths of power. By the one he could live to be the greatest mortal king. By the other, he might follow the path of renunciation. But, since the signs and the times were ripe for a new Buddha, it might be that out of the perfection of this union such a one would emerge. Thus, the king was strongly urged to be careful and concerned over the nurture and upbringing to be given his son.

The king was incredulous. He did not consider it a compliment that his son's two choices lay between power and renunciation. This was as bad as the traditional choices between power and inability to rule. It was reported that he responded by saying, "No son of mine, not of a royal Sakya warrior chief, can become a monk or a priest. I shall use all my power to see that he shall grow to love power, to seek it and lust for more power, more possessions and more material satisfactions."

Thus an ominous note and consequent dread of the future were injected into the royal rejoicing. But of this Maya knew nothing. She was sequestered high in the upper reaches of the palace where amid the rafters swans nested as do the storks on European steeples.

The months passed for Maya, contented with the thoughts of the growing infant within her, dreaming dreams of his future greatness as have mothers since the dawn of time. True to his word, the king respected her request for seclusion and she in turn would not move from her couch in the high eaves of the palace, where the soft breezes cooled her head. Then came the time for which she waited; she sent word to the King that her time was at hand.

A Prince is Born

Following the custom of the Sakyas, Maya started with her vast retinue of ladies-in-waiting, eunuchs and slaves, gaily bedecked and jewel encrusted, for her parents' home to give birth. They moved toward the river Rohini across which lay the kingdom of Koliya which her father ruled as king.

However, it was not to be that she should reach her parents' home. The royal procession stopped and encamped in a pleasant grove called Lumbini. Here her bier, flower laden, was lowered gently to the ground as her moans indicated the increased pains of her labor. Thus the future Buddha was unexpectedly born. Maya, with the newborn infant, was carried back to the palace of Suddhodana but the queen's strength never returned. She languished and died on the seventh day.

The site of the birth was to be remembered as a holy shrine. The great missionizing king, Asoka, in the golden age which followed, erected an inscribed pillar to commemorate the blessed event. Falling in disrepair, the pillar was rediscovered by British archaeologists in 1898 and may be seen there today. The year of birth was 563 B.C.

The infant prince was entrusted to Maya's sister, Prajapati, who henceforth became the foster mother whose love, compassion and vigilant care were to see the young prince Gautama, grow into a strapping, brilliant, handsome youth loved by all who looked upon him.

But the death of the mother brought a two-fold sorrow and concern to the noble Suddhodana. He had lost not only the most beloved of his wives, but lost her on the seventh day, and this was a second cause of great concern and fear for the King. For following the birth prophecies by the wisemen, swamis and yogas, the fear had not been dispelled that his son might choose the life of a holy man rather than a ruler. Indeed it increased, for there was an Aryan tradition that the mother of a Bodhisatva, or a Buddha, always died on the seventh day following birth.

Suddhodana now felt compelled to resist the destiny which unfortunately seemed to be emerging for the young prince. Of what use is power, and a kingdom, if it will be inherited by strangers or distant relatives? At all costs his son, Gautama, must be reared to rule and inherit this pleasant, prosperous land.

In a time and place where many believed in destiny and signs, King Suddhodana was to set himself courageously and also stubbornly against that which the heavens ordained. His was to be an epic struggle to circumvent the will of the gods and the incarnation already made manifest. Can the edicts— the will of an earthly king—overcome the edicts of the stars?

The struggle of Suddhodana, once seemingly the most favored of kings, was so titanic and futile that he may well have become one of the most disconcerted and unhappy of rulers.

2

A MOOD FOR CHANGE

The religious atmosphere surrounding the palace, and indeed the early life of Gautama, can be understood only in terms of the religious culture and expectations of those times. There was both a general air of expectancy and of acceptance of a vast religious tradition that stretched far back into the remote past of Mother India. Much stratification and petrification of religious belief and practices, locking in certain priestly excesses, had led to a mood for change. Religious experiments were being conducted by many throughout the vast Indian sub-continent. Hence it was, for instance, that the new school of Vardhamana was attracting many converts at the time of the birth and youth of Gautama. It sought to purify and free the old practices, through a process of asceticism and self-mortification, and the Jain monks were honored for their self-discipline, devotion and courageous self-denial.

Why had such schools, or cults, arisen in this land, and what was it they were reacting against? Understanding the reasons should lead us to better understand why the times were ripe for a new reformer offering a more enlightened rule for self-fulfillment.

Between one and two thousand years before the birth of Gautama, Aryan warrior tribes broke through the passes of the Hindu Kush Mountains from the Iranian Plateau. From this cradle of the white race, the Aryan people pushed eastward into India, westward into Greece, Persia and Rome, and northward into the Slavic countries. Those who crossed the Hindu Kush Mountains to the east were henceforth isolated from their brethren beyond the mountains. Prisoners of the Indian peninsula, they were to develop an essentially peninsular life. Here they found a dark skinned people, settled herdsmen, whom they considered to be inferior and more backward than they were with their warrior life style.

As they moved into the Indian land mass, they followed the great rivers which ran from the mountains through the plains toward the sea, and as they pushed further and further southward, some settled at choice locations. Thus developed the many petty provinces, or countries, each ruled over by first its family chieftain, and then in time the rajahs, or kings, as social stratification occurred. These people brought with them their ancient religious beliefs in many natural gods, each controlling some force of nature or representing some powerful emotional drive apparent in the lives and struggles of people.

They developed a singing religion that was expressed in sublime form in the Vedic literature—poetic and memorable stanzas of deep beauty and lofty insight about the powers of the great master gods, or spirits, which ruled the earth and the passions of mankind. Chief among these gods was Indra, identified with the elements: wind, rain, thunder, lightning and storms. There was Dyauth Pitar, the sky-god, and Asura, the spirit of heavenly virtue and tranquility. Agni was the god of fire, and Mithra of the sun. Soma was the spirit of intoxication. The names of many of these gods indicate the close relationship of the original religion to that of their distant cousins who had migrated into Persia, Greece and the Euro-

Asian world to the west. Later Brahma, Altman and Vishnu became combinations and refinements of these earlier gods, and still later Krishna became the greatest god of all.

A priestly class, known as Brahmans, arose to interpret the religion, to recite the Vedic Hymns, to explain the symbolism and the mysteries of this evolving religious tradition. Such occult power elevated the priests in time to rival the rajahs or kings, but the materialistic greed and corruption of the priests hastened the decline of the ancient Vedic religion.

These Aryan peoples, of whom the Sakyas are a prime example, settled on land once owned and occupied by a black people, the earliest known residents of India. Often these primitive natives were pressed into service as their servants, herdsmen, and workers. The Brahmans were concerned with keeping their faith pure and unsullied from contact with theirs. Likewise, the Aryan chieftains wanted to keep their proud family clan intact. As a result a caste system developed, with several levels of social acceptability. Originally based on a division of labor, it later was simply inherited. The aborigines, who were the lower class of workers, became the "untouchables," and the Brahminic priests became the highest caste. The other divisions of the caste system lay in between.

But the system failed to stop intermarriage and intercourse, social and physical, between the peoples. No longer is there a possible distinction genetically between the various castes, nor are there any white Aryans left in the Indian population. In this regard, the caste system was a failure. But in the elevation of the Brahmans, the priestly class, we see proof of the usurpation of power by the priests, and the misuse of the secrets of the mysteries of religious interpretation to perpetuate themselves rather than to be servants of the people.

During the century before the birth of Gautama there was widespread dissatisfaction with Brahminism, an awareness of its corruption, and widespread belief that religion was being used by the priests to accumulate wealth rather than interpret religious truths. Hence many people were seeking alternatives.

Some turned to asceticism in rejecting the practices of the

Brahmins as the way to find religious truth. They withdrew, apart, forsaking not only the market place, but the temple with its wealth, greed and selfish opulence. These ascetics took to the woods, and the river banks, and caves in the high hills, where, withdrawn from life, they sought by self-denial to find the path to Nirvana. During the several decades before the birth of Gautama, the ascetic monk Vardhamana had many followers, who called themselves Jains.

Others were to interpret the ancient literature for themselves. They delved into the mysteries of the Vedic Hymns, and wrote the Upanishads. In discourse and argumentation, this path led to philosophizing upon the meaning of life, a tradition long since forgotten. Some of these men traveled from court to court, offering their wisdom to the rajahs or kings. (Undoubtedly Suddhodana called upon such wisemen to explain the mysteries of the events surrounding the birth of the young prince.) To prepare themselves these men drew apart, as did the ascetics, to the wilds, the woods, the river banks or mountain groves to discuss and meditate upon the religious way of life. Out of their experience was to grow a new conception of meditation, as they concentrated upon the meaning of the divine, or the transcendental principle. In logical disputation they sought to discipline thought and discover the primordial meanings of all things and of life itself. At the time of the birth of Gautama the movement for writing the Upanishads, the sacred texts, was well underway, subject to critical analysis and deep reflective meditation. Wise men, holy men and philosophers were to be found throughout the lands of India.

Concepts were emerging that were to play an important part in the future of the various religious movements which have been native to India. Chief among these concepts is that of reincarnation. In all cultures there is some meaningful and coherent explanation of ultimate affairs, a generally agreed upon and accepted explanation of death which cannot be explained apart from life. There is a persistency and obstinacy about life which has emerged over and over in the cultural pattern of many peoples. An explanation is found by which life is held not to end but to continue. This may take the form which it does in the Western world that there is a spiritual side of life which does not die, but continues through the soul. We find this concept in Judeo-Christian-Islamic thought pattern. It is likewise closely related to the Greek concept enunciated by Plato that there is an ideal form for all earthly appearances, which continues forever. Among Christians, this is the belief that the immortal soul survives death, and following the return of the Messiah will go to Heaven. Paradise for the Muslim is somewhat similar to the Christian Heaven.

Many faiths include belief in the transmigration of souls—that when a person dies the soul migrates to another life entering the stream of existence at that moment, or thereafter. In the Brahmin faith this transmigration became the basis for the concept of Reincarnation. The soul of a person, or his spirit, continues on, indestructible, carrying with it the merits and demerits of the previous existence. Thus, in the righteous mills of the gods, all evil must be compensated for and all virtue rewarded, so that the treasury of deeds (merits and demerits) is always accounted for. A good person, if he has fully compensated for the evils of all past incarnations, and has lived an upright life, will be reborn in a more favorable station. But woe befall the person who has given in to greed, appetite, and deceitfulness: he will be born into a lower form of life. For the Hindu, this can take the form of rebirth as an animal, or worse, an insect, a worm, or an amoeba. (Hence, the sacredness of all animals—all life—in India.) Then will begin the long climb back up the ladder of progressive improvement.

Fortunate is the one who can master his senses and control his appetite! He may well be on the road to enlightenment. Little wonder that so many turn to an ascetic life in which they rigorously discipline their appetites, feelings and instincts. To many this seems to be an assured way of earning a higher life in the next incarnation.

But life is not a tortuous treadmill to be gone through forever. It can come to an end, an end of the most blessed peace, of total rest, of complete quiescence, a state highly to be desired. This state, which is call Nirvana, is reached when one has become perfect. Perfection itself is achieved in a succession of lives lived without flaw. Eventually, according to this belief, when one reaches perfection one is prepared for the final level of existence, and passes beyond the state of the Bodhisattva to that of the Buddha.

A Bodhisattva is one standing at the threshold of Nirvana. Those who go through this life as a Bodhisattva, if they are proven worthy, following death will be born again into a life in which they may become a Buddha. Thus, according to the common religious heritage of India, there are many Bodhisattvas, some of whom may become Buddhas. The holy men, the ascetics and the men of wisdom all aspired to this end, and sought Nirvana, the state of restfulness when all restlessness would cease; of peace, when all striving would end; of fulfillment when appetite would no longer entrap; and of quiescence, when all life's striving would be stilled. This is the fulfillment of the goal of all life: the extinction of self, the attainment of final truth, the enlightenment, peace of mind, bliss and glorification which carries one beyond all experience of life.

Gautama was not to be the first Buddha, nor the last. But he became by common consent The Buddha, the greatest, and within his own lifetime was recognized as such. It is clear that this recognition came within his lifetime at least partially because the people were prepared for such a coming, comprehended and expected such a person to appear among them.

It is said that great persons do not emerge in spite of their times, but because of them, and this era of religious ferment of which we are speaking created the conditions for a Buddha. It is likewise said that persons do not create great ideas, but that such ideas exist and they seize people (or people seize them) and this makes for greatness. In Gautama's case, we are not prepared to say that this was so, but to note here that the stage was set for the emergence of a transcendent Buddha who would be supreme over all earthly persons, and would set an example that would be an inspiration to countless millions throughout the passing millennia.

A Mood for Change

In the century before the birth of Gautama, the redefining of the Brahmin faith was underway through the creation of the Upanishads, and this continued for the several centuries following his death. During this time, while the reforming movements of Jainism and Buddhism, and others, were to make inroads, the Hindu faith was to reorganize and survive, reincorporating back into its fold many elements which seemed to be slipping away. The great god Krishna became ascendant at this time, superseding the earlier gods, and the Karma of Indian life was redirected.

Karma refers to the intrinsic nature of any essence, substance, element or being. Everything has its unique essence or quality, its necessary action or reaction to exterior forms, and this is its Karma. Karma is the essential internal elements that give uniqueness and individuality to any person, substance, essence or being. Life fulfillment, the path to Nirvana for all persons, is dependent upon being true to one's Karma. And Dharma is the way.

Dharma is the way to the divine, the essential procedure that one should follow. It may differ for persons at different times or under different circumstances, but there is a correct way, internally perceived, which leads to Nirvana. If it is true that "there is a way that makes for righteousness," then such a way is Dharma. It is the path which one should walk. In the Western world many talk about "a Christian way of life," which would be the Dharma for them; or they may speak of "the Jewish way," which would be the equivalent to what the Indian recognizes as the Dharma. The Torah of the Jew, known as the Law, is probably similar to Dharma. In China, during this same era, Lao Tze presented the religion of Taoism, or the "religion of the Way," written out in the *Tao Te Ching,* or *Book of the Divine Way.* In India, Dharma, "the way," is somewhat similar to a universal religious manifestation, though, as in other traditions, it has its own unique ramifications. One scholar describes it as "the universal, cosmic law," and several others suggest the element of law, as well as way, is implied in Dharma, which has no exact English language equivalent. Some say it may best be called the universal law of life. Such a concept is probably found in most religious systems. Indian religion cannot be understood without an awareness of the importance of Dharma.

However, as we turn our attention to the religion of Gautama, the Buddha, we must note that he will give a specialized interpretation of the cosmic way. For clarification, in this study, when we talk about the concepts of Nirvana, Reincarnation, Karma, Dharma, Bodhisattva and Buddha in Buddhistic terms as related to the teachings of Gautama, we shall follow Buddhist custom and capitalize these terms.

We can now see the type of culture into which the young prince was born in 563 B.C. We are better able to comprehend the way he was seen in his own time, and to understand the nature of the forces which played upon his mind, the court, and those with whom he subsequently came in contact.

3

PROPHECY AND FATE

Gautama, the young prince, grew in the seclusion of the palace, following the pattern of most heirs apparent to a throne. Here, reared under the watchful eye of his aunt, Prajapati (the Mahaprajapati, as she was often called), he was given both love and formal training as befits a prince. The greatest of teachers were brought in, and it is told how he excelled so in his studies that at least one swami reported that it was as though the gods had favored him with supernatural powers to acquire all knowledge by more than human means.

Yet the life of a prince can be a lonely one. Companionship was mainly from the women of the court, since the men, including his anxious and doting father, were involved in affairs of state. Although there was a strong bond of affection between father and son and a solicitation for each other's well-being, they seldom saw one another, and in many ways it might have appeared that they were strangers. They lived in different palaces on the royal estate, and apparently an appointment had to be arranged for a visit between father and son. King Suddhodana was simply too busy, or too involved, with the practical concerns of managing his province to be a companion to his son.

Yet he sent for reports on how the boy was progressing, and invited the visiting teachers to report to him. Then he would question them concerning the boy's inclinations and aptitudes.

The king repeatedly insisted that everything the youth desired befitting a prince and future king should be provided, and that nothing should be allowed to becloud his mind or upset his temperament. He would also send for Prajapati to hear her reports of his activities and discuss with her Gautama's nurture and training. In all these things the king thought he was fulfilling the role of a dutiful father. When he saw his son his heart swelled with pride, sheer ecstasy overpowered him, and he thought that surely Gautama was the most striking of all boys. The two would fall into an embrace and relish the brief encounters.

He was pleased that his son learned so rapidly and excelled in athletic activity, so important in the warrior caste of Gautama's family. The king could not, however, quite forget the strange experience of the visit of the greatest of the kingdom's yogis, who appeared in Kapilavastu on the fourth day following the prince's birth. This yogi, known as Asita, approached the throne and asked if he might see the young prince. Suddhodana received the venerable sage with reverence and instantly sent for the prince, who was brought forward in the arms of his mother, the Maharani Maya. Gently and reverently the ancient yogi beheld the young child in her arms, and then tears welling up in his eyes, his voice choking, as the queen stooped to place the child at the master's feet, he said, "Stop! It is I who should do him homage." The ancient sage looked at the face of the young child as the tears trickled down his cheeks, and the assembled court trembled.

The Maharajah could contain himself no longer and he fell in alarm at the feet of Asita calling out, "Oh holy one, tell me why you are weeping. Is my son doomed? Am I to lose this most precious possession? I plead with you to tell me what misfortune you see in his future."

The ancient ascetic raised the king from the floor, explaining, "Fear not, Oh king, it is no ill omen I see, but great joy and rapture which this prince shall bring to all the world, for he is honored among men, and will be called blessed. I behold before me a future Buddha, and I weep for myself for my days are numbered, and I will not live to see this wonder and majesty unfold."

Then, holding his bowed head in his hands while tears gushed forth and his body convulsed with sobbing, the Swami departed the court and the city. The king and queen trembled as he left, while all others marveled at the sight and message they had witnessed. This was to be the last public appearance of Maya who died on the third day following.

Such were the memories that troubled the king's mind, but of which he no longer spoke, although he remained ever vigilant. He was pleased that his son excelled in the manly arts and in worldly knowledge, and he determined to make him relish the pleasures of the world so much that he could never be satisfied with the more austere life of the holy man. Thus he ordered two palaces to be built for the young prince: one for the summer season, of cool marble and waterfalls, and one for the winter with cedar paneling and thickly carpeted floors, filled with light from the sun. Here lived the prince and his retinue—composed of his guardian, Prajapati; his companion, Chandaka, or as he was often called, Chanda; his teachers, servants, eunuchs and court attendants. Here, in these abodes, the prince grew up in relative seclusion.

The king, concerned by the earlier prophecies and the brooding, introverted moods of his son, ordered that everything be done to make him cheerful and happy. Nothing touching the serious side of life was to be taught him; he should be encouraged to seek happiness and indolently satisfy his every wish. Thus the youth grew, pampered and seemingly without an awareness of the facts of life and death.

Yet, he would withdraw from the constant round of pleasures, entertainments and luxuries that surrounded him to sit for long periods alone, disconcerted, and pensive. The king, learning of this, and that such periods increased as his adolescent years advanced, called his private chaplain, and to the Brahman expressed his concerns. He told the priest he feared that his only son might withdraw entirely from life, so that then he would be without an heir and worse, his proud family would die out.

"Oh king," responded the priest, "fear not. These are the moods of youth in puberty. Let us find for your son a fitting bride, and when he has a family of his own, he shall be bound to the world by bonds of iron."

The king was pleased with the advice of the Brahman, and promptly sent for his son to tell him of his plans. In the meantime he instructed the Brahman to have all warrior caste families surveyed to locate the most suitable bride for the prince.

"Go," said the king, "Go, Brahman, and visit all the homes in Kapila, observing the young girls and question each, and then report back to me who are the possible brides for my son."

To his son, the king said, "My child, you are now of an age when you should think of marriage. If there is some maid that pleases you, tell me; and if not, then we shall have a great gathering and choose the one who most pleases your eye and catches your fancy."

The prince replied, "Give me seven days to consider this matter, my father. Then I shall give you my answer."

Gautama then mused, "Endless evil comes of desire. That which grows in the forest of desire has its roots in the soil of strife and struggle. Desire burns like a fire and cuts deeply like a sword. I am not one who has such desire, nor have I sought the company of women, for I prefer the silence of the woods and the meditation of my own soul, for there alone do I find peace. Yet the lotus grows among the swamp grass, and many who have both wives and children have found wisdom. It is my lot in life to be the son of the great king, and a member of the warrior caste. Therefore must I seek to strive within the prison fashioned by my birth, yet hope that in this

life I, like the lotus, shall find the sun and bliss of existence."
These thoughts grew in his mind as he mused for a week, and
then on the seventh day he approached his father.

"Father," he said, "She whom I shall marry must be a person of rare talent and disposition. If you can find me one
who meets the qualities I shall enumerate, she will I marry.
These are the qualities I wish in a wife:

"She must have the bloom of youth, the flower of beauty,
be chaste and modest, gentle and kind, living not by a proud
vanity.

"She must have a sister's affection, a comrade's concern,
and a mother's tenderness for all living creatures.

"She will be sweet and truthful, and know no envy. She
will be delicate and of good manners, and yet not haughty or
superior to any.

"Yet she must be loving and loyal, one who will never
think of another man except her husband, holding this the
highest virtue.

"She will not be selfish or greedy, nor shall she be ambi-
tious and jealous of the possessions or lots of others.

"She must care nothing for wines, and sweets will not
tempt her, desiring neither perfumes nor song, dance nor
frivolity.

"She must be the first to awake and the last to fall asleep.

"And most of all, she shall be pure in body and speech and
thought."

The king listened gravely and said, "My son, you have described your mother whom you did not know, who in her
day was alone so virtuous. We shall seek for another like unto
her, and you shall have your wish."

Again the king sent for his chief Brahman, and said, "I have
sent you forth before, but now send I you out with a special
commission to find a bride like unto the late Queen Maya,
virtuous in all her ways, unaffected in the ways of the world,
superior in her virtue and gentle and loving in all her relationships, aristocratic in her bearings. When you find such a one
bring me word."

The king's chaplain replied, "Oh Lord, there is such a one

and we have found her; she is the daughter of the Sakya warrior, Pamita."

But the king in his wisdom thought, "Even the wisest of men may make mistakes. This Brahman may exaggerate her virtues, or misconstrue the wishes of a young man's heart." So he instructed the chief ministers of the realm to plan a great party to which all the suitable young women would be invited, where all would meet and be met by the prince. Thus there was planned a great ball, and the king told Gautama of the arrangements. Further he told him that he would provide jewels mounted in gold and silver settings, and ornaments made from precious metal, which the prince would present to the maidens. Therefore did the word go out: "On the seventh day from this day shall Prince Gautama, son of King Suddhodana, present gifts to all the young girls of the city invited to attend the royal ball."

The day arrived and the prince sat on the throne in the great hall of the palace, as the young women came forward and curtsied before him. The performance of this rite was an outward form to which the young prince had resigned himself, expecting neither pleasure nor discovery of such a person as he had indicated. For he longed not for a wife, believing none would meet his expectations. One by one the maidens came forward to meet the prince who presented baubles from the table in front of him. At last the final one was given, and none of the young ladies had aroused his interest. He was about to breathe a sigh of relief, when another young maid approached, and to his dismay there was no jewelry left.

He looked at the girl who approached him, fearlessly and without the self consciousness that marked the demeanor of the others. When she reached the table in front of the throne, she saw that the prince's hands were empty, and smiling she said to him,

"Have I offended you by coming last?"

"You have not offended me," he replied.

"Then why do you treat me with disdain?"

"I do not," he explained. "But you are the last and all the

jewels have been given away. May I give you this ring from my finger?"

But she would not accept the ring, saying, "Must I indeed take your ring?" But he insisted, and the king, seeing the look in their eyes, was delighted and asked who was the maiden.

"She is Yasodhara, daughter of Pamita," he was told.

Thereupon the next day the king sent his Brahman to Pamita to ask her hand in marriage to the prince. Much to the Brahman's surprise, the father said, "Take this message to the king: The noble young man has lived all of his life in luxury, confined within the palace walls. But we of the warrior caste can only intermarry our daughters with men of like breeding, men of courage, stamina and fierce competitiveness. First show me evidence that your son is a worthy suitor for a warrior's daughter, and she shall be his."

The king was not sure that his son could so prove himself because of the life of luxury and seclusion in which he was reared, but he told Gautama of Pamita's response.

"Fear not, father, for I have been well trained, and would like to compete with the finest horsemen, wrestlers, archers and runners. Let me test my skills against the best the realm has to offer."

Thus a great field day of games and contests was scheduled by royal edict, and word went out for all young men of skill and training in the realm to come to compete.

In the contests Gautama surprised all by his skills, sportsmanship, athletic powers and competitive spirit. He excelled in all events, and won victory after victory. Pamita, who was there to judge the events, sent word to the king that Gautama was indeed worthy of his daughter's hand. So the wedding was arranged.

There began a new phase in the life of Gautama. He and Yasodhara were exceedingly happy together, enjoying their life in both the summer palace and the winter palace. They were now surrounded by many dancing girls, servants, attendants and young friends. They spent much of their time revelling in the greatest luxury the court could provide. The king now felt he had successfully outwitted whatever fates and preordained directions were set for the young prince's life. When word was brought him that he shortly would be a grandfather, his joy knew no bounds. Now, as his chaplain had said, the prince would be bound to this world by bonds of iron.

Here in their lovely homes the prince and princess drained the cup of pleasure. They had known many weeks of celestial joy. They had led a life of voluptuous ease, spending languid hours listening to music played by the princess and her maidens. Now that the princess was to bring forth a child, and according to the custom of her people be secluded, the king was once again concerned.

Suddhodana was an upright and righteous king. His standards were the highest. Since the death of the lovely Queen Maya, he led a life of celibacy, austere in all his ways, giving his attention to matters of state and the welfare of his people. He honored the wisdom and the rules of the Brahmans and swamis, and his self-discipline was exemplary. Yet such are the strange contradictions of life that he sought to corrupt his son with the temptations of the flesh, the avarice of the selfish and the self-satisfaction of the indolent. For many years he had lived a life based upon such a double standard: upright and rigid in his own existence, while heaping every temptation and urging easy virtue upon his son.

Hence it is not surprising that during Yasodhara's confinement he sent the most beautiful dancing girls and courtesans he could find to the palace to entertain his son, instructing his ministers to seek out the most enticing and exciting maidens in the realm. With furtive glances, their eyes boldly inviting his attention, drooping their lashes and suggesting ineffable delight, these lovelies sought to lure him into the pleasures of the flesh. But he remained content to merely observe the pleasures of the dance, the joys of youthful beauty and the magic of vitality expressed in these alluring joyful maidens.

And yet, the king himself never yielded to indolence and pleasure. Rather by subduing his own passions, he surpassed his countrymen and was the noblest in the kingdom. He spent hours in study, and the knowledge acquired he placed at the service of his people. Indeed, it was said that he not only sought the welfare of his own subjects, but was concerned for all the world. He purified his body with the waters of the sacred pools and he purified his soul with the sacred water of virtue. He did not sacrifice truth to utility, and yet his tongue was so civil that when he spoke he never gave offense. Instead of punishing with death those who deserved it, he instructed them in the ways of virtuous living, and offered them freedom.

What a contradiction therefore that the king would so try to subvert his son and lead him into a life of selfish wantonness, into the paths of easy virtue out of fear of the birth songs of passing troubadours and the stories of soothsayers seeking to entertain. And what a tragedy that the king did not recognize that in spite of all temptation his son was a model of decorum, living by the same virtues and self-discipline as his father. Truly the son was in the image of the father, and it was a shame that his qualities were not called upon to help guide and rule the kingdom where his abilities, virtues and insights would be put to constructive use. His ability to discipline himself, and his detachment from selfish concerns, would have made him a prince and ruler equal to the deepest yearnings and highest dreams of the father. In not recognizing this the father failed. Such are the contradictions of life.

4

THE FOUR SIGHTS

In due season the beautiful Yasodhara bore a son, and he was given the name of Rahula. Great happiness now filled the hearts of Gautama and his father, and to the king it seemed as though his fondest wishes were ensured.

But while the new family found much joy together, the prince was not completely satisfied. The need to find a serene sense of being continued to dominate his thoughts. Only when he was preoccupied with the affairs of his personal life, and had no time to think, was he at all composed. But activity cannot be continuous and the periods of withdrawal returned. Chanda his companion and those about him noted his increasing contemplation, which they described as a moodiness, bordering on despondency. Their reports to the king upset and worried him.

When the moments of moodiness occurred he was usually not with the beautiful Yasodhara or his infant son. Rather, these occurred when, following the social customs of the times, he frequently withdrew into the prince's own quarters, essentially a bachelor's quarters, where he was with his male companions. It was here that his deep moods were most pronounced. Yet there were times with Yasodhara when, as a cloud crosses the sun, his countenance would change and deep despondency swept over him, making him listless and unattentive. Then she too feared for him, and felt as though she might lose him unless she could penetrate the deep veil which masked his withdrawal. She too began to worry over the deepening crisis in the internal life of Gautama which pierced the outward joys of the summer palace.

Chanda related the facts as he saw them to King Suddhodana who, disconcerted, consulted his chief advisors. It was proposed that Chanda on an upcoming spring holiday should escort the prince to the lovely botanical gardens some distance from the summer palace. He was admonished to assure the prince that here he would behold such beauty personified in nature as he never before suspected existed. At this season a multiplicity of flowering plants, many in their full bloom, made the gardens an enraptured wonderland. Perchance this would soothe the prince's aching soul and bring composure to his troubled mind.

"It will gladden his eye and raise his spirits," the king suggested, "and if it should not, we will have the most beautiful dancing girls present, with musical instruments, to make it a festive and joyous occasion. See that all is done which can be done to make the prince forget his concerns and worries and revel in the beauty of nature and the joys of human pleasures."

The prince agreed to accompany Chanda on the trip to the botanical gardens on the forthcoming holiday, and together they set forth through the woods to the secluded bower in question. Here, as the king had promised, was the most gorgeous array of flowers and plants imaginable. Here, under the azure sky, amid the green grass, the bubbling brooks and singing waterfalls, the radiant beauty of the flower beds was a delight for the soul. Joining the occasion were numerous dancing girls and the loveliest courtesans to be found in the kingdom. But to these the prince gave scant attention.

Chanda accused the girls of not using all their feminine wiles on Gautama, and urged them to be more forward and suggestive in their advances to him, assuring them that great prizes awaited those who were successful in seducing the prince and currying his favor.

He also chided the prince for ignoring the lovely girls who had been trying to please him, and told him he appeared ungrateful and snobbish, unbecoming to one of royal birth. Rather he should give pleasure to the girls, make them feel that their efforts were appreciated. "Bring joy, Oh my Lord, bring joy, into their hearts. Take hold of them and make them one with you, even for an hour, and you will find joy as you give it," he was cajoled. "Of what good are your graces and beauty, if you do not share them and extend your pleasures to others?" he was asked. "Spare them the shame of being spurned," he was admonished.

But Gautama, content to relish the delights of nature and the beauty of the gardens, paid no attention to the dancing girls.

Thus did the prince live the life of virtue, seeking after beauty and truth in close communion with the wonders of nature and the love of his family, straying not from the path. Yet the great cloud of despondency seemed ever ready to envelop him, and so the king proposed to him the exciting adventure of riding forth to behold the realm over which the king held power and which in time would be ruled by the prince.

When Gautama agreed, a magnificent chariot with the royal arms and gilded with precious gems and metals was prepared, to be drawn by Kantaka, the great white stallion which was the pride of the royal stables and Gautama's favorite. Chanda was to accompany the prince and serve as his escort and charioteer. In the meantime, unbeknownst to Gautama, the king's courtiers had gone out with a decree from His Majesty that the route should be cleaned and painted, that flowers and decorations should abound.

All was in order as commanded, and as the great gates swung open, the prince and his attendant burst forth in dazzling array drawn by the great white steed, Kantaka. His subjects were joyful to see their resplendent prince ride by, his happy face and proud countenance, illuminating the scene like the passing sun. People dressed in their finest clothing were in the streets cheering. They shouted, applauded and showered the prince with flowers. Gautama was happy in return and he thought, "How fair is the world, and how good is life with its endless joys and pleasures."

At this very moment the horse reared up, for stumbling across the road in front of them was an ancient man, enfeebled by years, his limbs lame. The prince, thrown forward by the sudden stop, leaned over to look at the spectacle in front of them—the old man desperately trying to pull himself erect with the aid of a staff, fear in his eyes, and short of breath. His clothing was filthy, tattered rags; his face unshaven; his straggling hair mostly gone; his cheeks hollow and his mouth toothless. His bony frame was almost devoid of flesh and his skin wrinkled and dry. To Gautama, who had never laid eyes on a beggar or tottering elderly person, he appeared ugly and uncouth. "What is this?" he gasped in astonishment, looking at Chanda for an answer.

"My prince," responded Chanda, "this is an old man. This is the fate of all who live out their years. Sooner or later, old age conquers youth, the bloom of youth and vitality of strength is sapped. Many, like this ancient become homeless wanderers and beggars, unwanted anywhere or by anyone. Unhappy is the day when old age conquers youth."

"Does this happen to all people?" asked the incredulous Gautama.

"Indeed it does, my lord. It is the human lot," responded his companion.

Stricken with horror at this revelation, Gautama said, "Turn the chariot around and let us return home. There can be no more joy in this ride. What is the lot of man that it ends in such despair? How can we sing and dance and play as though all life were an eternal garden of youth?"

Silently they made their way back to the palace, and when the chariot entered the great gates, all could see the forlorn countenance and depressed spirit of the prince. Word spread rapidly of what had happened and both the king and the princess rushed to his quarters to comfort the prince. But this could not be, for he responded bitterly to his father, "You have fed me with lies and surrounded me with all this shallowness, lulling me into a false sense of happiness. You have raised me as a deceived youth who would believe the world a place of beauty and all mankind happy and carefree as are those within the palace. I trusted you, and today I have perceived the truth of life."

Days went by and the prince continued to brood. He had seen the end to which all life moves, and it grieved him deeply.

But with the passage of time the depth of the shock began to wear off, and a fresh perspective that placed age as a remote possibility began to grow in his mind, encouraged by the court, the gurus and teachers now ever present. When the king heard that his despondency was lessening, and he was becoming more attentive to the life and events around him, particularly that of his immediate family, the king decided to try again. Was he not all powerful? Could he not command that no such incident occur again and that the aged, the sick, the halt and the blind be removed from the streets until after the royal procession returned to the palace? Such orders were given, and the king came to his son and said, "My boy, you saw an unfortunate sight, but consider how good life is for the vast majority. Go forth again and assess life more fully. Behold the people and the spirit and joy of life that dominates all. You shall then see that in the balance wheel of life, there is much cause for rejoicing, and goodness abounds on all sides." The prince agreed to the excursion for he too wanted to see more of the outside world.

When the people saw the prince on his second trip, they did not cheer as loudly or sing as gaily for they beheld that he now lacked the look of fresh innocence of his earlier excursion. But it went well, the people were happy and the day lovely; all seemed serene. The procession continued on its way until suddenly Gautama caught sight of a diseased person, tottering in exhaustion at the edge of the road, trying to hold himself erect, but barely able to stand. He was repulsive in his filth and feebleness, unlike anyone on whom Gautama's eyes had ever fallen before. The diseased person coughed convulsively, spitting up blood and he cried in agony. This was a far worse sight than the ancient person previously seen. This man was wracked by pain; his open sores attracted vermin and lice.

"What is this we see, good Chanda?" asked the amazed and incredulous Gautama.

"This, O prince, is one of the unfortunate ones, sick unto death, his body worn out and diseased, his spirit shattered, his pain great, and his outlook without hope. Such unfortunates are not known by us who live in the palace, but such are found in the world beyond the garden walls."

"After the first sight, I am not surprised," whispered the prince. "The deceit continues, and misery abounds. Let us return to the palace grounds so that I may reflect upon what we have seen. O vanity, vanity, that this is the lot of humanity, and yet people do so little about it, and live as though such would not be their fate! Oh, the shallowness of man, that he blinds himself to that which in time he must endure!" And so saying, the prince dropped his eyes and sank into a deeper mood of depression than on his earlier trip.

Again, the king was furious when he learned that his orders had failed to clear the street of diseased, sick and elderly persons. Again, he and his court, their teachers and wisemen, the swamis and priests, tried to comfort and explain away the fact of sickness and disease, but the shallowness of all explanations was too obvious to the prince.

Impatient with the words of comfort and explanations offered, the prince sent word to the king that he must go forth again to see if sickness and old age were the common lot of the people. The king was delighted that he would have still another chance. Couriers went forth to prepare the way, and the palace guard was dispatched to see that the orders were carried out, that all old, sick and diseased, halt, crippled and blind were confined to their houses. Thus the prince set out on a third excursion.

All was as the king had ordered, the ancient ones, the cripples, the sick and diseased were all confined. But one event had not been anticipated. At the very hour of the princely excursion a funeral procession was in progress. The prince, in horror, stared at the funeral bier on which lay a corpse, carried by four men. Following the ancient Indian custom, the lifeless body, stiff and expressionless in death, was followed by the mourners, beating their chests and rending the air with their wails and lamentation. This was a strange new sight to Gautama, who shuddered as he stared at the lifeless corpse and heard the sorrow in the voices of the grieving family.

"What, good friend, is this we see?" he questioned Chanda, who with downcast eyes responded, knowing that in all their years together in the palace Gautama had been shielded from death.

"O sweet prince," he said, "all who live must someday die, and this is the face of death you see. When the breath ceases, all consciousness, pain, joy, thoughts and feeling flee from the body. This abode in which lived a person is now a worn-out shell, useless and decaying, and it must be disposed of. Where or what happens to the life, who can say; but the body is now a decayed husk to be consumed by the flame or the sun. Men and women mourn those whom they loved and see no more."

In spite of his strength, the prince felt a cold shudder pass through his body; he felt faint, and murmured, "So this is the destiny toward which life leads! And yet man, without fear or thoughtfulness, lives his foolish life frittering away his time and opportunities while his loved ones and friends are consumed. There can be no joy until I can overcome these dreaded fears discovered in recent months. It is the end of joy."

Chanda understood, and without instructions slowly turned the chariot around to return to the palace. The trip was so short that King Suddhodana knew something again had gone amiss and rushed to talk with Chanda and Gautama. Yet what could he do? The damage had been done. His son had seen and learned of aging, disease and death, and now knew toward what man's destiny impelled him.

Nevertheless every effort was made to sooth the downcast prince. Many were brought to talk with him, and seek to bring him out of the deep mood of despondency which had settled over him. Long he sat in silence, hardly noticing those who expounded to him concerning the meaning of life and the ways of the world. They sought to encourage him to accept with good grace the happiness, pleasures and good fortune which befell him as the most comely prince in all of the kingdoms of India. But his spirit would not be uplifted, and he sat dejected paying little heed to the words uttered by those seeking to alter his mood.

At last the prince looked up at the assembled teachers and friends, and uttered these words:

"I have seen old age for the first time. I have learned that it comes to all creatures, and in time to each of us, if as you say, we are 'fortunate' to live so long. Old age destroys memory; it defaces the beauty of youth; it saps the strength of man and the vitality of women. Yet, the world is not frantic or overcome with terror. I would like to think that this is courage, but to me it seems like the shallowness of those who live for the moment only and heed not approaching destiny.

"I have seen sickness and disease for the first time. All my life I have been sheltered from this knowledge, and yet it is a great reality which each should be prepared to face. Disease is the universal lot of all men, for some it will come early, for others late. To some it will come with great pain and suffering which they feel in their body, for others it will touch those whom they love, and the pain and anguish will then be in the heart and the mind. People see suffering and sickness, and yet they go forward as though it will not touch them. Oh, the shallowness of life that one can close his eyes to this knowledge and not cringe in terror. But for one concerned for the life about him, there can no longer be joy and pleasure once he has looked into the face of sickness.

"Finally, I have looked into the face of death. Death is the ultimate end of all living creatures, and yet we pass our days in singing and dancing, in playing games by the brookside and useless learning while the greater secrets of life and death remain hidden from view.

"Woe be to youth which is the sport of many maladies! Woe be to life, which is only a single breath! Woe be to the idle pleasures which debauch humanity!

"That person is blind and ignorant who courts not the future, while knowing that the body is the abode of old age.

"That person is but the sport of a dream who nurturing the health of the body lives without fear in the coming evils too loathsome to contemplate. Thus is his life anguish and pain, and he knows it not.

"That person who fears not death is not prepared for living.

"With these thoughts clear in my mind, let me go forth to the city and see it as it really is. No time for preparations. Come, Chanda, afoot we will walk to the market place, and let no messenger go before us."

Thus it was that Gautama entered the market place. Here he saw and heard the frenzied buying and selling, the cacophony of sound and voices, wares and produce, of buyers and sellers, of beggars and merchants, and he was amazed at the fretful, anxious fervor of the people in quest of the day's substance and the hope for profit of a good barter. He saw the fear in the eyes of the mother unable to pay for the rice, and the anguish of the young maidens unable to buy the longed for dowry dress. He saw the workmen with their handmade wares anxious to sell the product of their hands and skill, and the fear in the back of their eyes that they may not earn this day the pittance needed to buy the kernel of grain needed at home. For the first time, he saw the great insecurity which was at the heart of the life of the city, and he was amazed that these people could live and find joy in spite of it.

But one sight caught his eye and held him spellbound. There in the midst of the clatter and clutter, the hurry and fervor of the market, he beheld the serene countenance of a monk in a saffron robe, sitting there, imperturbable, calm, uninvolved, patiently awaiting the occasional alms that fell into his nearly empty basket.

"Who is he?" the prince asked Chanda.

Chanda replied, "That, dear prince, is a holy man, a monk, who has forsaken the things of this world, in search of a better life. He seeks alms not for his own use, for he has conquered want, but to bring deliverance to those who share with him. By their sacrifice they unwittingly aid their own souls, he thinks, and so he comes to this market which has nothing he wishes so that his presence may touch the lives of others."

"I covet such a life of serenity," thought the prince as he gazed on the serene countenance of the monk in the frenzied atmosphere of the market place.

5

RENUNCIATION OR LIBERATION?

The prince and Chanda returned to the palace. Gautama could not free himself of the image of the serenity of the monk in the midst of the market place. He did not wish to. It brought him joy and inner peace just to recall his countenance. But he tried to reinvolve himself in the affairs of the court, and most of all, in those of his family. He had not heard the words of the Brahman to the king, "When he has a family of his own he shall be bound to the world by bonds of iron." Yet the fair Yasodhara and the tiny Rahula now seemed the most important considerations as he weighed what course of action he should follow in the search for serenity.

Perhaps he could find it here, in the palace, and live a life of serenity apart from the cares of the world outside the palace gates. Here he could enjoy the best of two worlds: of the lovely family which he adored, and of the freedom for reflection and meditation within his private quarters here at the palace. At all events, he was not pressed to make a hasty, ill-considered or ill-conceived decision. He continued to live his pensive, thoughtful life, interlaced with periods of carefree pleasure with his family. Always he would withdraw again to think over the deeper issues of life, either sitting quietly, or silently stalking the halls and grounds of the palace. Thus his solitariness and apparent moodiness were noted by others.

There was a futility to living, a lack of purpose, if all endeavor led but to slow disintegration with advancing age, the infirmities and sickness brought on by disease, and final termination in death itself. Of what good was life? It disturbed him to think that the golden moments of youth were like the passing bloom of flowers—seen today and withered tomorrow.

Yasodhara was concerned over her husband. Knowing so well his moods, she understood that he was moving toward a great change in his life. As he slipped further and further away from her in his thoughts, she began to realize that in time she might lose his bodily presence as well. Nevertheless, she was grateful for the moments together, and spared no effort to show her affection, devotion and reliance upon him.

Once, in the middle of the night, she awoke from a nightmare, and called him, trembling, as she recounted a terrible dream, seeking his comfort and reassurance. She told how in the frightful moment of an apocalyptic cataclysm she had beheld the world destroyed, but she was outside of it, looking at it. The whole earth shook, the winds roared and rent the mountains, shattering the rocks and uprooting trees. The sun was eclipsed and the moon fell from the sky while the stars shattered and were extinguished. Her own diadem fell from her head, her beautiful pearl necklaces and golden chains crumbled, and she was stripped of her clothing by the elemental forces. She went to reach out with her hands, but they were cut off; she tried to run but her feet were severed from her body. And then she saw that the diadem, scabbard and clothing of her husband were scattered about the earth, destroyed or in disarray. In the darkness of the night lurid flames arose from the cities of the earth, the great gates of the cities and palaces were flung open, while the ocean was boiling like a giant cauldron. Then the whole earth convulsed and shook and shook and shook, as she awoke and came crying, running to her husband.

Gautama took Yasodhara into his arms and comforted her, assuring her that these were indeed good signs, not evil omens. The destruction and passing away of the physical universe and the dismemberment of her mortal body were good omens, for they symbolized the end of earthly, worldly attachment, and that she, like he, would soon be freed from the hold which bound her to material things.

"Rejoice, dear Yasodhara!" whispered Gautama, "If you saw the earth shake, then you are one with the gods. If you saw the sun and moon fall, then you shall defeat evil. If you saw the trees uprooted, then you shall overcome the forest of desire. If you were dismembered, then you are freed from bodily passions. And since you saw my robes and jewels cast about, I am on the road to deliverance. Out of the darkness of the void shall come a new light, and the ignorant ways of the world and its blind direction shall be corrected. I who am on the path to deliverance will find the answers I seek. Be happy, darling, drive away all fear. You, as well as I shall be singularly honored, and both of us shall find deliverance. I am now free of my fetters, for I was held back by fear of losing you. But now I know that each of us shall find the path of deliverance and each of us shall achieve serenity."

So did they return to their sleep, both supremely happy and reassured. In the morning Gautama awoke, feeling very relaxed and at peace with himself. Now he knew his decision was proper and that a sign had been given to him through Yasodhara. He lay in bed and thought about the fulfillment opening before him, and knew that it was to begin with the renunciation of this life which at times he greatly enjoyed. He recalled the words that had come to him as he returned to the palace on his last outing, spoken by a young woman seated by the gate. As Gautama approached she bowed before him and murmured, "She who is your bride will know supreme blessedness, Oh prince." These words had remained a refrain in his mind: Yasodhara, his loved one, must also know deliverance before he could seek it alone. Now he knew it was foreordained that as he found it for himself, so would she in time also.

That day he was in an ecstasy. The time with his wife and the young prince, Rahula, was idyllic and the tender moments would remain in Yasodhara's mind for weeks to come. The young child seemed so gifted, and the dream promised that he too in time would find his own destiny. The couple were entertained by dancing girls and soft music, and the day passed quickly.

Gautama returned to his quarters, but could not sleep. High expectations were swarming through his mind. He walked through the corridors and halls of the palace, coming to the great salon where the dancing girls had retired. He looked in, and instead of seeing lovely, delicate and feminine forms, saw the disheveled, misshapen, exposed features of the dancing girls without their makeup and graceful manners. He could hardly believe his eyes, as, held in a trance, he looked at them reclining where they had fallen. All was in disorder: their clothes, their hair, their jewelry. Beneath the carefully prepared cosmetic faces of the daytime, he saw the wrinkled, dry skin of reality. Some had blemishes and other deformities that were exaggerated as they slept, and some in dreams were in contorted positions unbecoming to their feminine charms. Still others, their corsets unlaced, appeared grotesque and ugly. Smiles were now grimaces. Scattered around these debauched maidens lay their finery and their silent musical instruments.

"Oh, what a graveyard!" he muttered. "Verily I am beholding a graveyard. These are the living dead, dead and they know it not. There is no life in the palace, only the appearance behind which dwells the reality too hideous to perceive."

The prince returned to his quarters, anxious to greet the new day, for now there was no question. He must see his father, to seek release from his obligations as the crown prince, next in line for the throne. The crown was no longer tolerable to him, and he hoped his father would understand and release him. The importance of this day was tremendous; he had seen, heard, and learned enough. The course he must follow had been narrowed and determined. Inaction remained the greater crime.

When the king was prepared to receive that morning, Gautama was waiting. His father saw his radiant face, so much like the carefree, happy youth of former days, radiant with expectations. He was glad to see the changed countenance, and embraced his son. "Oh, my son," he said, "I see the cloud has passed, and you are now sure of yourself and comprehend how good life really is."

"Indeed, the cloud has passed, my father, and the way is clear before me. Grant my request now that I may go forth, leaving the palace, to walk the path of deliverance. Give me your permission to renounce the throne so that I may go in solitude to the mountains and the groves, and there abiding in peace find the everlasting happiness which I crave."

At these words the king trembled, fear overwhelmed him and tears welled up in his eyes. He answered when he regained his composure,

"Son, give up this idea of a religious life. You are still too young to enter into such a calling. Your thoughts in the youth of life are not yet certain, and change with each new experience which comes to you. Do not begin an irreversible course from which there is no withdrawal. You cannot now renounce the throne and never return to it. This is too great a sacrifice to make in youth. With it you are everything; without the promise of the throne you are nothing. Believe me, you have too much to lose and little to gain by such a proposal. I would not do justice by you if I were to submit to such a request.

"Rather let me, who has known my youth and lived so much of my life, make the sacrifice in your stead. Gladly will I don the saffron robe and go forth a meditant and a recluse if you will assume the throne today. The time has come for me to leave the palace and to embrace religion. The time has come for you to rule and use your high ideals, your sense of sympathy for the people, the knowledge of your deeper insights to exalt the kingdom and bring relief to the suffering subjects.

"O my son, reign in my stead. Be strong, be courageous. Your family and your people need you. Oh, how they have loved you, do love you! Know the joys of accomplishment, taste the sweet fruits of achievement, the joys of youth, and then in time your turn will come when, wise with the wisdom of the world and experience, you can go forward into the woods to live the life of a hermit and a religious one.

"Listen, O son, to a father's deepest wisdom, I plead with you, for you have so much to offer, and nothing else remains for me but to see you on the throne," concluded the king with tears still in his eyes.

"Dear father, how can I ever thank you for your kindness and willingness to sacrifice for me? But you yourself had said it, and called it a sacrifice to go forth as a religious seeker. To you it would be a sacrifice, and that makes all the difference, for to me it would not be sacrifice but great joy, deliverance and exaltation to seek the way of the religious calling. I do love you for your offer, and I am pleased to be the son of such a father, but no man can do for me the things which I must do for myself," the prince replied and then continued:

"Since you are so honest with me, and have been so deeply moved, I must reply that it would be impossible for me to stay in the court, unless you could promise me four things, and those I doubt any person today can do."

"What would you ask?" responded the king.

"Promise me that my life will not end in death. Promise that neither sickness nor disease will break my health. Promise that old age and infirmity will not follow the flight of my youth. And finally, promise that misfortune cannot destroy my prosperity." The prince stated the conditions that troubled his life.

"You are right; no man can make such a promise, for this is

asking too much. It is contrary to all the laws of life. There is no reversal from the human process, the universal process, which touches all that breathes," the king replied.

"If neither you, nor any mortal, can promise these four things, then there is no hope, no help for me or for all the people to be found in my staying. I am pledged to find the means of deliverance from such destruction as life provides. O father, do not hold me back. It would be like trying to stop the occupants who would flee a burning house. The day inevitably comes when we must part, but what merit is there if the departure is not of one's own choosing? Let us agree that I can depart now, and perhaps I shall find the answers that insure continued existence, not alone for myself, but for all mankind.

"If I should delay and death separates me from the quest, then all I have to offer is lost. Perchance my ardor will lead to the conquest of death, and that is worth the effort. Perhaps I can raise the lamp of wisdom before what has been the darkness of ignorance. Perhaps there is a better way, and I can find it. This is the kingdom I seek, and without pride, without station, without protection, I long to go forth. The world has raised the wrong banner, and followed the lesser course. The world is troubled, the world is in turmoil, and I myself must live in turmoil until I find release for all who live in the world. This is the kingdom to which I am called."

The king embraced his son and said, "The hour is late, go sleep upon it, and return tomorrow and we shall talk further about your destiny, for mine is wrapped up also in yours." And so they parted.

Gautama was a fair and sensitive person. He had tried to please everybody, and to do what was expected in every instance. But the reality was finally becoming clear: his choice, his decision could not be accepted by others. To seek acquiescence led merely to a strategy of postponing. He could procrastinate no longer. It grieved him to think that he must take action without his father's blessing and release, but he understood, too, that now it was impossible for his father to grant it. Now he knew that he and his father understood each other better than ever in the past, and that nothing constructive would come from lingering or talking longer. Back in his quarters he paced back and forth, pondering the steps to take and the finality of the decision made.

He wished to see his wife and Rahula one more time. But dared he risk a further postponement? He might creep in while they slept and take one last look; but that too would be risky, for what if either should awaken? No, now that he was prepared he must go at once! And so, renouncing the opportunities for final farewells, he summoned his faithful companion Chanda.

"Fetch my steed, the good Kantaka," he told his friend. "Before the sun rises we shall ride forth, so bring also the horse of your choosing." Thus, guided by the morning star, the two companions rode out from the palace.

Gautama turned for one last look at the palace, and murmured, "Until I conquer old age, disease and death, I shall see you no more!" Hours later, as the first rays of the sun began to appear on the eastern horizon, they came to the edge of the great forest. Here Gautama reined in his horse and dismounted. They had ridden forty-two miles, crossed the Aumi River, and stopped at Vaisali, the modern town of Besarh. Gautama stroked the face of the great Kantaka, and said, "O noble beast, my father rode you victoriously into battle, and today you have carried me into battle against the forces that imprison all life. Companions we have been, and I shall not forget what you have meant to me."

Then, turning to Chanda, he said, "Surely a horse has the strength and speed of a god, and his loyalty is above reproach. Take good care of Kantaka, for we shall miss one another. But you, dear friend, surpass the gods and steeds in your devotion and loyalty. You knew why I wished to venture forth tonight, and you alone did not hinder me. Although we shall be torn asunder, you had a higher loyalty, and that shall nourish me in some deep moment of agony. Take the horse and return now to the city.

"Take also my necklace and jewels and give them to my father and tell him what I have done. Tell him I could wait no longer, that we had said all we could to one another, and further discourse on so unhappy a subject would merely bring him more distress. In our last talk we came to understand one another, and no further farewell could profit either. I go in search of a hermitage not because I am turned against family and friends, but only to more fully serve them and myself.

"Therefore do not grieve, good Chanda, and tell my father and family not to grieve."

Chanda cried out in protest, asking him to think of his father, the just and merciful king; of Prajapati, his foster mother who loved him; of Yasodhara and his own flesh and blood, Rahula. "If you will not think of yourself, think of all these who love you more than life," wept Chanda.

"Fear not, I think of them. But in the wisdom of my heart I know that what I do is what I must do if I would be true to my own life," answered Gautama. "Perchance the day will come when I may return, but first there will be much testing to prove myself worthy. When I return, if I ever shall, it will not be as prince or nobleman, but as one who serves a higher goal.

"We must part, Chanda, for there comes a time when persons bound by the closest ties must each go his own way. My time has come, but you can bring hope, and help bring peace to those who love me, for they know and trust you. Tell them what you must, but urge them not to pine for me, for I have made no sacrifice. I go in sorrow only for the grief I temporarily cause those who love me, but I go in rapture and joy for this is my great adventure, my true testing. I may at last be awakened to a new glory as yet unknown! Take Kantaka and return to fair Kapila and do not look back, nor shall I look backward as I go forward into these woods."

And so the two friends parted, going in opposite directions and neither looking backward.

Shortly Gautama met an early morning hunter and offered to exchange his fine garments for the coarse robe of the outdoorsman. After exchanging clothing, Gautama took hold of his sword and severed his hair as close to the roots as possible.

He handed the sword to the astonished hunter and walked quickly into the woods.

Here he would begin his solitary search for the meaning of life and follow whatsoever paths became evident to him.

Little was he to know of the anguish in Kapilavastu, particularly in the palace. There the king, the Mahaprajapati, and Princess Yasodhara, joined by Chanda, the chaplains and advisors of the king talked over the incomprehensible events which had led this most glorious and noble son to desert the court for the life of a recluse.

An ancient Brahman summarized it succinctly, and none dared disagree: "The saintly Asita at the birth of the young Prince beheld a destiny that would lead him away from the court to a greater kingdom. Who has the power to alter the course decreed by the gods?" And thus did the court of King Suddhodana mourn.

6

THE QUEST FOR SERENITY BEGINS

Alone. Gautama was now alone. He had cut all ties with the past. Stripped of his royal raiment, he stood almost anonymous and indistinguishable from the masses of people with whom he had had so little recourse. In the distance he heard the final faint sound of horses' hoofs, and with them the last possibility of withdrawal from this strange urgency which had become the obsession of his life. His head shaven, his garment a coarse peasant's robe, his hands empty and his being without identification, he entered the woods.

In this forest, he had heard, there were hermits living in caves, and swamis with their disciples, meditating upon the way to salvation, or deliverance. Men came here to be instructed in religion and to seek out spiritual answers. Here he hoped that he might learn the disciplines of the meditant, and uncover mysteries unknown by the populace and palace alike.

What were his thoughts at such a moment? He was as one obsessed by some strong inner compulsion which allowed him no peace. A marked person from the moment of birth, if not before, he now had shed those markings; formerly a person of assured means of support and protection, he fled those protections; formerly living by certain comfortable beliefs, he now was stripping himself clean of all presumptions and going forth empty to refill the cup of life, perhaps of wisdom. This was the state he now was in. He had turned aside from all previous experience except the knowledge of the four sights. Only the consequent strange obsession to find the riddle of life and death remained. Now he was on a quest to find if there is a purpose, so that humanity could accept the infirmities of age and disease and the eventual ending of life in death. Did death really end it all? Was it true that all of life was wrapped up in this brief interlude between birth and death? Was there no enduring reality, or only this passage from birth, to youth, to strength, to slow deterioration by either sickness or the aging process?

Although his father had steered his instruction away from religious and philosophical subjects, he nevertheless was a child of his culture and knew in a general way the expectations of birth and rebirth, of the transmigration of souls, and of the compensation for evil and the reward for good deeds in which the Brahmans believed. How this faith held the answers he sought, or if it did, he was not prepared as yet to say. His mind was a blank page as he entered the woods to be lost in the dim shadows under the trees. Now he must first cope and survive, and following the time-honored customs of this land seek the religious truth which comes only through meditation and self-discipline, unless he could find a better way.

The birds were singing as the sun arose, and the coolness of the early morning forest urged his feet along their course. He knew he must travel deep into the forest, far away from the eyes of his father's guards in the event they sought to follow, and he felt that the deeper he ventured within the woods the greater distance he would put between his new life and the old. Thus he moved on. He who had never known want, or been without servants and the abundance of the palace, now possessed nothing that went beyond his finger tips, the soles of his feet, or the rough garb that touched his skin. This marked more of a transformation than many throughout the ages have fully comprehended. He was one, alone, without props or supports or reserves. That is, he possessed none, unless his mind and its turmoil, with its driving urgency and consequent high exhilaration, gave him greater possessions than those from which he had escaped.

He might have thought as he made his way forward that now he stood at base zero, brought down to the absolute minimal point of life. But he was to learn that there are lower levels to which life could sink, and he was to taste suffering, despair, want and the borderline between existence and non-existence far beyond what he himself could then realize. At all events he went on into the woods. How long he was there before joining a group of meditants is uncertain.

The Chinese version of the life of Buddha relates that he went on until he came into a community of yogis and Brahmans who were encamped in a sprawling, squalid community. According to this ancient account, some of them lived in a cemetery and wore hempen robes, deerskin hides, or the rags taken from corpses. Paradoxically, their search for beatification began in filth and squalor. They fed on the fruits and berries of the woods, and drank water from forest brooks. They received milk from cows, but also used these cows in sacrifices. Some practiced yoga and had initiation rituals which were harsh and cruel. Some always faced the sun as it made its journey through the sky from east to west. Some kept their arms above their heads at all times, until their arms became useless, withered limbs. Some never left the cemetery and some sat in the cow dung, covering themselves with it. According to this account, in the midst of the babble of desolation and human degradation, Gautama began his meditation. Listening to the oracles and spokesmen, learning what the Brahmans and yogis had to teach, he became caught in the cross currents of argumentation, speculation and the confusion of the different positions advanced.

According to another account he entered the community headed by the holy man, Arata Kalama, where he studied his philosophy, sitting for long hours before the master, listening to the doctrine set forth. Here he was exposed to thorough examination of the doctrine of renunciation and of reincarnation. He paid strict attention and asked probing questions, for he found this concern sympathetic to that which drove him forth and brought him hither.[1]

Arata taught from the Vedas and Upanishads, and he and his disciples had prolonged discussions concerning the meanings therein. They found contradictions over which they could not agree, and they differed in their interpretations.

Whichever version is correct, or whether he spent time with two separate groups, it is clear that Gautama entered into the experience with immense joy and found the pure quest for religious truth to be a most meaningful challenge. He listened; he asked questions; he made comments; and as he gained confidence, he participated fully. Whether it was the unwashed community of the Brahmans and yogis and their assorted following of religious seekers, misfits and oddities sitting in cow's dung in the graveyard, digging for roots in the forest, or the more organized ashram of the great guru and swami, Arata Kalama, it is evident that their disdain for conventional living patterns only helped the young neophyte, Gautama, to feel they were really committed seekers. At first he did not doubt that they placed spiritual truth above all material considerations.

Only with the passing of time did he come to see that some of this was meant to draw attention to the religiosity of the practitioner, was an effort for peer approval, rather than a way to enlightenment. He found that filth was not a means to detachment. He saw that philosophical expostulation was often meant to be heard rather than understood. With the passing months he came to see that much of the excitement that came with first joining the group was wearing thin, and that the talking and arguing were circular, arriving at no conclusions. Finally, he became aware that many of those who spoke the most often were not concerned for the fate of humanity, but merely involved in their own fulfillment and self-gratification, like cats licking their own bodies.

Their rules and regulations often seemed foolish, and the time for meditation was interrupted too much, lacking in proper understanding. The ecstatic meditation of the Brahma and his world had deteriorated. Finally, Gautama came to feel that his answer lay elsewhere. One morning after the practice of yoga, after the prolonged meditation, after the deep contemplation of his inner feelings, he said to the guru: "You have much to give, teacher, and from you I have learned much. However, of your own experience there is that of which you have not spoken to me."

"My son, my life is an open window. What you do not see may be found by entering into my mansion. I am like a tree bearing fruit. The fruit is there, but it must be plucked. Knowledge is not to be given, but taken; not to be parceled out, but to be entered into."

"Master, I would know this about you. Your wisdom is immense, and from you I have learned more than from all other sources of life. But my scope is limited, and I have traveled only a short distance, and have far to go. My own light has been kindled by the embers from your flame, but I wonder did your light come from a single flame, or many? And did you not travel far, and stop at many lamps to have become so enlightened?"

"Yes. Your question is clear, and though you sought to hide the intent, your purpose is transparent. But not your goal. You have taken from me much, and perhaps in time I shall be able to give you more. But first you must draw water from other cisterns. You must broaden your experience and deepen your knowledge. Your time has come to move on if you would fulfill your destiny. Long have I waited for you to see this. Perchance when next we meet I shall be able to learn from you also. But go quietly without disrupting the ashram. Farewells are not seemly to those who meditate and seek after an inner light."

With the swami's blessing, Gautama arose and went silently into the woods. He possessed nothing except the clothes on his back, a bowl, and the thoughts in his mind. He traveled lightly, moving on without being missed until long after the sun had set and arisen and set and again come up.

He parted politely and quietly from Arata, without disturbing the harmony of the ashram, as was his custom, for he had become the gentlest of men, who wished no harm, no hurt, no dismay to touch the lives of those with whom he had sat for so many days. But he had wearied of the disputations and logical wrangling that took place between the various disciples. He had grown tired of the philosophical hair-splitting of the brethren. He had had no great insight yet. He now suspected that the enlightenment he sought would not come through talking or philosophizing or dogmatizing about the nature of truth. Memorizing the Vedic literature and the Upanishads, singing, intoning, and discussing the passages of other men's thought were not the key. They were merely shackles to hold one back. He was glad to be on his way. His head was full of knowledge, but his quest would lead him elsewhere.

He had heard all his life that there were deep in these woods, as elsewhere, the followers of Mahavira, the Jain. These holy men had organized their own ashrams and withdrew from the world to practice the austerities and rigors of personal discipline which would bring release and enlightenment. Others lived as hermits, in caves dug out of the sides of the mountains, or in trees (on rude platforms), while some dwelt along the river banks. Gautama would sit and talk with these mendicants who, though owning nothing, still often seemed possessed of much. Often the young neophyte envied them their equanimity and composure, realizing that such envy was a mark of his own imperfection. A few would deign to answer his questions, but frequently the communication was non-verbal as they sat and meditated together. Gautama would sit with such a holy man for a full day, and leave to sleep in the grass with thanksgiving in his heart for the spirit of composure and oneness shared without a sound.

But he felt that he had not yet found the answers, and so he continued on his way. He was a wandering mendicant, in search of an answer, perhaps of himself, in search of those who had discovered the true meaning of life. This he had neither perceived nor yet heard enunciated. For some unexplained reason however, he found that fasting was easier when he was in the company of others—there were the shared experiences that came through the common practice of yoga. So he was always glad to be in the company of other holy men seeking similar ends.

The long periods of silence led him to appreciate the talking which had overwhelmed and dismayed him at the ashram of Arata Kalama. There were times when he longed for a human voice, and the exchange of views with explanations and considerations as well as the expression of doubts or the searching for reasons. Accordingly he was relieved when his journeys finally brought him to the banks of a tranquil stream where there were many ascetics, some singly, some together, some in ashrams (or communes), some forming classes around a leader, and some looking for kindred spirits able to assist and help them.[2]

Here it was that Gautama tarried, and joined many groups, talking, listening, asking questions, giving answers, raising doubts and probing for meanings. Gradually some of the ascetics came to look up to him and give special attention to what he had to offer.

Gautama found here the sage Uddaka, and sat at his feet for a time. So thoroughly had he learned the message of the Vedas and the Upanishads from Arata, and so adept was he in the interpretation of the philosophies of the popular ascetics of the time, that he was listened to attentively even by Uddaka.

It was the custom of these ascetics to go into the city to beg for alms. They went to the city of Rajagaha, and word spread rapidly that there was a mendicant with the appearance of a royal god. The news even reached the ears of King Bimbisara, ruler of the kingdom, who came out of the palace to see for himself. He called to Gautama, "Why are you who are young and handsome and in good health a beggar?" Then he was asked to come talk with the king.

"Stay here in the palace with me," the king is reported to have said, but Gautama in humility thanked the king for his generosity and answered,

"O king, I am the son of King Suddhodana, and have already renounced a throne and kingdom to follow the religious way. I have chosen to forsake the ways of power and enjoyment for the austerity, meditation and self-sacrifice which leads to religious truth. I search for peace and enlightenment and until I find the answers never known before, I shall not rest content."

"I pray, my son, that your efforts shall bear fruit. I know and honor your father and would be proud to have such a son as you. Promise me one thing: when you have found the path of enlightenment, come and bring me word of it, for I too would know the answer. You and your companions are welcome indeed to stay in my kingdom."

Gautama thanked the king, promising that he would come here if enlightenment were to be revealed, and the two men parted. When he returned to the woods, touched by this encounter with King Bimbisara, he increased his fasting. As a result his body began to take on the appearance of a shadow of its former self.

There were in the woods five Brahmans who were in search of a master. They heard Gautama's responses and discourses when he sat in the circle of Uddaka's disciples. Now they saw him in his solitary practice of yoga, and his deep meditation, and noted the serenity of his countenance in spite of the rigorous fast by which he disciplined and controlled his body. They came and sat with him, and so it was, that without seeking, Gautama came to have five disciples. He opened his mouth, and addressed them, and found they were willing, eager students anxious to learn the secrets previously denied to man. He talked of the great mystery of life, and of the cruel destiny which lay in store. He talked of liberation and the thought that through stillness and silence it might be found; through the practice of yoga and abstention from all thought it might be found; of the Vedas and Upanishads and that through knowledge from the elder philosophies it might be found; of fasting and abstinence through which it might be found.

He told how he had tried the ways of the world and they brought no ultimate answer. Philosophizing brought no ultimate answers. Meditation had not yet brought the answer, nor had yoga exercises. Hence it appeared that through fasting and the adjuring of alms, through abstinence and humility, one should seek ultimate answers. He proposed that they become rigid ascetics in the hope that the cleansing of the body of all impurities would open the mind to spiritual insights not possible when one was contaminated by materialistic accretions.

His disciples agreed that this was a path worthy of following and they began, with Gautama, the ascetic practice of fasting. None however was so thorough, and so determined, abstaining from food and drink as was he. His appearance rapidly changed. Gautama, once so handsome and well-proportioned, so muscular and well-built, became quite skeletal. A few months after having dazzled King Bimbisara, Gautama would not have been recognized. No longer appearing youthful and beautiful, Gautama was a sagging bag of skin and bone. His deep sunk eyes lacked luster, and his hollowed cheeks were covered by shrivelled skin like that of a prune. All who now looked upon him thought he was close to death.

No longer was he able to walk or even to stand, and he lay at the edge of the stream moaning in pain. He had reduced his diet steadily to just a few grains of rice and a small portion of water. Still no spiritual message came; still he was without a beatific vision; and still the meaning of life, death and human destiny remained an undisclosed secret. The conundrum of human frailty was still unanswered. He had failed to find enlightenment for himself, and he was no longer able to be of service to suffering humanity. All had been to naught; this alone was the emerging message. No longer could he stand, or reach for food; he was no longer able to gesture to his disciples, who watched from a distance, to bring him sustenance; he could not crawl to the river's edge for a drop of water to cool his parched and swollen tongue. He closed his eyes and knew the end was at hand.

At this time a young woman, named Sujata, who lived near the woods entered to fill her pitcher at the stream. She saw the miserable husk of a human form lying still and lifeless by the stream. Gently she raised his head and poured a small amount of water into his parched mouth. She gently stroked his feverish brow and massaged his swollen tongue. With her fingers she put a small portion of food from her bowl deep into the back of his mouth, and with soft strokes of the throat helped him ingest what his condition would not permit him to do voluntarily. She spent the long morning with him, and slowly forced nourishment and water into his system, and then placed him in the shade so he could sleep through the heat of the day. That afternoon she sent back her maiden, Punna, with more food, and when Gautama stirred she offered it to him. Slowly he looked about, and then took the food and ate. For the first time in many months he enjoyed the taste of milk and rice and sat there contentedly.

The five Brahmans who had been watching their master's noble effort at asceticism now said, "Look! He is weak. He has succumbed and given into the ways of flesh, for he is eating; he is no fit master for such as we." They arose and left him there.

But Gautama had other thoughts passing through his mind. He recalled as in a dream the appearance of Sujata at what he believed to be the very moment when his life's spirit was fleeing the body, and he said to himself, "For three years I sacrificed everything to learn the ways of philosophy and of the holy men. I lived in the filth of a cemetery, and ate the crust and roots of the earth, studying the Vedas and Upanishads, but it brought no enlightenment. All I learned was that the words of men are vain, and pass like the wind without enlightening.

"Another three years I have denied my body every pleasure and practiced an unrivaled penance, wishing to master my passions. I hoped to find the divine peace of Nirvana, but it never came. All that approached was death, and I found myself without hope, losing all strength and possessing no will.

"From these six years I have learned little. I can recite words but they do not enlighten me; I can meditate but it reveals no mystery; I have fasted, and found no meaning in life. Then a stranger, an unknown human being, in passing by, had compassion on me, and offered me food and drink, ministering to my feeble and feverish body.

"This have I learned: there is no hope in words alone; no hope in ascetic practices alone, but there is hope in human kindness. I have been a fool and found a path."

With these thoughts Gautama smiled for the first time in many weeks.

7

ENLIGHTENMENT

Gautama, recovering in health, deserted by his disciples for ending the fast that would have cost him his life, now wandered off alone until he came to a great mucalinda tree,[1] whose vast head of foliage and many trunk-like roots offered protection from the fierce rays of the sun and the cool breezes of nighttime. Here, once again totally alone, the weary, recuperating mendicant sat. He meditated on all he had heard of his childhood before his days of recall; on all that has transpired since his earliest memories; on life in the palace which he could not fully enjoy, and the terrible wrenching discovery of the contrast between the good life within the royal walls and the bleak existence beyond. He recalled his wife, the fairest of the fair, his tender young son, Rahula, and of how long it was since he last saw them. He thought of the good King Suddhodana, his father, so just, upright and forceful. Then he thought of his childhood friend, Chanda, faithful to the very end; of the great steed, Kantaka, and of his mission of escape. There were those first bewildering days in the great woods seeking to become a meditant and a mendicant, and of the confusion and distortions he found among so many. He thought of the magnificent passages from the Vedas and of the uplifting thought of the Upanishads in which he had immersed himself. There were memories of his first voyages forth as a mendicant, practicing *pindapāta*, the art and necessity of alms gathering. There was the practice of yoga, of deep meditation, and finally of asceticism, in which he had persevered to the very brink of death, when he was saved by the compassion of a kindly shepherdess.

He thought of the moods of despondence he had felt in the palace and of the deep-seated depression which so often gripped him. He recalled how he had enjoyed the good life, but always found some shadow or dimension that made life fall short of his expectations. Even as a youth these shortcomings brought sorrow to him, and he could not explain it.

Then had come the harrowing experience of discovering the presence of disease and sickness which brought anguish, pain and anxiety into the lives of the people. This awareness had followed the discovery of old age. Then came death, not simply soothing and peaceful death, but the death which comes at the end of suffering, when in anguish one passes beyond life and others must mourn and feel bereft. In addition, he had discovered that life is filled with uncertainty, futility, disease and grief. And what were the answers? Perhaps to give in to greed and grasp as much of life for full enjoyment and saturation in as brief a time as possible, so that one could go into the shadows with the satisfaction of having tasted life to its fullness? He had observed those of his caste and the palace community who so lived. No. The only answer was to escape the tensions and fears of life through a path which led to serenity. But no such path had been known to the palace chaplains, Brahmans, teachers, swamis, yogis and wisemen. All answers given were so shallow they could be easily overturned.

Hence he had come to the woods to find the answers from other seekers, but here too he found only seekers without answers. Some felt the answers lay in ancient literature or contemporary philosophy, but all their answers were only a restating of the questions in unresolvable form. No known philosophy offered a solution. All offered only quandaries, or directed one to give up the search for wisdom and fall back on ritualism and faith—to desert the search for truth.

Others had followed the path of asceticism and the mendicant, and he too followed these paths, but found no serenity, no solutions, no peace of mind—only meaningless involvement that led to no constructive end. No vision had come even as he lay dying. Only the affective action of a simple shepherdess from the fields who came to draw water at the river and leave her offering to the gods. Upon seeing him, she took compassion on his weakened condition and nursed him back to health. Even those who were his disciples and friends watched from a distance as he lay dying, lifting not a finger to bring him succor. Then they condemned him for accepting the nourishment which saved his life. They had gone off vilifying him for breaking the fast. So here he sat today, destitute of human companions, every avenue he had explored now closed to him. The only glimmer in the darkness of his mind was the compassion of a fellow human who took pity on his weakened condition.

Was all for naught? Is there no hope, no answer, no path to follow? Perhaps human compassion? The simplicity of that thought at first seemed too naive to accept: yet, the practice of ethics might hold a solution. Surely more must be required if there was a way—Karma—leading to light and life?

As he sat there under the mucalinda tree meditating, and day gave way to night, Gautama had the temptation to renounce it all. Perhaps power, the political power of earthly kingdoms, such as his father's, or greater kingdoms created by uniting many smaller kingdoms, would bring the peace of mind he sought, and give an opportunity to elevate the conditions of the people. Yes, this was possible. It was an intriguing idea. Why had he not seriously thought of it before? He could renounce the holy life, accept the power offered and reign supreme, thereby having a worldly opportunity to do good. It was a tempting thought. He meditated on this for a long period of time, and then put down the temptation.

He sat in silence as the night wore on. His mind was churning, and he had no thought of sleep. Gradually came the first rays of a rising sun, and a second temptation arose to haunt him.

He never stirred as he sat there, thinking about all the objections to the life he had led these recent years. Doubting, he faced anew a temptation by admitting the futility of the life that self-awareness brought to the fore. Introspectively, haltingly, self-consciously, he re-examined the path over which he had walked in recent months, and of the alternatives to his chosen course. These self-doubts were like the tempests and the turbulence of a great storm swirling about him and through his mind. He was shaken and blinded by the thought of the uselessness of his renunciation and striving. No, it could not be meaningless! He cried out, he covered his eyes, he clutched the dry earth to hold himself firm, and sobbed convulsively. No! No! No! It could not be without purpose, without direction, without meaning! Suddenly a great stillness overcame him. Of course not. There was a meaning, a purpose, a message, a value. And in serenity he suddenly knew he had for the second time, in as many watches, been tempted. He breathed easily, slowly, happily, and settled down, a growing calmness quieting his so recently restless spirit.

But this was merely a self-hypnotic trance, he told himself. He was finding a false calm, and the reality of his own human frailty overwhelmed him. He had come so close to death, had been at the mercy of evil powers and faulty reasoning, and had been deserted by those who should have been his colleagues. They seemingly had become his adversaries by their very inaction. Confusion again was rearing its tempestuous head, and he suddenly jerked his own, knowing that the despair and inner turbulence he felt was but the reaction to the awareness of his own frailty—similar to that which he observed in all life. The arrows of fear and anger were now seeking to turn him away from whatever lesson there was to learn, and he must turn these missiles back upon their own sources. He was not to be so penetrated, so vulnerable, so weak. And suddenly he knew that in the third watch he had been tempted for a third time.

These experiences were now behind him. Great temptations, deep doubts, strong fears had sought to overwhelm him, but he had been steadfast and resisted all. He had rejected the thought of worldly power; he had overcome the self-abasement and self-doubt that sought to break his faith in himself and his mission; he had denied the accusatory posture of blaming both his mortal weakness and his erstwhile companions for his nearly fateful end, and proven himself strong in the face of adversity. He sat there again in deep meditation. He had come through the slough of despondency and had overcome the deeper depression of futility and self-negation. What then was the meaning of the message not yet discovered?

For many days and nights he sat there thinking on this subject. This was the heart of the problem which had driven him forth and brought him through so many experiences, through periods of growth and days of frustration until at long last he had stripped life down to the barest level of subsistence. What now lay ahead? He sensed that he was coming closer to the all-elusive answer.

For days he sat in meditation. Not only all the events and circumstances of this life passed before his mind's eye, but other experiences and thoughts welled up from deep within his subconscious mind, breaking through for brief moments. Life after life seemed to pass before him; many existences of which he had been a part passed in review. If he had not lived previously and actually experienced the events, how was it possible for him to have the recollections, the distant memories, the sensations and responses that passed in parade as he sat transfixed in meditation day after day?

Deep within the culture of this land was a belief in a wheel of life, in which there was a transmigration of souls from existence to existence, life after life, and he thought of its possibility. However, the soul lacked memory. It seemed to him that what he recollected was the continuation of life itself, of being itself. Gradually there dawned in his consciousness the idea that the wheel of life was not the transmigration of souls but of being. Life itself is reborn! The continual round of striving, of suffering, of yearning and seeking, yes, even its inevitable slippage and shortfalls, was being reincarnated in body after body after body. This began to make sense to him for the first time, bringing into understandable terms much of the teaching of Arata Kalama and of Uddaka. Passages from the Vedas and from the Upanishads reinforced this growing concept. The days passed while he meditated on.

It was as though he left his body now and traveled the world over, going to strange places unknown to him in his studies, and never traveled by him in his journeys. Now he found himself at the distant outposts of the earth, moving about the universe through space. He saw the abode of the gods and the distant realms of the immortals. He traveled far and beheld the universal suffering, striving, anguish and sorrow of humanity, and perceived that no one had ever found the answer to relieve the suffering world of its yoke of pain. He had heard from Arata of those who leave the body and travel through space, returning to the abode of their human frame, but he was not conscious of such a separation, merely of the mind's sighting as far as life itself.

He sat as one transfixed beneath the mucalinda tree. His trance continued and he recalled the temptations that came at the beginning of his meditation. Now it was as though evil spirits had been the instigators and tempters he had faced. Indian culture abounded in tales of such. Chief among the sources of evil was the god, Mara. Now, face to face with Mara, he was confronted with one more temptation, one supreme proposal: "You, Oh saintly one, have achieved a perfection and goodness never before achieved by men. You have beheld the nature of evil and sickness and pain and death, from which there is no escape. In your perfection you can escape this chain of fate, this wheel of life, and enter directly into the blessed peace of Nirvana. Why should you, now that you are perfect, continue to struggle? Enter immediately into Nirvana, and you will be at peace through all eternity."

With resolute will, Gautama shook off the temptation, responding, "No! Until I can bring release to all humanity; until the least of the people have found deliverance; until all who are sick, or mourn, or die can find salvation, I shall not enter Nirvana."

With this decision, clarity came to Gautama's mind. Thus it was that he gained enlightenment under the mucalinda tree, henceforth to be known as the bodhi tree, or simply as the Bo Tree, which means the tree of enlightenment. Here, beneath its branches Gautama came to the vision that was to change the course of existence, not alone for him, but for countless thousands in his own lifetime and for millions during the millennia which were to follow.

He thought of the suffering of all forms of life, evident on every side. All of life was caught up in suffering; humanity found no escape from the reality although it chose not to face the inevitable consequences of the maturation process. Sickness, enfeeblement, loss of appetite, loss of abilities and of organic functions bring with them varying degrees of suffering. The life of pain and anguish becomes unbearable until death itself brings release.

He knew that penance did not bring release; nor did philosophy; nor fasting and alms gathering. The ascetic practices of the monks in the woods did nothing to overcome the suffering he found on every side. Only in the clarity of the insight of the inner mind did he find the answer. Suffering is the root of all evil.

People suffer because they hold on to this existence too tightly, and believe that all life is inscribed in this one temporal existence. They see themselves as bounded by the finite limitations of their bodies, and of the brief years of growth, maturity and aging, ending in death. Out of the illusion that this comprises all of life comes the sense of suffering. People cannot let themselves ride freely in the great whirling wheel of existence, which gives them not only this life but many others. Hence they are striving for success or subsistence most of the time, and pressing for fulfillment now. The result is the unhappiness seen on every side.[2]

They suffer from the moment of birth. They enter the world in pain both for the mother and the newborn infant. There is suffering because there is old age and death. Old age and death occur because there is birth. Birth occurs because there are desires. Desires occur because there is sensation. Sensation occurs because of the senses by which we touch, feel, smell, taste and enjoy contact with the world about us, and, most particularly, of other people. These exist because there is perception. In consequence there is both form and name. Hence there is impression, and impression exists because men live in ignorance of reality. Ignorance is the root cause of the suffering in the world.

Gautama, having thought his way through this chain of related concepts, now saw that ignorance lies at the root of death and infirmity. To suppress ignorance one must overcome impressions. To eliminate impressions requires the suppression of name and form. This in turn requires the suppression of perception. Perception can only be suppressed if one overcomes all sensation. This can only result if one eliminates desire. Desire cannot be eliminated while one has false impressions of existence. Hence to correct the false idea of existence, one must eliminate existence itself, which means to eliminate birth, which in turn overcomes suffering. Accordingly, Gautama now saw that all begins with the false conception of life itself, and the suffering that flows from it.

Buddha understood that to eliminate unhappiness selfish cravings needed to be overcome, which was now possible through the chain of reactions which he had seen. There was a path by which one could overcome that which demolished the goodness of life. He was ecstatic. To think that for so long he had followed difficult, painful prolonged paths of suffering which led but from sorrow to unhappiness, never bringing release!

Yet was not the striving better than the shallow joy of those people in his father's city, and all other cities, who did not strive, but shut their eyes to the approaching horrors which life would bring? Yes. But both extremes were bad. Somewhere between would lie the proper path, and so it was that the doctrine of the middle path began to take shape in Gautama's mind. New concepts were now whirling about Gautama's mind.

His was no beatific vision of secret communion with the gods, or even with the one eternal almighty God. Rather his meditation was that of a philosopher, analyzing all concepts and every possibility. Through a rigorous logical discipline he tested and compared every concept as it emerged in his mind, keeping what stood the test of a rational analysis, and discarding what fell short. The result was the development of a religious faith, or a philosophical system, which was proven point by point, like a building resting upon a sound foundation and built from the base upward, so each element stood secure and sure, not to be shaken by the winds of doubt or the storms of confusion.

He founded a system like none established before. It did not rely upon the outward authority of divine revelations from a god. It was not dependent upon the practice of sacred rituals guarded by either Brahmans or a new priesthood. It did not rely upon the sacred texts of the past to give it authenticity. It was proven true by no outward symbol or great prophetic event. Rather it was a faith that was meaningful because it made sense, was logical and could be tested by each person.

This faith was to call for the practice of moral principles in living, and the measuring up to universal standards, inwardly revealed. One cannot be concerned with his own salvation, or liberation, unless he assisted his fellow companions with their own release. How to clarify what was in his mind? He could see it all there before him, but he needed to articulate it, to codify it, to give it concrete form so that others could comprehend what was now clear to him.

The one point that was most clear was that now he had found a great peace. The anxiety, the fearfulness, the depression and despair that had haunted him for so long had now dropped away and for the first time a new serenity had entered his life. This was the great experience brought to him under the bodhi tree. He had found release from the chains that fettered him and which bound him to his present earthly existence. He was moving beyond a sense of the importance of this earthly life, for there was the great wheel of life, and as it turned so had his many existences, yet all were but as one. Now he arrived at enlightenment; the path of Nirvana, of an inward peace, was his. Yet there remained that vision in his mind, that dim recollection, of his final meeting with Mara the great arch enemy of Nirvana, assuring him that now since he had won peace and release, he could give up all striving and enter into the bliss of Nirvana. But not until he spread the message, and made it possible for all who wanted to enter, would he proceed. Thus he never doubted, as he stirred to consciousness, that just as his physical life had been saved by the compassionate Sujata, he too must carry his own balm to suffering humanity so that they too could be saved, and enter into the great inward peace which brings release, the peace of Nirvana.

His victory had not been won without a loss. He saw anew that he had wasted many years in a fruitless and meaningless search. However, this experience was required to reach the lower levels of subsistence, before he could have been spiritually, psychologically, morally and humanly prepared to accept the new vision that finally emerged in his own mind. Without the degradation of living in the slovenly cemetery among the callous self-styled seekers; without the babble of confusing arguments that came in the ashram of Arata; without the years of solitary wandering, living in caves and eating roots and berries; without the practice of *pindapāta* when as a mendicant he collected alms and learned the true meaning of humility and self-debasement; without the practice of asceticism and the life-defying fast that nearly brought his death; without all these experiences, perhaps he would still be without the enlightened vision. It appeared necessary for him to go to all extremes, and break his heart at every boundary, before he could venture beyond. Perhaps this more arduous side of the coin had to be experienced to balance the ease and bountifulness of his early life in the palace. Perhaps this experience was necessary to make him truly human, able to relate to all sorrowing and downcast people, not as his subjects but as brothers and sisters. Perhaps without all the other experiences he might never have been able to appreciate the importance of human compassion and loving kindness to a stranger given by Sujata. This went far beyond any *pindapāta*, far beyond any alms giving, far beyond the practice or response to mendicancy. It was the saving balm of human concern, and without this life is beyond salvation.

Thus as he sat under the tree and meditated on all these happenings, much became clear to him, far beyond the written and spoken word. Through these experiences, alone, the great message was revealed. Each had helped prepare Gautama, the prince, to become Gautama, the monk, and now Gautama, the enlightened one—the Buddha.

The psychological and emotional experience through which he had passed was too great for him to break its hold. In lethargy his body sat there while his mind raced on and on. A cloud burst had come up and still he sat there. Two merchant brothers, with many carriages laden with goods, were returning to the northern countries when the storm struck. They sought shelter within the carriages, and after the storm found that the wheels were sunk deep in the mud and would not move. They went in search of help, or for logs to sink beneath the wheels, and came upon Gautama seated beneath the Bo Tree.

First they thought he was a monk, but as they approached they felt he might be a god, even Brahma. He sat so still, like one transfixed, and there seemed to be a light that glowed from him. In his ecstasy he was radiant. They approached hesitantly, and then decided perhaps they should bring an offering, and so went and prepared food, which they brought to him, "Oh Holy Man," one said, "will you do us honor by partaking of our food?"

"Eat, saintly man," said the other. And the two brothers, Trapusha and Bhallika, offered their food.

Gautama turned his eyes upon them, and asked, "What day

is this?" When they told him, he took the proffered food and ate with pleasure. Then he told them that he had been to many places without moving from under the tree; he told them of the great insights that had come to him, that he would tell many people of what he had now learned, and that they were the first to come to him in his enlightenment. "May the blessings of the gods go with you, and your journey know no problems," he said.

They returned to their carriages and found that the sun had dried out the mud and the wheels rode easily out of the dry sand. They drove forth saying to each other, "Truly, he is the Buddha, the Enlightened One, who is expected."

And Gautama, now knowing that he had been enlightened, prepared to go back toward the cities of Magadha, particularly those where he had been a mendicant—to Rajagaha and also to Benares. He was ready to proclaim the new message, the message of the fourfold truth, and the path of deliverance, and the way to Nirvana. But first he must find the way to Benares.

FIVE DISCIPLES

It was good to have food again, and after Bhallika and Trapusha moved on, he sat there thinking about the course he
should follow. He must be up and about his business. But
what was his business now?

He recalled the vision of his encounter with Mara, when
that legendary tempter had urged him, now that he was enlightened, to enter directly into Nirvana. He thought of his
obstinate refusal to enter until he had carried the message to
suffering humanity. But what was that message?

Again a chain of thought followed. He had begun by explaining it to the two merchant travelers, and they seemed
impressed, and indeed found his explanations inspiring and
helpful. Yes. He could express the message which had come
to him during his long period of meditation—dare he say
trance?—under the bodhi tree. They had proclaimed him the
enlightened one, and claimed that he had enlightened them.
Dared he make the claim himself?

Yes! It was true. He was now enlightened. He had found the answers for which the ages waited. Now he must codify them, systematize them, bring them into readily understandable terms, and then expostulate them to the people. But where to begin?

While the two merchant brothers had been impressed, it would be difficult to go to others like them, whose goals in life were not primarily religious but commercial. He might better begin with those who were already seeking religious answers, a better way. Yes. That was the place to begin. Then he remembered his five disciples, and how critical they became when he had ceased his fast. They thought he had failed them. He would go and find them and they would be the first to hear his message, the first to be enlightened. That was the place to begin. Had he not heard that they had gone to the deer park in Benares? He would go there and find them.

Arising, picking up his bowl and scant supplies, Gautama now turned his face toward Benares, and set off along the dusty road. He walked alone, but now with a new certainty. He was still overpowered by the reality of the great personal discovery, that generating and explosive vision which brought him to the ecstatic awareness of a fresh new approach to the meaning of life. How could he put it into words? As he walked along, he thought of the message he would reveal.

It was clear to him, that for the second time a great change had occurred in his life. Just as surely as the transition which began when he fled the palace riding the great steed, Kantaka, with the loyal Chanda at his side, saying a final lonely farewell before burying himself in the woods, a solitary seeker, he was now undergoing another transformation. That time, he had changed from prince to pauper monk. Now he was changed again: from monk to the enlightened one—the Buddha. That was what he had become.

In later years countless people would dwell upon the Bo Tree vision and upon his reception in Benares. But perhaps the most important event of all was this long walk alone, nearly two hundred miles, when he came to grips with the realities of his new life, and fortified himself for the prophet's role. The merchant brothers had perceived the change in him, and by his countenance and the glow of his personality they recognized he was no longer a simple monk. He knew it. Now it would be up to others to test him. Yet the greatest test was of himself. It is not without significance that this message would be presented in one of his first dialogues: the importance of finding himself.

He was sitting alone beneath the shade of a tree for rest when a band of traveling musicians passed by. They were in disarray and disturbed because a young female companion had run off with some of their goods. "Have you seen a young lady pass by?" they asked Buddha.

"Why do you look for another person?" responded the Buddha. "It is much more important that you find yourselves." This answer at first dismayed the frenzied victims in search of their deceitful erstwhile companion. One of them said, "You are a holy man. You do not understand the ways of the world."

"Play your lute," said the Master. And the musician obliged. There was no doubt that he was skillful and excelled in his art. When he finished, the Buddha complimented him, expressing great pleasure in the music heard. Then he asked if he might borrow the lute.

After he played, the musicians in their turn were dumbfounded. They never expected to hear such exquisite music coming from the lips and fingers of the holy man. They heard sweet melodies such as they had never dreamed, and when he had finished they in turn were lavish in their praise of his playing. They asked if he could teach them the musical principles he knew that made it possible to so excel in his playing.

"Once you were masters of your art, but now think your knowledge is superficial," he responded. "So you think also you know yourselves, but your knowledge of yourselves is also superficial. Look at you, a group of musicians, running about willy-nilly trying to find a strumpet who has taken some trinkets from you! Is that the point of existence?"

The musicians, chastened, sat before him. As he began to talk, they listened while he queried them on the importance of the possessions carried off by the dancing girl. He showed them that what they had lost was exterior to them. Goods that could be taken away were of transitory value only. To find the girl and regain their possessions would not help them much in their confused wanderings.

Then he discussed with them the true purpose of life, and how easy it was to run about hither and yon, going no place and accomplishing nothing because one did not know who he was, why he lived, or what purpose he wished to fulfill. They went off a sober group of men, pledging that they would heed his teachings and be a different group when next they met.

So it was with Gautama. He had come to know himself as the Buddha. He knew with a certainty, never before experienced by himself, who he was, what his destiny was, and who he had become. All the self-doubt of three and a half decades had been cast aside. A new certainty possessed him, and most glorious of all, out of that awareness had emerged an all-encompassing serenity. He was at peace with himself, and peace with all the world. One purpose alone seemingly motivated him now: to share the glad tidings and good news which embraced his life with his fellows so that others could share in the new spirit of serenity now possible.

He had been Prince Siddhartha Gautama, who had laid aside the title of prince and the familiar personal name to become simply Gautama the monk. Now that too was to be laid aside, as he became the Buddha, the enlightened one, the serene, the blessed and the opener of doors for those who had the eyes to see beyond the present. He had found himself.

So he thought his life out as he walked, or sat, or slept. He considered how he would teach his new wisdom to his old monks when at last he joined them. What were the basic points and concepts he wished to present? How should his telling points be made? How to clarify rules and laws as they had been elucidated to him in his mind's eye? How to make concrete the principles of a life of liberation, the way of deliverance, to those who were seeking?

All with whom he would be talking knew of Karma, the

way beneath the law, supporting life and the orderly, proper management of life, which was part of the Brahmin tradition and the culture of India. Karma was the law and the way. It had been simplified for easy understanding by the people: evil produces evil and good produces good. Out of evil comes evil and out of good comes good. Evil thoughts lead to evil consequences and good thoughts to good consequences. Evil deeds bring evil and good deeds bring good. The law was clear. Karma was clear. If only one lived by it, how much better life would be! This was the starting point for the Buddha's insight. Karma held the key.

But for Buddha, Karma was to take a special significance. If our lives are the inevitable consequence of all we do, or say or think, why should one live by paradox? The extremes of life—of the search for worldly comfort and gain on the one hand, and for masochistic suffering and privation on the other—are both contradictions. Extremities are followed by hosts of men and women, but deliverance does not come.

It was simple. There was a middle way. The first great principle arrived at by Buddha, the axiom on which all other postulates hung, was the Doctrine of the Middle Path. He would begin his teaching with this principle, so simple that it left one dumbfounded!

In modern times it has been said by many scholars that Buddha took the main concepts of the Brahminic culture and redefined them. He did this not only with Karma, but Dharma and Nirvana, the transmigration of souls and reincarnation. Hence it was not a radically different idiom he offered the people, but a refinement of ideas already held. For instance they all believed, to some degree, in the transmigration of souls and reincarnation. These are seen by Buddha in a different light. He did not reject them, but rather purified and clarified their realities.

"The Buddhist movement was the revolt of the higher Brahminism against the lower. It was led by one of the most searching reformers that ever appeared upon the pages of history. Buddha conceived that the only remedy lay in awakening the spiritual life of the individual. The bloody sacrifice, caste, the costly tank pilgrimages, must be swept completely away," wrote Lillie.[1] With such a verdict the modern reader is inclined to agree. He reformed the older religious culture and in a sense struck the death knell of Brahminic religion. (At a later date, Hinduism was a counter reformation to Buddhism, after the centers of Buddhism moved from India to other countries and cultures in Southeast Asia and north of the Himalayan Mountains.)

The teachings of the Buddha were oral, and his method was what we call in the Western world the Socratic method. He seldom indulged in long discourses, but participated in a question and answer dialogue with inquirers. These questions often gave him the opportunity for a fairly full explanation. It has become customary to refer to them as sermons, although in actuality they were dialogues. Often, too, he resorted to a parable procedure, not unfamiliar in the West, in which he illustrated a point with a simple story. He had a tendency to make such stories, or parables, first person accounts, applying them to himself and the questioner. This device led him to speak in another idiom of the culture. He was a Buddha who had been a monk and previously a prince. Most stories or examples he desired to use did not involve either a monk or a prince, so he resorted to the device of speaking about situations that occurred in "a previous existence," when he might have been an artisan or any necessary occupation or character that suited the story for the point he tried to make. Those who heard him appeared to accept such stories as literal truth, and perhaps he did too.

At all events, Dr. Edwin A. Burtt, Sage Professor of Philosophy Emeritus, at Cornell University, an American scholar whose appreciation and interpretation of the Buddha's teachings introduced him to many Westerners, noted that "much, if not all, of this material was first committed to writing several generations after his death. I believe that it expresses the substance of his major doctrines and authentically discloses his keen and winsome personality."[2] One can study a lifetime and rarely discover significant exceptions among ranking scholars to this conclusion. Accordingly, the substance of all available evidence is that there is a reality to the teachings themselves, and that the Buddha's life emerges through the writings eventually recorded.

While Buddha walked along the roads to Benares, he continued to think about his message. Gradually the way of expressing it became firm in his mind. There was, in addition, to the Middle Path, the Four Noble Truths that had been a new revelation to him, and from these there followed the eight steps to the path leading to deliverance. He repeated them to himself as he walked along. Yes, he knew the basic message which had been an enlightenment to him!

On the way he met a Brahman, Upaka, whom he knew from earlier days. Upaka was astounded to see the striking bearing of Buddha, and asked him, "Whence comes it that thy form is so perfect, thy countenance so lovely, thy appearance so peaceful? What system of religion is it that imparts to thee such joy and peace, Oh Gautama?"

To this question the new Buddha replied that he had overcome all worldly influences, ignorance, error and passionate craving.

Then the Brahman asked him where he was going, and on hearing that he was going to Benares, asked for what purpose. Buddha responded in a verse still remembered:

I now desire to turn the wheel of the excellent Law,
For this purpose I am going to that city of Benares
To give Light to those enshrouded in darkness,
And to offer the ambrosia of the gods to men.

To the further questioning of Upaka, the Buddha responded that he was now the enlightened one, who had completely conquered all evil passions, rid himself of the remnants of personal being, and that he desired by the light of his religious system to disperse light to all, even as a lamp enlightens a house.

But the erstwhile fellow monk and fellow seeker could stand no more of Buddha's high-flown pretensions, and curtly concluded: "Venerable Gautama, your path lies that way," as he pointed in one direction, "and mine lies there."

He abruptly turned on his heel and, with his back to the Buddha, stalked off.[3]

Nothing daunted, Gautama, after reflecting on this encounter, realized that he would face the incredulous, the distrustful, and the envious, but there was no choice but to proceed and to persevere in expounding the religious truths revealed to him. If anything, the encounter with the Brahman reinforced his decisiveness and awareness of his own Buddhahood.

At last he came to the outer limits of the city of Benares, and made his way to the Deer Park where the monks were most likely to gather. As he approached, his five former disciples saw him coming from a distance, and said to one another, "Look, here comes our fallen teacher. He is weak because he could not maintain his fast. Let us ignore him, for we have been diligent ascetics while he succumbed to the weakness of the flesh and satisfied his appetite." They agreed they would disdain him, showing their superiority over him. They would make plain they would have nothing to do with a master who had broken his vows.

The five ascetics continued to sit in silent resistance but as he came closer they became uncomfortable. It is suggested that a lifetime of habit made them uncomfortable as he approached, for he was of a higher caste than they and custom forced them to be polite and offer a seat to him when he reached them.[4] Thus they all stood in spite of their protestations and agreement among themselves. Or was it because, like Upaka, they saw the regal splendor and divine bearing that now set him apart from others? Tibetan lamas say it was the astral aura that radiated from him that made him so prominent and commanding a figure.

"I found the most holy of the laws, which we were seeking without success, when I finally broke the fast which led us nowhere," Buddha said.

"But you failed us," said one of them, almost beneath his breath.

"No, it was the law we were following that failed us," responded the Buddha. "We all know the law of Karma: out of evil comes evil and out of good comes good." There is no value in extremes which go counter to the law of Karma. Karma does not teach that abuse of self is good and partaking of sustenance is bad, but just the opposite. This is where the ascetic practice fails.

"There is a middle path on which all are enjoined to walk. This is the secret of Karma, but men look for mysteries in the spiritual and do not see what is obvious. Therefore the obvious becomes a secret, and men have failed to understand it. I say to you that both extremes are equally abhorrent. We must always find the Middle Path. Asceticism does not lead to deliverance. Have ever you seen an ascetic who became a Buddha, or even a Bodhisattva, by extreme abstinence? Tell me. Which of you have, and who was he?"

The Buddha was seated in their midst, and talking to them. He now looked inquiringly at each and waited for the answer that none could give.

"Yet, I, who tried in vain the path of total philosophy, failed. And I tried the path of total abstinence and that failed. And then, under the bodhi tree, I found my enlightenment, and have become a Buddha. I was challenged by Mara, the evil tempter, to desert this life and enter directly into Nirvana, but I declined, saying I would first grasp the wheel of life and roll it for all men to see. I have come first to you, because you were my students, and I wished first to share with you the answers we sought so long without avail, and which now are revealed through me.

"We begin, as I have stated, with the doctrine of the Middle Path. From there we go on to the reasons for humanity's failure to find release. I can explain it through the Four Noble Truths which all must first learn. Out of these will come understanding of the path of deliverance. And that path is revealed by the Noble Eightfold Path, which leads to deliverance.

"Listen carefully and I will explain to you the mysteries of the path to deliverance, and when you understand these, then your quest will be ended and you too will find deliverance.[5]

"Now this, monks, is the noble truth of pain. Birth is painful. Old age is painful; sickness is painful; death is painful; as is sorrow, lamentation, dejection, depression and despair. All are painful. Contact with any of these unpleasant objects, ideas or sensations is painful. In short there are five relationships which when we grasp them are painful. Know this: the ceaseless cycle of births and death is painful. Therefore the first Noble Truth is that existence is painful.

"Now that you have heard the first Noble Truth, Oh monks, listen to the second: the cause of pain, of suffering, is found in desire. It is the craving, combined with pleasure and lust, which leads to rebirth. It is the search for pleasure here and now. This is the second Noble Truth: unhappiness is caused by selfish craving.

"Now, monks, you know the first two Noble Truths: existence is full of pain and that pain is caused by selfish craving. Listen now, Oh monks, to the third Noble Truth: the end of pain is found in the end of desire, the end of craving, the ending which comes without a twinge of appetite. This is the third Noble Truth: deliverance from pain is found through non-attachment.

"Thus, monks, you have heard the first three Noble Truths: existence is full of pain, pain is caused by selfish desire, and deliverance from pain comes through non-attachment to the things of this world. Listen now to the fourth Noble Truth: there is a way which leads to the cessation of pain, and wise are those who walk in that way. The way is simple if one but follows the Noble Eightfold Path. This Eightfold Path is so-called because there are eight steps to be taken; namely, right views, right intention, right speech, right action, right livelihood, right effort, right mindfulness and right concentration. These are the eight stages of the Noble Eightfold Path of Deliverance.

"Now, monks, tell me what is the doctrine of the Karma, not previously understood.

"You are right, it is that there is a doctrine of the Middle Way; avoid all extremes; know of a certainty that right produces right and wrong produces wrong.

"And what, monks, are the Four Noble Truths?

"Sear these into your minds, Oh monks: Existence is full of suffering; this suffering is caused by selfish desire; selfish desire can be destroyed by non-attachment; and this is accomplished by following the Eightfold Path.

"What now is the Eightfold Path? Pay attention and I will teach it to you, step by step. This path is the way to moral cultivation. By walking in this path, one frees himself from the ceaseless round of births and rebirths, of birth and death, of death and rebirth, world without end, life without end. And what are the eightfold steps?

"The first is right views. One must have the right understanding of the Four Noble Truths, and so be able to correctly view the true nature of life. The right view of the Middle Path is important, as well as the right view of Karma, which is the moral energy for persevering on the path to deliverance. This is not possible unless one has right views of the message which I, as the Buddha, offer.

"The second step of the Eightfold Path is right intention. One should renounce all sensual pleasure, intend no evil, perform no harm, do no wrong, bear malice toward no other being, and keep oneself pure in thought and deed. This is the necessary measure, for what one wills, and carries forward, determines the true nature of one's becoming. It is more important than one's being.

"We now come to right speech. This is the third step. It is not enough to be pure in thought and purpose. One must not defile his tongue by false or evil words. Right speech is an indication of the nature of life, for what comes out of the mouth shows what is within the person. One should be courteous, kind, compassionate, thoughtful, and free from inciting others to evil action. What one urges upon others is one's own guilt, and the responsibility remains the instigator's.

"Likewise we must ourselves take right action. It is not enough to know or think or speak the right way. We must perform the right way. What we do determines that we are more than all pretension, and shows the nature beneath the surface. Therefore by one's action is one known.

"Right livelihood is the fifth step. One must live a clean

and morally acceptable life. Accordingly, persons must not degrade themselves by their actions, their vocations, or their search for sustenance. One must avoid that which is harmful to life. One must not earn a living by harmful activities. Therefore one cannot be a warrior or a butcher, a hunter or a fighter, or perform any other deed of violence. To do so casts one from the road to deliverance. Deliverance is offered not alone to those in the holy brotherhood of monks, for all persons may partake. But to do so they must live without doing violence or harm to any living creature.

"The sixth step is right effort. One must endeavor at all times to avoid any evil state of mind, and produce every possible good state of mind through the practice of morality. Effort is motivation and one must persevere to achieve deliverance.

"From right effort, it therefore follows naturally that we move into right mindfulness. We must now come to study the deeper levels of philosophy which lead to deliverance. We shall spend a lifetime delving into right mindfulness. But remember that one's thoughts should never be controlled by one's emotions.

"Finally, we come to the need for right concentration. One must keep the mind set on the most important fact of life itself: the fact of suffering, and the means of overcoming it, through the practice of the Middle Path. Only by such concentration can one achieve Nirvana.

"The three final elements of achieving deliverance are first the practice of wisdom; then the practice of morality; finally the practice and achievement of meditation.[6] We need to stress these attributes. Meditation is known to all of us, but by meditation we mean the concentrated thought that deals with specific considerations. One's meditation must not be half-hearted but intense and rigorous, and it will open doors to the mind. The achievement of wisdom comes only through the practices of morality and meditation. Only then can one come to know the Ten Universals, the Ten Impurities, the Four Sublime States, and therefore be able to reach the calmness and insight which opens the gate to Nirvana.

Five Disciples

"There, monks, you have in its barest essentials, the elements of the enlightenment which came to me. We can spend more time talking about all these elements and the means to deliverance. But first what are your thoughts and your questions?"

After they had talked for some time, Kaundinya asked him, "These precepts, the Four Noble Truths and the Eightfold Path, are wonderful in themselves, but do they answer all questions that one needs to live by, master?"

"The answer is yes and no, for they can be the guide for a lifetime, but during one's life there will be many other laws or rules by which one should live. There is, for instance, the Five Commandments of Righteousness. They are: do not kill; do not steal; do not lie; resist sexual temptation; and refrain from the use of intoxicants."

Then Kaundinya, the most outspoken of the five, said, "Surely this is the wisdom for which I have searched. You are indeed the Enlightened One, the Buddha, for you have set in motion the wheel of life, the Karma that teaches that the world is ruled by justice and wisdom. Behold, I have faith in you as the Buddha, and wish to become your follower. I will live according to the precepts you have established. I have perceived that you have the power to tame human beings as one tames a wild bull, and that both gods and men must heed the message you bring. I would join in establishing the knowledge of that wisdom."

"You have understood well, Kaundinya. Stand here beside me, and together we shall preach the law. Lead a goodly life and have done with suffering."

They clasped hands, and then the other four came forward and likewise expressed their intentions. Thus did Bhadrika, Mahanaman, Vashpa and Asvajit become disciples, and so Buddha now had five to stand with him in spreading the message of enlightenment.

INTO THE TOWNS
AND CITIES

With his new found followers the Buddha, the Enlightened
One, remained in the Deer Park for some time. Here he
preached and instructed his disciples and all others who
stopped to listen. Many were the hours spent in discussion as
he explained his approach to wisdom. The crowd of idle
watchers expanded for more and more people came to hear
the rishi[1] who was expounding a radically new doctrine in
the Deer Park.

They perceived that he was more than a swami, a guru, or
a wiseman. They saw that he had transcended his earlier role
of a monk, and many marveled at his golden aura and the supreme confidence which radiated from him. He seemed possessed of a sense of serenity that brought relief as one beheld
his visage and composure. Accordingly, some who came to
observe remained to listen, and those who were attracted out

of curiosity often bowed low in reverence. They came to observe a unique guru, and remained in wonder as they beheld a Buddha. Truly, he was the Buddha, the murmur ran, the Blessed One. Others who gathered asked for instruction, and some joined his company. Thus was the holy order of the Buddha formed. It became known as the Sangha.

But those who were not monks had many questions: Was his message meant for the laity, for those still in secular pursuits? Did he not have a message for them? Was his path meant only for holy men who renounced the world, traditional family life, and the ways of commerce and statesmanship? As he explained, his message was for all. Likewise his heart was filled with compassion for all of suffering humanity. The human race was not evil, nor should it be looked upon as corrupt. It was simply that misery abounded in the world. The Buddha's compassionate heart reached out to all who suffered, whatever their caste, sex, clan, trade, position, or station in life. All were bound together by a great inconsolable need.

The Buddha now spent his days teaching his doctrine to his five disciples, talking constantly with them, and answering their questions. Together they became as one in their understanding of the Dharma and the new insight of Karma which became known to him. They were able to expound, each one himself, the truth concerning the way which led to enlightenment.

They now understood that just as the Buddha was enlightened, so were they likewise, and through persevering in his teaching they too could earn their own release, their own freedom from the suffering of this world.

The Buddha made it clear to them in many ways that right knowledge is but one avenue to enlightenment. Right deeds were equally essential and were to begin in the humility of the mendicant. The sacred art of *pindapāta*, of alms gathering, of going forth into the city, door to door, begging for sustenance was a daily requirement. But the Buddha did not merely send them forth; each morning he took his own bowl and led the way into the city, going from door to door, begging for a morsel of food. Thus by concrete, cooperative action was a true brotherhood formed from the first day, in which the master was not set apart from the disciples, but led by setting an example, never saying, "Go and do as I command," but rather suggesting, "Come, let us go together into the city and bear witness to our human needs." He is thus described:

> One slow approaching with his head close shorn,
> A yellow cloth over his shoulder cast,
> Girt as the hermits are, and in his hand
> An earthen bowl, shaped melonwise, the which
> Meekly at each hut-door
> Taking the granted dole with gentle thanks
> And all as gently passing where none gave.
> Two followed him wearing the yellow robe,
> But he who bore the bowl so lordly seemed,
> So reverend, and with such a passage moved,
> With so commanding presence filled the air.
> With such sweet eyes of holiness smote all,
> That, as they reached him alms the givers gazed
> Awestruck upon his face, and some bent down
> In worship, and some ran to fetch fresh gifts,
> Grieved to be poor; till slowly group by group,
> Children and men and women drew behind
> Into his steps, whispering with covered lips,
> "Who is He? who? when looked a Rishi thus?"[2]

His disciples went their various ways throughout the city seeking their own alms. It was the Buddha's pattern to go in silence from door to door. He neither knocked nor began a conversation, standing meekly with his bowl in hand, and spoke only when spoken to. His eyes were downcast and he was in meditation throughout, contemplating the Four Noble Truths and the path to enlightenment. This the Buddha demonstrated and taught his followers. *The Dhammapada,* a sacred book of Buddhism, succinctly summed up the proper attitude in this stanza:

> Better it were to swallow an iron-ball,
> Red-hot as the blaze of a fire,
> Than to eat the alms of the people
> As an immoral and uncontrolled man.[3]

He reminded his followers that at all times right mindfulness was necessary, that one prepared himself for accepting alms by proper meditation. The schedule of Buddha and of the Sangha, as his group was known, was to rise early, meditate, enter the city for alms, and eat at noon. The afternoon and evening would be spent in dialogue and discussion.

The appearance of the Buddha as a mendicant, or rishi, in Benares, became a sensation and great numbers of people began to follow him. As Edwin Arnold describes it

> . . . . Then our Lord,
> After the manner of a Rishi, hailed
> The rising orb, and went—ablutions made—
> Down by the winding path unto the town;
> And in the fashion of a Rishi passed
> From street to street, with begging-bowl in hand,
> Gathering the little pittance of his needs.
> Soon was it filled, for all the townsmen cried,
> "Take of our store, great sir!" and "Take of ours!"
> Marking his godlike face and eyes enwrapt;
> And mothers, when they saw our Lord go by,
> Would bid their children fall and kiss his feet,
> And lift his robe's hem to their brows, or run
> To fill his jar, and fetch him milk and cakes.
>
> . . . . But he
> Passed onward with the bowl and yellow robe,
> By mild speech paying all those gifts of hearts,
> Wending his way back to the solitudes
> To sit upon his hill with holy men,
> And hear and ask of wisdom and its roads.[4]

The Buddha, the Enlightened One, or the Awakened One, became known by several other titles of veneration, used in one sense or another in the many works concerning his ministry and teachings. He was often called, the Blessed One, or the Lord, or the Tathagata. Tathagata means one who has achieved perfection, or has achieved the perfect state, although some writers translate it simply as "the Perfect One." Since Buddha had no doubt of his own enlightenment and arrival at a state of perfection, or of the perfect knowledge by which he was resolved to live, this description seemed a simple, not immodest one to him.

A disciple of his is frequently referred to as a bhikshu, which is a Sanscrit word; or in the Pali language, in which is so much of the early authentic writings concerning the Buddha, as bhikkhu.

> Not therefore is he a bhikkhu
> Merely because he begs from others.
> Not by adopting the outward form
> Does one truly become a bhikkhu.
> He who wholly subdues evil within,
> Both small and great,
> Is called a bhikkhu so long
> As he lives his life in meditation.[5]

By the very act of right action as practiced in the daily alms gathering in the city, Buddha attracted a wide following which wended its way outside of the city to the Deer Park and there heard his discourses. There was a special aura, a charismatic quality about him, which made Buddha stand out, attracting crowds to him.

Among those who came was an aimless youth of wealth, Yasa, disconsolate and at loose ends with his dreary life. This young man, the son of a merchant, possessed everything that money could buy. In addition he was loved by parents, family and friends. Yet, not unlike Prince Gautama of the Sakyas, he was depressed and restless, seeking something which he did not possess. Tossing uneasily in his sleep one night, he dressed himself and went for a walk, overcome by the futility of his existence. His aimless steps led him to the

Deer Park, which perhaps he subconsciously sought, although he did not know it.

That morning the Buddha had arisen earlier than usual and was strolling in the park when he saw the distraught youth approaching. As he walked with downcast head, Yasa thought of the meaninglessness of his life, and said to himself, "Oh, my heart! Surely it will break if I do not find release."

The Blessed One immediately understood the wretchedness that tore the youth's life, and perceived his own youthful self in the forlorn figure of this distraught, well-dressed youth. He therefore approached Yasa and said, "You find your life unbearable to live. Come with me and I will teach you a law which will set your mind at ease and free you from the shackles which bind you to the misery you see about you. Behold, you are tired of the wasted pleasures of the world, but I can open your eyes to joys of which you will never tire."

Yasa was drawn to Buddha by the extraordinary beauty and serenity of his presence, and listened intently, with joy in his heart, to the words of the Enlightened One.

As the dawn broke, he had already heard the true meaning of Karma—that out of evil comes evil, and that good comes only from good—and he had been instructed in the Fourfold Path, learning of the misery of existence, which could be overcome only through non-attachment to worldly goals and goods.

"My former life is dead within me," he exclaimed. "I can never return to the life of luxury in which I have lived. You have liberated me, beloved Master, and I must join your group. Please, say that you will accept me."

And the Buddha, wise in the ways of the world and of the eternal order, did so.

Now that morning the parents of Yasa were greatly disturbed to discover him gone, and when he did not return shortly, sent out search parties to find him, for they understood how serious had been his depression and they were fearful that harm had overtaken him. After searching in the city the father came out to the Deer Park, and there he saw his son sitting at the feet of the Enlightened One. As he approached, the Buddha drew him also into the circle of those whom he was addressing, and soon engaged Yasa's father in dialogue. As he spoke, his words so impressed the father that he was glad for his son, and invited the teacher and the Sangha to come dine with him the next day. Then it was that both Yasa's father and mother asked if they could become the Buddha's followers, even though they could not desert their obligations, both civic and commercial, to become monks.

Buddha thereupon welcomed them as lay members of his order, who, though living in the world, would abide by the principles he had expounded of the Four Noble Truths and the Eightfold Path to Deliverance. They gladly accepted, and from that day on there were many who became followers of the Buddha without withdrawing from the world as bhikkhus. After Yasa had joined the order, and his parents accepted the new Dharma of liberation, four friends of Yasa came to the park, hoping to bring him to his senses so that he might return with them to the gay social life of the city. These four were Vimala, Purnajit, Subahu and Gavampati. As they drew near, Buddha began a parable instructing his disciples with this tale:

"There once lived a hermit who dwelt in the woods high in the mountains. His was the frugal life of an ascetic, living with only bark and leaves for garments, eating only roots and wild fruit, and a hare as his only companion. The hare could speak like a human and so conversed with the ascetic, learning from him many things.

"One year there was a terrible drought so that the forest pools were dry, the trees and plants failed to flower, and there was no food. All the animals moved to the lowlands seeking water, but the obstinate ascetic and his faithful companion, the hare, remained.

"At last came the day when the ascetic realized he would die if he remained any longer in the forest wasteland, and he told the hare he would return to the city, where he could beg food at the houses.

" 'No! No! No! Do not go!' exclaimed the hare. 'Wait another day and all will be better. You have taught me that the city is a place of evil and corruption, and it is better to live the life of solitude. Do not betray your faith by fleeing this sanctuary.'

"The hermit thought that since rabbits were good foragers the hare would bring him food, so he agreed to remain one more day. But though the hare spent the day and the following night scavenging for food, he found none. In the meantime the hermit, who held Agni, the god of fire, in great reverence, had kept his fire glowing both for warmth and respect to Agni. Thus the hermit was at least warm, although famished beyond human limits.

"When he saw the hare return in the morning without food, his despair showed on his face, and the poor hare realized that his friend felt he should not have listened to a simple hare.

" 'We animals lack the proper sense, and I am sorry to have failed you,' said the hare to his friend, and leaped into the fire.

"Instantly the hermit shrieked, and grabbed the hare and pulled him out. 'What are you doing?' cried the hermit.

" 'I do not want you to fail in your vows by leaving the woods, and so I would gladly give my body to the flames so that you can eat, my friend; put me back in the fire and feed on my flesh.'

"The hermit, deeply moved, cried, 'I shall not take the road to the city, but shall stay in this refuge, even if I must die.' The hare was happy, and at that instant the sky opened and rain fell, and the drought was ended."

After a moment of silence, the Buddha said, "At that long ago time, my friends, I was the hare. The hermit was an evil-minded young man who had just joined our circle, hoping to entice one of our members back into the city. I see you there, Vimala, and recognize you. In following generations I

have progressed and evolved so that today I am the Tathagata, and you are still on the treadmill leading nowhere. I
saved you then, and again I offer you a new chance to liber-
ate yourself from human bondage, so that you may join Yasa
and me and the other bhikkhus who have freed themselves
from human chains."

Vimala bowed before the Holy One and proclaimed his desire to follow him as had Yasa. He quickly was joined by
Yasa's other friends. Steadily did the Sangha thus acquire
new members, and before many days there were sixty
gathered together in the Deer Park as followers of the
Buddha, and the word was spreading rapidly.

Following his morning of alms gathering, the Buddha continued to teach publicly each afternoon in the Deer Park.
Soon he was sure that the converts were able to understand
and expound the truth that he unfolded before them. He told
his followers that each should take his bowl and go out,
singly or in pairs, to bring the enlightenment to others. He
charged them to return to the Deer Park for the next rainy
season, when once again they would be together.

So another pattern of the Sangha was established: the com-
munal gathering during the rainy seasons followed by the period of private witness, when each went out to walk alone
(or in pairs), telling of the Eightfold Path leading to enlightenment. There was a coming together each year at the time of
the monsoon, and a period of dispersal, of diaspora, as they
scattered to the four winds, carrying the message of liberation from suffering to the villages, towns and cities, along the
highways and the byways throughout the country. As a result
the message was spread far and wide from the very first, with
sixty bhikkhus to carry the word of freedom from suffering.

The bhikkhu, serene and full of hope and guided by an
inner peace, moved quietly along the highway, humble and
ready to talk to any wayfarer he met. He wore his simple
outer robe, his undergarment, and carried an alms bowl.
Some carried a razor, a needle and a water strainer. He never
carried more. This was sufficient for one who had attained

non-attachment to worldly goods, and more would burden him down, stripping him of his freedom.

He would enter a village in the morning with his bowl, stopping in front of each door, eyes down, spirit subdued, his thoughts turned inward in meditation. If spoken to, he answered softly and with courtesy. He would explain he had found freedom from the cares and worries of this world by following the path to enlightenment of the new Buddha. That afternoon and evening he would explain the Buddha's teachings and the law as he understood them. His was the power to invite others to join him and to follow on the footpath which led to deliverance from suffering and to Nirvana. He came not to deny the old faith, but told those who believed his message that they might find a new light. In the Blessed One the ancient faith was at last fulfilled. This was the engaging invitation offered.

It was an uplifting and promising new encounter with faith, apparently neither radical nor negative. A fulfillment of the faith, something to learn about. Certainly the example of these monks made it most attractive.

After the disciples had departed, Buddha remained a while longer, meditating in the Deer Park. Then he decided the time had come for him, also, to go out. He recalled the promise he had made to King Bimbisara that when (or if) he became enlightened he would come to Magadha and share with him his insight. The time to go there seemed at hand, so gathering his few possessions, the Buddha began the long walk to Rajagaha, the capital city. He started out on his serene way, walking quietly, following the paths and the signs that led toward the familiar city, where as a novitiate he had sought the proper path. But he was in no hurry, and there was no pressure that drove him on his way. He stopped often to converse with travelers on the journey from birth to death, from life to life, from being to the end of existence.

It was his constant hope that his words might offer liberation from the bondage of this life, bringing his hearers closer to an understanding of Nirvana, to the true conception of

Karma and a deeper comprehension of Dharma. His destiny lay not in some distant duty or place where he was required to be, but in the full use of the present moment. This acceptance of the present was the greatest achievement which emerged from all the wisdom distilled through years of searching. This acceptance was the basis of his serenity and wisdom. The full savoring of the moment was the key to that majestic, overpowering presence that captivated almost all whom he met: the full flavor of life lay in the present moment, and consisted of the basic principles that good brings good; and evil, evil. Out of the appreciation of the present came the knowledge that there was no haste to move hastily ahead; no anxiety to reach a distant goal; no requirement for accountability for his passing moments, other than to live according to the law of Karma and the fourfold truths through the Eightfold Path. Sufficient to today was the fulfillment of its opportunities. He had summed up this wisdom in imperishable words:

> Better than a thousand useless words is one single word that gives peace.

> Better than a thousand useless verses is one single verse that gives peace.

> Better than a hundred useless poems is one single poem that gives peace.

> If a man should conquer in battle a thousand and a thousand more, and another man should conquer himself, his would be the greater victory over oneself; and neither the gods in heaven above nor the demons down below can turn into defeat the victory of such a man.[6]

> Better than a hundred years lived in vice without contemplation, is one single day of life lived in virtue and in deep contemplation.

> Better than a hundred years lived in ignorance, without contemplation, is one single day of life lived in wisdom and in deep contemplation.

Better than a hundred years lived in idleness and in weakness is a single day of life lived with courage and powerful striving.

Better than a hundred years not considering how all things arise and pass away is one single day of life if one considers how all things arise and pass away.

Better than a hundred years not seeing one's own immortality is one single day of life if one sees one's own immortality.

Better than a hundred years not seeing the Path supreme is one single day of life if one sees the Path supreme.[7]

This was the wisdom which brought serenity to the Master's life. Many speak of the greatness of the Buddha's teaching, but from the very first, it was the example he gave those teachings, the integrity of his life which proved the reality of the teachings. He understood this principle, saying:

If a man speaks many holy words but he speaks and does not, this thoughtless man cannot enjoy the life of holiness: he is like a cowherd who counts the cows of his master.[8]

The principle was so simple, but people lived in ignorance. He stated it thus:

Many do not know that we are here in this world to live in harmony. Those who know this do not fight against each other.[9]

Thus could he walk in serenity the path set before him. And he was content to walk alone, even when there were companions by his side, for he knew:

Hidden in the mystery of consciousness, the mind, incorporeal, flies alone far away. Those who set their mind in harmony become free from the bonds of death.

But he whose mind in calm self-control is free from the lust of desires, will have risen above good and evil; he is awake and has no fear.

> Considering that this body is frail like a jar, make your
> mind strong like a fortress and fight the great fight
> against Mara, all evil temptations. After victory guard
> well your conquests, and forever be on guard.[10]

Through the mind, which is to say his knowledge of the
mind, he had won liberation, founded on a serene detachment. The great key to survival was that of liberation, found
in the principle of freedom from possessions and worldly
relationships. Upon this principle so much depended. It
brought freedom and a truly creative personality, a spirit able
to flow with the conditions and circumstances of life, and
one therefore able to attain Nirvana. The conquest of appetite was a key, whether it be bodily, material, social, political
and, yes, even spiritual appetite. Craving lay at the root of all
failure. Appetites conquered people, turning them into glut-
tons, drunkards, and those who coveted the goods of others.
Craving overcame the priest, the ascetic, the guru and the
swami when they took pride in position and title, and it conquered the powerful and the rulers who cherished their
scepters and might. This accumulative and possessive urge,
this uncontrollable, insatiable appetite, was the undoing of
spiritual powers. The ascetic who prided himself on his rigid
discipline and the regime of his austerities was as much a glut-
ton as the drunkard or the over-eater. Only the principle of
moderation, the middle way, set one free to be oneself.

Now the Buddha, secure in this knowledge, walked the
dusty roads on his way to Rajagaha. In time he came to the
Jatila monastery at Uruvila. This monastery was presided
over by Kassapa and his two brothers. The Jatilas were an
ascetic group of Brahmans, whose matted hair, oblations to
spirits or gods (both good and evil), and strange diets made
their group well known in this area. Their monastery stood
on a promontory overlooking the Neranjara River.[11]

In this region the Jatilas were much admired because of
their obviously difficult ascetic practices and the forceful
way in which Kassapa[12] preached and taught. Accordingly,
there was much discussion between him and the Buddha.

Kassapa was unwilling to admit that the Buddha had found a truth greater than that which he and his fellow ascetics were following. Much as he may have admitted to himself that the practices of his cult failed to bring personal equanimity, he felt compelled to challenge Buddha, which he did with a certain amount of hostility.

Here the serene nature of Buddha proved to be a good defense and example of the superior way he followed. With a quiet voice, Buddha, always gracious, responded to questions, and offered interpretations. Told of the evil spirits and gods which inhabited the monastery, requiring the oblations of the Jatila rites, Buddha calmly replied that such were unnecessary. He stood liberated from the control of all such spirits, and could show Kassapa and his brother monks the way to freedom from such powers. He talked without concern for the terrible retribution of the spirits prophesied, and as the days went by, his visit extended, and the brothers came under the spell of Buddha's serene way.

At last Kassapa admitted to Buddha that he could now see the superior way offered by him. He stated he was pleased to have heard from Buddha's lips how he had tried metaphysics and asceticism before he came to discover the new Karma leading to liberation. He, Kassapa, had followed a similar course, and now knew that the ways of Jatila asceticism were shallow, leading away from serenity and fulfillment. He said that the Buddha's way of the Fourfold Truth and the Eightfold Path to enlightenment were the proper course for one dedicated to the religious life. He wished to renounce his present orders and become a follower of Buddha.

The Buddha was pleased to accept him. Shortly thereafter his two brothers also joined the Sangha, as did many of the monastery monks. Thus, when the Buddha resumed his journey to see King Bimbisara in Rajagaha, he no longer traveled alone. A large group of monks was now following him, and Kassapa became a pillar of the Buddhist brotherhood.

Great excitement swept through the capital city of Magadha even before Buddha had entered the gates of Rajagaha. Word spread rapidly that a new Buddha was approaching and that Kassapa, his brothers, and many of his monks from the monastery at Uruvila were also coming. However, Buddha camped at the outskirts of the city in a great woods overnight, and the next morning meekly entered the city and, as was his custom, went from door to door with his alms bowl.

When word reached the king, he and a retinue from his court made their way to the forest where Buddha had returned following the morning's *pindapāta*. The people were astonished to see the king come to the woods, but surmised that he came to see the renowned Kassapa. As the king approached the Buddha and did homage to him, some thought that he had made a mistake, intending to honor their country's great holy man from the monastery at Uruvila.

Sensing the situation, Kassapa stepped forward and did homage also to the Buddha, crying out that the people of the city were to be a witness that he acknowledged that his teachings and his quest had been in vain until the Buddha had enlightened him. He publicly proclaimed the Buddha to be the bearer of the greater message of enlightenment.

Then Buddha expounded the Middle Way, the Fourfold Truth and the Eightfold Path. When he had finished, the king stepped forward and said, "When I was young there were five goals I set for myself: first to be a good king; second to have a Buddha visit my kingdom; third, to see that Buddha; fourth, to have him teach me the path to Nirvana; finally, to be accepted as a follower. I now ask that you accept me as a follower so that these goals may all be realized today."

The Buddha said, "I have returned as I once promised you. Gladly I accept you as a seeker after the path of enlightenment."

The king then invited Buddha to dine at the palace the next day so that they could talk further, and the Buddha agreed.

The next day Buddha appeared at the palace gate. Great was the pleasure of the king, who now recalled their earlier meeting. He was full of gratitude that the Buddha had kept his promise to return. "Stay in our city and make this your headquarters," urged the king. "There is a fine bamboo grove near the heart of the city which I will give to you if you accede to my wish."

The Buddha agreed, and then Bimbisara had a golden bowl of incense and water brought in. Taking some from the bowl in his hands he poured it over the hands of Buddha saying, "As this water passes from my hands to yours so does the bamboo grove pass from mine to yours."

Buddha received the bamboo grove which for a long time was to be one of his major centers. Here he would return many times. And thus did the work of the Enlightened One prosper.

10

THE VICTORIOUS RETURN

Great excitement now reigned in Rajagaha as word spread that King Bimbisara had embraced the new faith taught by the Buddha, as had Kassapa, the famed holy man of Uruvila who had left the mountain to follow Buddha. It was also reported that the king had turned over to the new order the bamboo grove which would be a home to Buddha and his disciples.

Each day the followers of Buddha, and the Awakened One himself, were seen entering the city to beg for alms, and each afternoon the various bhikkhus held forth in the bamboo grove where small earnest groups would gather. The larger groups were those about Kassapa and Buddha himself. On one such day Buddha gathered all the groups together to hear a discourse on the five hindrances to liberation. These "five hindrances" were memorized and often repeated by the various bhikkhus who had heard them expounded in the bamboo grove.

The Buddha began by reciting the Fourfold Truth: misery is the law of the world; the basis of misery is found in desire; there is a means to free oneself from misery; the way is found through non-attachment to the things of this world.

He went on to the Eightfold Path of liberation from misery or suffering. This path is succinctly summed up as right understanding, right purpose, right speech, right conduct, right work, right effort, right alertness and right concentration. One cannot falter if one follows these rules. They are all based upon the underlying Karma of the Middle Way: avoid extremes; out of good comes good; from evil comes evil.

They are so simple, these rules. Why then do so many fail? Because there are hindrances to their practice. The Tathagatha proceeded to list five as follows.

The First Hindrance is sensuality. It is a lure that traps many persons. There is a desire to follow the five senses. The enticement of giving oneself over to the gratification of the body and the pampering of the emotional desires leads some to seek sensual release. Anyone who so acts is bound to fail in his quest for liberation from suffering.

The Second Hindrance is that of ill-will. Hatred, envy, anger, a suspicious nature and a critical attitude show the bad temper; they are snares that have entrapped many a hopeful holy man who thereby never attains Nirvana. Goodwill is the only course to follow, for ill-will destroys the self.

The Third Hindrance is lethargy. Those whose spiritual and physical energies are allowed to dry up never attain liberation. They are overcome by a torpor of mind and body, like one drugged or intoxicated or lulled into a false sense of laxity. They miss the greater goals of peace, serenity and the bliss of Nirvana by this illusion of nothingness.

The Fourth Hindrance is that of worry. Those who are overanxious and agitated by a false concern for achievement betray their own failure to detach themselves from human cravings. When one has overcome desire, has overcome craving, has overcome appetite there is no longer a need for worry. But the worrier will not stay long on the way leading to freedom.

The Fifth Hindrance is that of indecision. He who waivers on the path, who has doubts, or fears, or is enticed by other longings, soon departs from the true path. He is not apt to be among those who find the way to Nirvana.

These Five Hindrances should be memorized and recalled, for each is a serpent that arises like the image of Mara the evil tempter, to block your path and turn you aside from the way to deliverance. And then he said:

"When these five hindrances have been put away, he looks upon himself as a free man, freed from debt, rid of disease, out of jail, and secure. And gladness springs up within him on this realization, and joy arises to him thus delighted, and so rejoicing all his frame becomes at ease, and being thus at ease he is pervaded with a sense of peace, and in that peace his heart is stayed."[1]

Then he continued, "Rather, let one take the positive path I have proposed, for know this of a certainty:"

"O let us live in joy, in love amongst those who hate!
Among men who hate, let us live in love.
O let us live in joy, in health amongst those who are ill!
Among men who are ill, let us live in health.
O let us live in joy, in peace amongst those who struggle!
Among men who struggle, let us live in peace.
O let us live in joy, although having nothing!
In joy let us live like spirits of light."[2]

Another verse by the Buddha that sums up the freedom, or release, from the five hindrances is this:

"The wise man who by watchfulness conquers thought-lessness is as one who free from sorrows ascends the palace of wisdom and there, from its high terrace, sees those in sorrow below; even as a wise strong man on the holy mountain might behold the many unwise far down below on the plain."[3]

These noble sentiments, spoken by the Buddha in Rajagaha, not only attracted followers, listeners and students, but disturbed many others. Not all people were ready for the higher path. After seeing the attraction of many to a noble path of ethical living and the quest for serenity, others became hostile to Buddha and his followers.

Some were distressed at the number of persons deserting the secular life to become his followers. Others saw in the growing ranks of monks a loss of workers and consumers. Some were irritated by the increasing numbers of persons who were now going from door to door seeking alms.

As a result angry voices began to be heard in public about the growing menace of the Buddha's strange new doctrine which was disrupting the life and commerce of the nation. "Why has this son of the Sakyas settled in our midst and drawn our people away from industrious pursuits?" some began to ask, suggesting it might be a conspiracy—or perhaps he had been disgraced in his own country and driven forth. A growing campaign of malicious gossip began, and the Buddha's disciples soon found that some of the populace greeted them with suspicion.

Others noted with alarm that children were deserting their families, forsaking their employment or craft, so that parents were deprived of the expected support from their offspring. Even more disturbing was the number of men who were leaving their families to go to the bamboo grove to become bhikkhus. "More and more women are becoming widows! Children are left fatherless and ill provided for!" lamented others.

The disciples were often taunted as they walked along the road by others saying, "The great monk came to Rajagaha and conquered the bamboo grove; does he now intend to conquer the entire country?" "A plague would do less harm to the city than an infestation of the Sakya monk's followers," they heard cried out as they passed. "The Sakya monk has come to Rajagaha and stolen the disciples of our own gurus; what will he steal next?"

The monks became aware of the growing anger in many quarters, and some became fearful that violence might break out against them. Perhaps, they said, even against the Master —although because of King Bimbisara's support this seemed unlikely. At last they began to talk at the Sangha meetings of the growing hostility and their fears.

"Be not afraid, disciples," replied the Buddha. "It will soon stop. Turn away their wrath with gentle words. Those who would insult you, accept their words without offense, speaking quietly when such is possible, hoping to point out to them the error in their fears. Say simply to them, 'It is because our people speak only the truth, and the people who follow seek for the truth that some have followed the Master. What offense is found in this?' and you will find they will be silent. In a few days, if we turn away wrath with kindness, the hostility will cease of its own accord." So did the teaching of serenity overcome the fears of many.

Among those teachers whose pupils had turned to Buddha were the followers of Sanjaya, some who were prominent persons from the city of Rajagaha and from even the more distant parts of Magadha. Returning to the city was Sariputta, the son of an important village elder. He had sought for release from the anguish, discontent and despondency of life, hoping that the teachings of the great Sanjaya would bring peace and understanding, but so far they had not. While he heard there was a new teacher in Rajagaha, he gave it little thought, because he had seen and listened to so many, and was content that he had attached himself to the greatest in all the country. He felt it was not the teacher who had failed him, but he that failed to grasp the essential truths and was unable to practice perfectly the faith of Sanjaya.

Upon entering the city his attention was attracted to the gentle demeanor and serenity of a bhikkhu. He remained calm under taunts, and quietly, with a grace and compassion never before witnessed, went about his daily duty of *pindapāta,* standing silently before each door, alms bowl in hand, a kindly and reverent look upon his face. He was above the storm of resentments Sariputta felt rippling through the air. In time, as his gentle demeanor broke through the resentment about him, he received his alms and then softly began his walk back toward the bamboo grove. Sariputta could not take his eyes off this man, and followed him, at a respectful distance, as he went from door to door, and then out of the district as he walked toward the grove.

Sariputta, feeling compelled to talk with him, caught up and said, "Friend, I who have followed the holy way, have watched you this morning as you went from house to house. There was something wonderful about your way. Your face was calm, your spirit at ease, and there was an aura of inner peace that no one could disturb. I have known several teachers, and traveled with many monks, but never have I seen one as much at peace as are you. Who is your teacher, and what is the secret of his message that gives you the inner calm?"

"My name is Asvajit, and I cannot tell you the message, for I only am a new student, following the greatest of the masters, the Awakened One of our day. I was fortunate to know him before he was enlightened, and I was one of the five he sought out at the Deer Park in Benares to preach to us his first sermon. The message you would hear must come from his lips, but the essence that captivated me, and many, may be summed up in these words, known but to those who tread the path to Nirvana:

Whatsoever things are produced from causes,
Of these the Buddha has revealed the cause;
And likewise how they cease to be:
This is the greatness of the message he proclaims."

Thereupon Sariputta's heart leaped for joy and he exclaimed, "If this is the doctrine learned from your teacher, then indeed have you found the riddle that unlocks the secrets of sorrow and depression; that frees one from death; that which has been the hidden secret of many ages sought by many."

Assured that he could meet and hear the Buddha that afternoon in the bamboo grove, Sariputta, with rapture in his heart, went to find his friend and fellow disciple, Mogallana. He told him of the great discovery of the new teacher who would speak in the grove that afternoon, and of how powerful was his message. Mogallana confided that he too had heard of the discord in the city, and was anxious to meet the teacher who was able to rise above it, with kindness and serenity undisturbed. Thus they talked as they made their way to the bamboo grove.

The two men were enraptured by the presentation of the Awakened One, and came forward afterward to ask if they could join the Sangha. From the first meeting Buddha saw that they had special qualities; it was not long before they were among the chief bhikkhus. Indeed, Sariputta quickly became leader of the bhikkhus and the right hand of Buddha. He, Mogallana, Kassapa, and the original five disciples were for some time to serve as the inner core of the Sangha, assisting Buddha and acting as his lieutenants.

Traders from Rajagaha, as they traveled northward, made their way into Kapilavastu, and told of the remarkable Sakya holy man who had captivated so many people in the kingdom of Magadha. They said he was described by some not only as the Enlightened One, but a Sakya prince. Because of envy and suspicion some said that he should return to his own country, but they could not drive him forth for he had remarkable influence with King Bimbisara, who honored him above all the gurus and swamis of his own country, giving him the bamboo grove in the center of the city to use.

Soon the words of the traders reached the court, and great was the excitement of King Suddhodana, who instantly knew that this could be no one but his own son, Gautama. He sent for the merchants and questioned them, asking those who had seen him to describe this holy man, and they left no doubt in his mind. Accordingly, he sent an emissary to Rajagaha to invite the Buddha to visit his father in Kapilavastu.

The messenger arrived at the bamboo grove just as the Buddha began to talk. Listening to this prince of the Sakyas, his heart at first swelled with pride, but the more he heard the more his chauvinistic pride departed. Truly, he thought, this man is more than one of us; he is chosen of the gods, and speaks a message to be heeded by all men. Soon, he found himself enraptured. As he reflected upon the misery that surrounded his life and how suffering is caused by desire, he realized why the prince had deserted the court. With his own ears he was hearing a better way expounded, and he too wished to follow it. Humbly he went forward afterward to meet the Buddha, who recognized him as a countryman. After hearing his profession of faith and desire to follow the way to Nirvana, he welcomed him as both a cousin and follower.

King Suddhodana in the meantime waited impatiently for word from his emissary that he had talked with his son, but no word came. In desperation the king sent another messenger, but such was the power of the Buddha's truth, that each messenger from Kapilavastu became a convert; soon there were nine Sakyans in the bamboo grove.

The king was now truly impatient, so he summoned Udayin, a one-time playmate of the boy Gautama, and asked him to go to Rajagaha and see if the Buddha speaking there was Gautama. If so he was to tell him that his father was old, and desired nothing more of life than to see his son once more. He asked Udayin to implore his son to return to share his teaching with his countrymen.

Like all the others, Udayin listened with rapture to his former playmate, and like all the other Sakyan messengers, he too joined the Sangha, but he did not forget the message of the aged king. When the right opportunity arose to talk with the Awakened One, he told how King Suddhodana had implored him to urge the Buddha to come to Kapilavastu and spread the message among his own countrymen. "Recall, O Holy One, that your father is not so young as when you left him, but full of years and bounded with remorse. He too needs your message and the comfort of hearing your words. The kingdom is ready to receive you as the Buddha, and the season is right for travel. Therefore, O Lord, in your great mercy, visit him, for he is just and kind, and is ready for the truth you bring."

The Buddha was pleased with the words of Udayin, and responded, "Yes. The time has come to return. It is what I have wanted to do, and have not dared to do. You have shown me the better way. Ask the monks to prepare for the journey. We shall go to Kapilavastu and there see my father."

Udayin sped ahead to carry the news of his coming to King Suddhodana. In the meantime, the Buddha made plans with his disciples to travel toward Kapilavastu since it now was the dry season. There was excitement among the bhikkhus, and soon word spread into the city, reaching finally the ears of the king. As might be expected, King Bimbisara was somewhat dejected. Arousing his young son, Prince Ajatasattu, they went hurriedly to the bamboo grove. "Is it true that you are leaving?" asked the King.

"Yes, for the time being; but do not despair, for we shall be back. My father, King Suddhodana, has sent messengers to me, beseeching me to visit my homeland and share the blessed message of liberation with him, my family and people. What request could be more reasonable?"

"There is none more meaningful, Master. Take my blessings to your father, the king, my friend. And as you are his son, dutiful and loyal, so would I have you meet my son, Prince Ajatasattu."

"May he be worthy of your love, O king," said the Buddha pensively. Taking the youth's hand, he addressed him personally: "Ponder well my words, Ajatasattu. Cunning does not always succeed; wickedness does not always prevail."

Still holding the young lad, he told the parable of the two fish ponds—the smaller parched and drying up from the sun, while the larger had ample water. The fish in the smaller pond pleaded with the avaricious crane to carry them to the safety of the nearby deep pond, after hearing him extoll the wonders of its cool, abundant waters. But he ate each of the fish which he carried in his bill. At last he invited the wise old crayfish, who protested he could not fit comfortably into the crane's bill with his hard shell. "Let me hold gently onto your neck with my claws," he said. This done, the crane flew to the shore of the new pond and tried to shake the crayfish free. But when the crayfish saw the bones of the fish on the sand, he sank his claws deep into the neck of the crane until, his head dissevered, both of them tumbled into the water. "Thus," said the Buddha, "you see the cunning of the crane did not succeed and wickedness did not prevail. So it is throughout life."

Bimbisara thanked Buddha for his lesson to his son and for his services to his people. "While you are gone, we shall preserve the bamboo grove for your bhikkhus. But do me the honor of a gift by which I might daily remember you in my temple."

The Buddha responded, "My possessions are few; take which you will and keep them in your temple if you wish; but in your mind, keep what I have taught you. There is no greater gift than this, and no more sacred temple than the mind."

The distance to Kapilavastu was vast, and the Buddha and his retinue moved slowly along the way. With him were now a hundred followers, asking for alms along the way, holding their daily classes, resting from the midday sun, and traveling a few miles. Udayin had sped on ahead, and the king, overjoyed, sent out messengers with food to meet them each morning.

Still, sufficient unto each day were the needs thereof, and the leisurely pace of the pilgrimage home was not noticeably hastened. Perhaps it was as though the Buddha were in no great hurry to meet his past, to face the world of his renunciation. Perhaps there was need to spiritually fortify himself and prepare his disposition for what he would face. Perhaps there were inner moments of self-doubt, although none who knew the Buddha could believe such possible. Yet, since he was a man of depth of feeling and of a searching knowledge, great in wisdom and boundless in compassion, he knew that the homeward experience would be trying. Heavy demands would be placed on him, setting before him tests for which he must be prepared. Thus did he travel slowly, meditating often.

While he moved toward his former home, the king and his court waited impatiently; each bit of news of his approach was like a whirlwind as it swept through the court, raising anticipation of the arrival of the Awakened One who had renounced his rights to the throne to seek a broader kingdom.

There was such excitement that when the Buddha was camped only a night's journey away, the gates of the city were locked to keep the populace from rushing out and overwhelming the prophet. Pandemonium reigned as he entered the city.

The royal court was gathered in a great park, majestic with flowering plants and shrubs. As the Buddha came forward, his father, weeping, rose and advanced toward his son, falling at his knees. "It is not proper for the king to bow before the son," murmured the Sakya lords, jealous at the attention given this wandering son. A murmur of protest ran through the crowd, and as the Buddha saw the enmity of the people, he embraced his father and the queen. Immediately he began to speak, so that the crowd quieted and listened to his teachings.

This was a technique of the Buddha used throughout his ministry—to turn private discord into public discussion and to solve public issues in a personal way. Accordingly, as he sensed the enmity against him as a prodigal, he stopped personal dissent by a public performance. On other occasions he was to solve public disturbances by personal dialogue with carefully chosen individuals. In this way he usually prevented public controversy, so that he lived seemingly free of it although few shook the social foundations to the extent he did in his public ministry.

11

CONVERSION OF THE SAKYANS

The Buddha's return was not without its traumatic experiences. He was both a prince and a prophet, a son and a seer, a local youth whose universal acclaim placed him in an ambivalent position with those who previously knew him. How to accept him? How to treat him? How seriously to take him? All must have pondered these questions who had any contact with him or his family before his withdrawal.

Some had for years dismissed him as a wastrel who had rejected his inheritance, responsibilities and good fortune. They thought of him as a weakling unable to overcome his depression and therefore unfit to rule. They were prepared to be critical, to disbelieve, but also to try to subdue their latent hostility, and not offend the ruling family. Now he had returned with a vast motley retinue of followers: some unkempt, some from lower castes, and nearly all foreigners, though many were persons above reproach.

There were the Brahman priests, the swamis, the gurus currently in favor, who had a vested interest in the prevalent religious practices and customs of the land. How could they deal with the strange new teachings of this son of Sakyas? They must hold their counsel, walk softly and await the outcome before taking a stand. They must hope that he would either prove or disprove himself, sparing them an embarrassing controversy.

There were the military elite and the merchant princes whose power, methods and possessions were always to be defended against upstart religious fanatics. They must be prepared to deal with this most critical of situations created since the new spokesman was one of their ruling house's progeny.

Then, there were the sorrowing hearts of those whom he had left. Were they to welcome him with open arms, as though their aggrieved hearts were not worthy of solicitous attention?

If the people in Kapilavastu were to have such concerns, how much more must the Buddha have felt! He, with his infinite wisdom and sage understanding of the ways of people, must have approached his home city with great trepidation. He surely was aware of the mixed emotions which would greet him, just as surely as he sensed his own disturbing feelings. Joy and sadness, love and compassion on one side, duty and responsibility on the other.

Here were his father, the king and his step-mother, the Maharaja Prajapati, who raised him as her own. Most of all, here lived Yasodhara, the beautiful princess whom he had loved so dearly, and their tender young son, Rahula, from whom he stole away in the dead of night. How was he to treat them? How meet and come among them? How exemplify the transition which had taken place in his life?

He had deserted the material, practical world for a nobler world of the spirit. Could he return and not confuse the two? How to remain the spiritual leader, a role which for the first and only time in his life offered him fulfillment, and yet walk back into the old world? These problems vexed him, yet he knew he must surmount them. Only in doing so, could he maintain his own humanity. It was a tenuous path along which he must walk; it would be a test of his serenity.

The test began almost immediately. He felt the tension in the air as he entered the city and was so movingly greeted by his father. For that reason he cut short the salutations and preached his first sermon. He could not allow the pressures to build which would divide the king from his loyal subjects. After that first public greeting, there would be other, easier opportunities to meet, he thought. First he expounded the law of karma, and the reality of suffering which led to his flight eight years earlier. He told how suffering could be overcome by non-attachment to exterior possessions, and of the path to liberation from mortality.

Following the sermon and discussions that involved many of the bhikkhus, the king and his retinue, along with the nobles and populace, retired for the night. The next morning Buddha, together with his followers, arose and taking their bowls in hand entered the city. The people were astounded to see the former Prince Gautama meekly begging for alms from door to door. Word spread rapidly, and soon Yasodhara was informed of the strange happenings. She went immediately to the king, charging that the prince "shames us." The king was upset, and determined to go to see his son at once. With his palace guard, he went immediately to where it was reported his son was seeking alms.

"You shame us," he is reported to have said to his son. "Do you think it impossible for me to feed not only you but your followers? This I would gladly do. Have no such nonsense as this, my son."

"Dear father, it is not nonsense, but our custom. This we have always done, and it brings offense to none," replied the Buddha.

"It is not our custom," declared the king. "You come from an honored line of Sakyan warriors and princes, and never has one sought alms or begged for anything of any man."

"That may be true, my father, but you must understand that though you trace your descent from the Sakyan kings, I trace mine from the long line of Buddhas, all of whom found it an honored profession to seek alms, and this I do gladly."

However, the Buddha agreed that during his stay in Kapilavastu his followers would come to the palace to eat. Thus was this crisis solved by compromise and understanding. But there were to be many more tests to be met by Buddha. One such occurred almost immediately after his appearance in the city. His half-brother was to be married, and quite naturally Buddha was invited to attend the wedding and feast.

Nanda was the second oldest son of King Suddhodana, child of the Maha Prajapati. Following the renunciation of the throne by Gautama, he had become the heir apparent, next in line to the throne. He was much in love with Princess Sundarika, and it was with delight he looked forward to his coming nuptials. The Buddha attended the feast on the eve of the wedding day, and when the time to depart had come, he handed his bowl to Nanda, saying, "Come with me." Nanda carried the bowl and walked with Buddha until they came to the edge of a park. Here he expected to return the bowl to the Master and bid him farewell.

However, as they walked the Buddha asked Nanda if he was truly happy and received the reply that he really was. When asked why this happiness, the young prince replied it was because of all the good fortune that had been thrust upon him, including his succession to the throne, the lovely wife he was about to marry, and the deep love he felt for this most beautiful of women.

"You are then happy because you will be king some day if all goes well?" asked Buddha.

"Indeed, I am happy for that, but for much more. But, brother, I doubt you can understand, for this too was to be your happiness but you spurned the royal power," responded Nanda.

"Then that is why you are happy?"

"Yes, and because I love Sundarika who soon will be my bride. But you who deserted Yasodhara perhaps cannot understand the happiness I feel," responded the youth.

"Poor man," answered the Master. "You are so naive, and

do not understand that the love of possessions is but a shallow love, a tenuous joy that will not last. You have set your heart upon the acquisition of external things. From this comes misery and suffering! You are not approaching the first of the Noble Truths by which real happiness may be found. Have you not heard me expound the Fourfold Path, explaining that all creatures are born into this world in suffering and misery, and that the reason for that misery is the love of possessions? Then you must know that there is but one way to free one's self from this suffering. What you call happiness is but a will o' the wisp, an illusion, which at any moment turns into greater misery than you have ever imagined. What has been given to you can be taken from you. This is the most elemental law of Karma, misunderstood for centuries. Oh, my younger brother, I would spare you from this agony which surrounds your life."

"I do not wish to inherit the suffering you forecast," exclaimed the alarmed Nanda. "Take me with you, and let me become your disciple."

The Buddha took his young brother by the hand and together they departed. However, doubts assailed Nanda. Perhaps he acted too hastily. Visions of the loveliness of Sundarika danced before his eyes; thoughts of the suffering king and queen filled him with sorrow. But what was he to do? Should he live in torment for the sake of others and the joys of a passing moment? He dared not mention these doubts to Buddha. As they passed through the streets, he saw the party of the princess making its way to the palace. In shame he dropped his eyes and did not look at her.

She cried out, "Nanda, where are you going?" But he could not answer. The princess then called to the Buddha, "Are you taking him with you?"

And the Buddha responded, "No, he is coming of his own free will. Thus it must always be of those who would attain Arahatta." Thus did she learn that she had lost her lover and a throne.

Rahula was just eight years old when his mother took him to the great park where Buddha was eating with his disciples.

Pointing out her husband, she asked, "Rahula, do you know that man?"

"Why yes, that is the Buddha," replied the boy.

"He is much more than that, Rahula. He is your father. You should now go to him and tell him who you are. Say to him, 'Father, I am your son, and I come to claim my inheritance.' Listen carefully to what he says and report it back to me."

She had not yet spoken to Buddha, although she had been in the court when he spoke, and had hoped that he would come privately to see her. (It did not seem comely for her to approach him since he had deserted her seven years ago without explanation.) However, the thought having crossed her mind that he might quickly vanish from the city without seeing her, she was anxious that Rahula should be recognized as his son, and receive his inheritance. She had become something of a palace ascetic following her husband's flight. Withdrawing from pleasurable activities, she had a strong bent toward spiritual pursuits. Thus many have wondered whether it was a material or spiritual inheritance she sent her child to acquire.

Rahula dutifully followed her instructions, and approached his father, standing behind him until he had finished eating. Then it is reported that the youth addressed his father, "Father, I love standing in your shadow. I have come to claim my inheritance."

The father made no reply, as he arose to move on, but thoughtfully considered what the child had said. How should he treat this offspring whose birth had almost bound him to the materialistic existence of the palace? How should he recognize his own parenthood? How accept this child whom he had so dearly loved as an infant? Truly one passes through various existences in this life; for him there had been many. But Rahula also, a fine earnest boy, was so different from the tiny infant he had cradled in his arms. Yet it was the same life. He walked along pensively, the young lad at his side, still talking and asking for what he had to give him.

What was the inheritance he had to offer? Was it the jewels

and possessions showered upon him from birth at the court? Was it the jewels of knowledge and spiritual insight, which were the only possessions he now owned, or acknowledged? Surely it must be the later, the only worthy gift he still had.

"Child, you are right to claim your inheritance," responded the Buddha, taking the boy's hand. "But my gift is not worldly possessions. You would have to strive to protect them, and in the end they would be stripped from you, if not by other men, then by death itself. I can give you a gift that cannot be measured, and which will increase with use. Come with me; I will see that you acquire what it is I have to give."

Thus, taking the child by the hand he led him to the grove, and there called Sariputta, saying, "This is Rahula, my young son, who desires his inheritance, and so will come with us into the order. Take him, and teach him carefully, so that he will be worthy of what I have to give."

When word reached the palace that Rahula had become a member of the order, the aged king's remorse knew no bounds. Going to the Buddha, he accused him of taking advantage of the goodwill and courtesy of the court. "Out of love and kindness I asked for your return to bring gladness to an old man's heart, and now you take from me my most precious possessions, the heirs of my own blood to the throne," the father lamented.

The son comforted his father, admitting it was a hard blow for him to receive, but he urged him to think of his son and grandson, who now could find perfect peace which the world could neither give nor take away. "It would not be right for me to deny them this simply because they are of our flesh and blood," consoled the son. "For they too are deserving of the enlightenment I bring. Rather you must steel yourself, like a king going into battle on a well trained elephant, which under perfect control does not panic, stampede or wail. Restrain your own feelings, knowing that what must be must be. The true liberation of life is now within their grasp. If they had continued to live in the world, they would be tempted many times to evil deeds, from which no man escapes, and which in turn would return to unseat their equanimity. But their good deeds will leave the world to greet them in their next existence, like old friends waiting to greet the voyager at his arrival at journey's end. We live in perfect happiness, without hatred in a world full of hatred; we live in perfect happiness in a world full of sickness; we live without weariness in a world full of it; and we who have nothing possess life's greatest gift. Think of this when you think of your son and grandson."

"That is a comfort, my son, but think of the mother and grandmother, who have lost a tender young child before his wisdom is ripe. How can they be sure he is ready for the Sangha, can understand the law of Karma, and walk in the path of devotion? It is cruel to rip young children from their parents, whether it be as slaves, or as bhikkhus. Would my son be a robber of the cradle and destroyer of the home? Should you not wait until he achieves years of discretion and may be expected to know his own mind? Think of this, and answer me—is it right to take a young child without conferring with his parents?"

"No. It is not right, but I too am a parent to Rahula. However, this I pledge to you—henceforth it shall be a rule of the Sangha that no child shall be received without the parents' or guardians' consent." And the thought crossed the Buddha's mind that perhaps he should visit Yasodhara, the boy's mother.

She had hoped that he would come to her, but she remained discreetly in the background. He asked his father, the king, to escort him to Yasodhara's room. There he saw her, in a barren room stripped of all luxurious furnishings, clad in a coarse yellow robe, standing at the far end. The Buddha looked at her with eyes filled with compassion, and tenderly the two embraced one another. "See, I have tried to follow the holy law here in the palace," she whispered, "for I would be like you, and live the same life." He was overjoyed, and urged her to continue, saying that she was great in virtue, and great would be her reward. When he told her that Rahula had been taken into the order and would be trained in the holy way, she smiled with deep satisfaction. He told her how lay persons could follow the Four Noble Truths and the Eight-fold Law within their own homes, and urged her to continue. With tender touches the two parted, but she was to hear him speak again before he left the city.

It was unheard of in those days for a boy only eight years old to become a monk of any order, and Rahula's entry was startling to many when they first heard of it. However, Rahula's conduct helped smooth the way for he was cultured, sensitive and well-disciplined. He was glad that he would now be closer to his father, and eager to learn from his superiors. He would rise early in the morning, and it is told how he would take a handful of sand, throw it in the air, saying, "To-day may I receive from my instructors as much counsel as these grains of sand!"

His father helped in Rahula's instruction. In a discourse to his son on truthfulness we have some of his teachings. It is reported that seeing his son approaching, Buddha sat down, invited Rahula to join him, and had water brought that they might wash their feet. Pouring the water over his feet, the seer retained a small quantity of water in his basin. "Do you, Rahula, see this small amount of water left in the basin?"

"Yes, Lord."

"So it is, son, with the calling to be a monk, it is insignificant like those who utter lies."

Then the Buddha threw away some more of the water, saying: "Discarded indeed is the calling to those who deliberately lie."

Finally the Buddha turned the vessel upside down, saying, "Empty and void indeed is the calling of those who are not ashamed of deliberate lying." He now continued, "I say of anyone who is not ashamed of uttering deliberate lies, that there is no evil he who lies could not do. Rahula, thus should you train yourself, 'Not even in play will I tell a lie.'"

By such simple illustrations, Buddha helped with the instruction and upbringing of young Rahula in the Sangha. Another time, he showed his son a mirror asking, "Rahula, for what purpose is a mirror?"

"For the purpose of reflecting, father."

"So it is, Rahula, after reflecting should bodily action be undertaken; after reflecting should verbal action be undertaken; after reflecting should mental action be undertaken.

"Whatever action you desire to perform with the body should happen only after you reflect, 'Now this action which I desire to perform, would this action by my body be conducive to bodily harm, or to the harm of others, or to that of both myself and others?'

"After such reflection if you should realize that such bodily action would be conducive to your own harm or that of others, or of both yourself and others, then such action should you on no account perform.

"If, on the other hand, after reflecting you realize, 'This bodily action which I desire to perform is not conducive to my harm, nor that of others, nor of both myself and others,' then you may perform this bodily action.'"

He then urged the young monk to use reflection during and after all his actions, so that he always considered the consequences of his actions to himself, to others and to both himself and others. In the same manner he urged him step by step to consider verbal actions and mental actions, so that in all he did, or said or thought, he reflected both before action and afterward upon its effect on himself, on others, and on the relationship between himself and others.

He taught Rahula that constant reflection was always necessary for purity: "Thus must you train yourself: by constantly reflecting shall we purify our bodily actions; by constantly reflecting shall we purify our verbal actions; by constantly reflecting shall we purify our mental actions."

He also taught him the transitoriness of nature, that there are no stable or certain conditions of life to hold fast to except those set forth in the teaching of the enlightenment. Thus he taught his son to be non-attached to material possessions and emotional attitudes. He taught him restraint, so that he was liberated from the control of the five senses, and able to live a dispassionate life. He taught him to cultivate mindfulness so that he was not imprisoned in a human body. He taught him how to be composed and so learn the meaning of serenity. He taught him that at any moment and any time or in any place he could always contemplate the nature of the path and the law—hence he learned the secret of meditation.[1]

Though he took his son from his mother and from the palace, he enriched his life so that he would conquer suffering and live free of it.

In the meantime word was spreading rapidly that in addition to the many people joining the Sangha, others were being instructed by the bhikkhus to live holy lives outside of the Sangha. Those of the court and higher castes were moved, excited or alarmed when they heard that Nanda and Rahula had joined the order. Shortly thereafter two cousins came to the Buddha requesting they be admitted: one was Ananda, a prince of high regard, and the other was Devadatta, a playboy by reputation and something of a dandy. Both were accepted by Buddha. Ananda was known for his kindness and the simplicity of his life. He rapidly adjusted to the life of a bhikkhu, in time becoming very close to Buddha, and the most beloved of his disciples throughout the passing centuries. Though Ananda could not always comprehend the teachings of the Master, his love and simplicity were so pure that he constantly questioned, leading Buddha to deeper explanations of the message intended. Thus Ananda also grew in wisdom and knowledge.

Devadatta, however, for a long time remained a personal concern of the Buddha. The purity of heart needed did not come easily to him; his vanity and jealousy continued to plague the Sangha for some time. Indeed, some of the older bhikkhus wondered why he even tried to be a monk, and felt he should be dismissed. However, Buddha remained patient.

Not only did Devadatta create problems. The Buddha found he had to call Nanda aside and talk sharply to him, pointing out to his younger half-brother the vanity of well-pressed clothes, a bowl of glazed pottery, and the use of cosmetics. "Nanda, you and I are from the same family. You should not put on airs greater than do I. Like me you have forsaken the settled life for a life of homelessness, and like me must become a forest dweller. Forget the treasures of the past. Learn the pleasures of the present. Only thus can you overcome desire."

But with Devadatta the problem remained, and the Master was unhappy over reports of his jealousy toward his cousins, and apparent practice of guile by which he sought always to be compared or to excel his clansmen from the palace. In time this jealousy was to lead the insurgent monk to try to set himself up as a rival leader of the Sangha. But the Buddha thought that never had he expected the course of life to be without its trials and testings. Better that the problems be forced by those of his own family than by strangers.[2]

The king listened daily to his discourses, and in private audiences would carry on prolonged discussions with his son, who assured him that lay people could live by the Four Truths and follow the Eightfold Path. He taught both his father and step-mother the steps leading to liberation, and encouraged them to follow them while they remained to rule the kingdom.

At last the time came when the Buddha thought he had accomplished all he could in the city and that he and his followers should return to the bamboo grove before the next rainy season set in. Together, they left the city for the journey to Rajagaha.

But he was to return three years later when word reached him that his father was dying. In his final hours with the aged king, they talked about the instability of all things. They considered how all nature must change, and that there is a continuous stream of transition taking place. This being so, one should not be alarmed, but take with good grace the changes that life and death must bring. He guided his father's thoughts toward the peace of Nirvana which awaited him, and so it was that in quiet dignity the good king departed this life.

In the king's final year a great drought had settled over the valley of the River Rohini, and in consequence a dispute had arisen between the two nations which bordered it concerning their rights to water. After the death of King Suddhodana it now appeared that war would break out. The Sakyas and the Koliyas were preparing for battle, and the Buddha determined to go to their leaders. He was a son of both these people, since his father was a Sakyan king and his mother a Koliyan princess. He went to the great plain where the armies faced one another.

Summoning the leaders of the two armies to meet with him, he asked why the dispute required bloodshed. They could not give meaningful answers, and sought them from others. The princes turned to the generals, and they in turn asked the chamberlains of the kings. They were all nonplussed as to what the point in actual dispute was until the farmers came forward and said it was the right to use the water from the river.

"What is the value of water?" The Buddha asked, and it was answered that under normal conditions it is little, but now it was in short supply. He prodded them to give a monetary value to water in normal times and its cost now in a time of drought.

"And what is the value of land?" he asked. They responded that land was abundant, and of little value. Again he forced them to give him a monetary value of the land.

"And what is the value of princes, warriors and people?" he asked. They told him the value of persons could not be measured. Much as he persisted they could not place a monetary value on a human life.

"Then you would destroy that which is of highest value for that which is of little value?" he asked. Thus he brought about an armistice in which they agreed to share the water of the river.

Many in the armies saw that this wise man had been superior to their own leaders and the methods they had been taught; many from the armies asked to join his ranks. Others extolled his virtue saying that he who had declined to be king of the Sakyas was in truth a universal ruler.[3]

After the death of the king, and the ascension of a cousin to the throne, the widowed queen, the Maha Prajapati, became, according to custom, the Queen Mother. She had no longer a desire to remain in the palace, and determined to live in a hermitage. She, like the king, her two sons, her grandson, and Yasodhara, her daughter-in-law, had studied deeply the religious way expounded by Buddha which offered a new Karma. She ardently desired this now. She thought she was not too old to undertake such a venture, but considered herself too old to sit by and watch others manage the affairs of state which Suddhodana had handled so well. In talking about her wishes with her ladies-in-waiting, she found that many of them felt the same way. These included Yasodhara and many of the widows of the warrior chiefs who had joined the Sangha. Accordingly, they asked the Buddha to accept them into the Sangha, but he refused, stating the Sangha had been organized for men only. Much as he sympathized with their grief, he felt that they would find more useful lives in Kapilavastu. He urged them to consider other avenues of service.

On three different occasions she approached him with her following, and each time the Buddha sadly, but kindly, refused them.

After he departed Kapilavastu, she continued in her desire. Finally she and her followers determined to follow the Buddha at all costs. The Queen Mother said to her followers, "Children let us go to the Buddha's monastery as monks. Let us shave our heads, wear the garb of monks, and, taking nothing with us but a bowl for begging, let us make the journey to Rajagaha." Those who agreed with her accordingly shaved their heads, donned the coarse yellow robes of monks, and began the pilgrimage to Rajagaha.

They were a startling sight, this group of female mendicants, making their way along the dusty, rocky roads, practicing *pindapāta* on the way. They were not used to the hazards and fatigue of the road, and before they had traveled far, they came to realize the arduousness of the life of a homeless monk. Their dainty feet and light limbs were not prepared for the long walk; weariness, sickness, and despair overcame them. Their bleeding feet, cut fingers, and weathered faces bore mute testimony to the hardships they had endured.

When they arrived at Rajagaha they were received by Ananda, who cried when he discovered this aged, balded, bleeding female monk in charge was his aunt, the Queen Mother. On hearing why they had come, he was amazed, but promised to speak to the Master on their behalf.

However, the Buddha cut him short: "Enough, Ananda; do not try to persuade me to allow women to join the Sangha. I have never proposed that women should retire from the household to the life of the houseless. Under no doctrine that I know is this proposed."

Ananda was so moved by the dedication of the women and their plight after the long walk, that he could not accept easily a negative answer. But the Buddha responded: "All our rules and regulations are made for men. There would be problems and misunderstandings if women were admitted. A different type of rumor would rise against us, and charges difficult to suppress would circulate. These problems can be prevented before they arise."

Ananda would not be so easily put aside. "Are women not competent to attain liberation, Sire? Is the fruit of liberation to be restricted only to men? Are the messages and practices of religion for one sex only?" he asked.

"No, of course not. Women have equal opportunity to attain Nirvana," replied Buddha, whose universal message had never before been so assailed or so questioned. He placed no bounds against any living creature.

"But tell me, Reverend Father, are Buddhas born into the world for the benefit of men alone? Surely women too may benefit from their teachings and example. Everything you have said, and implied, applies equally to all people. These women have taken your teaching seriously. Would you now say no to them?"

At last the Buddha consented, for he would rule out no creature from the wheel of life that leads to final freedom. The logic of the argument could not be dismissed. But, he confided to Ananda, "If women were not admitted, the Order would stand for a thousand years, but now it will be fortunate to last half that time. When women are encouraged to retire from the household to the homeless life, the order of society is disrupted, and new confusions will be created. Yet it is true that women are the equal of men, and they have a corresponding merit which it is not my will to dismiss."[4]

Thus did his own family both strengthen the order, and lead to the extension of the rule to include men and women equally. The universalism of his rule was now complete.

12

JETAVANA PARK

After Buddha left Kapilavastu he returned to Rajagaha. The spiritual aid he had given his father and foster mother, the affectionate understanding and rapport which still existed with Yasodhara, must have brought satisfaction. Most of all, those who were converted to become either bhikkhus or lay followers of the path of liberation enriched his visit.

But he also realized that he was no longer simply a Sakyan; he found his loyalties went far beyond one people, or one kingdom. His mission in Kapilavastu was successful, but it was no more important in his eyes than his earlier missions in Benares and Rajagaha. His real country existed in the spirit and the light of truth which he taught.

He was not back at the bamboo grove long before he met a rich merchant, Anathapindika, who had come from Savatti. Upon hearing the words of Buddha he became an excited convert, and wished to become one of his lay followers. He invited Buddha to dine with him, and as they ate, Anathapindika extolled the honor bestowed upon him by Buddha in being his guest. How wonderful it would be if he could visit his native city of Savatti. The Buddha responded that he would be glad to present his message to the people living in that city. Anathapindika was so overjoyed that he promised to prepare a park for the Buddha's use, and immediately began making plans for the great visit of Buddha to his city.[1]

Indeed, as a rich man, Anathapindika now saw his opportunity to do something significant with his wealth that would benefit his community as well as helping in advancing the ministry of Buddha. Consequently, as soon as he arrived home, he surveyed the possible sites for the Buddha's encampment. None seemed as well suited to this purpose so much as the park belonging to Prince Ieta. Known as the Jetavana Park, it occupied a central portion of the city and was well laid out with trees, shrubs and flowers. The merchant approached the prince and asked if he might buy it for a teaching center for the Buddha and his bhikkhus, who would shortly visit the city. The prince was not interested in religious matters, but for a long time had envied the merchant his great wealth. He offered to sell him that portion of the park which he could cover with gold coins.

Immediately the merchant converted to gold coin as much of his wealth as he could. We are told that many carloads of coins were brought to the Jetavana Park, and there under close security of guards were placed on the ground. Alas, there was one small portion not covered. But Prince Ieta was so moved by the devotion of Anathapindika and by the great fortune which he would realize from the sale of the park that he donated the remaining section.

Excitedly, Anathapindika sent word to Buddha that all was now in readiness for his visit; the Jetavana Park would be his home in Savatti. With his wife, his son and daughter, and many of the wealthy people of the town, he went out to meet the Buddha and his followers, escorting them to the park.

"Here, O Master, is the Jetavana Park, which has been prepared for you. Take it and use it. May it be a place of refuge, rest, peace and joy to you, your disciples and the people of the city who shall come here to be instructed in the divine way of liberation." Thankfully the Buddha accepted the park in the name of his community, the Sangha. Over the years, this was to become a major stopping place, or monastery, for the Buddha and his followers.

While the Buddha was in Savatti, almost everybody went to hear him. Many converted and others began the study of his principles. People from the surrounding area came into the city, and as the name of Buddha spread, so did the name of Anathapindika. Long known as the wealthiest man in the city, he was now regarded favorably for having brought Buddha to the Jetavana Park, and for attracting so many outside people. Thus on every side, Anathapindika heard himself being praised.

"This is not right," he thought. "What I have done is for the benefit of my own immortal life, and I therefore do not deserve credit from the people. How can I correct the fault?" He thought about this matter, and finally arrived at a possible solution. "I have presented gifts to the Buddha and the bhikkhus, and for this I am entitled to a future reward; why don't I create a condition whereby the people of the city can do likewise? Then all those who join in gifts to the Buddha and the Jetavana teaching center will likewise earn a future reward. I will go through the streets of the city and ask the people for donations for the Buddha and his monks. I cannot expect them to give *pindapāta* to me, due to my favored position in the community, but surely I can do so for the Enlightened One."

He went to King Prasenajit, who ruled the city, to ask his permission. The king approved, and indeed sent out a herald through the streets to announce, "Listen, inhabitants of Savatti. A week hence the merchant Anathapindika, with the approval of the king, shall ride an elephant through the streets of the city, asking for alms for the Buddha and his disciples. Let each of you give whatever you can afford, and so you shall join the merchant in sponsoring the pilgrimage here of the Anointed One."

On the appointed day, Anathapindika, seated upon an elephant, with his servants going before him, passed through the streets asking for alms for the Buddha from all those who would join him in seeking compensation for their good deeds in the future life. The people crowded about him, offering gold, silver and jewels; those without such wealth offered produce or the work of their hands.

As they went through the city, they passed the door of a poor sickly girl who had not heard the king's herald the previous week. She asked what was happening, and it was explained to her. She had nothing except the dress on her back, but going indoors stripped herself of it, and threw it out of the window to the merchant's servants. When it was shown to Anathapindika, he realized that it must have come from a very poor person. He asked his servants to find out who she was and bring her to him. When it was reported to him that she had given the dress off her back so could not come out to meet him, he was greatly touched, and ordered goods from his stores to be taken to her; but alas, she died the following day. Possessing the serenity that comes in having performed a noble gesture, her death was celebrated later by the Buddha's followers as a perfect passage of one in a state of Nirvana.

The merchant, Anathapindika, now presented the gifts collected to the Buddha, and learned that Buddha was concerned over shelter for some of the sick and feeble among his followers. With this wealth and more of his own, buildings were raised in the Jetavana Park. Thus the park of Savatti became a monastery. Here he was to establish his favorite retreat and teaching center although he would continue to spend time at the Deer Park in Benares and the bamboo grove in Rajagaha.

The Buddha returned again to Rajagaha and rejoined others of his bhikkhus who were there. Immediately he found some matters which demanded his attention. One was of the condition of his half-brother, Nanda, whose grief-stricken heart showed that he had not successfully put out of his mind his sorrow and loneliness, perhaps guilt, felt at the desertion of his bride on their wedding eve. He had desired to find release from suffering, but now he found that he suffered even more. He had denied himself the joy and fulfillment which marriage to a beautiful girl whom he dearly loved would have brought. Was not this too great a sacrifice? Buddha had promised him release from suffering, but what man ever suffered more than did he? He was in agony. His Sakyan cousins who were with him tried to offer solace, but all words seemed only to lead into deeper depression.

Sariputta brought the matter to the attention of Buddha. Buddha had been concerned over his brother's dress and personal vanity, but now he understood that the life of abstinence, or non-attachment, was not fully accepted by Nanda. True, he might have agreed intellectually, but not emotionally. He had not made a full accommodation of his total being to this principle. After all, Nanda was at a time of life quite different than most, if not all, other bhikkhus. Who else had rejected sensual and material gratifications at the very moment of their achievement, as did Nanda? To leave a loved one while the coals burn hot is not easy; it is indeed more than a matter of the will. If he had doubts about the wisdom of his marriage, or was not ready for it, that would have been one thing, but Nanda was very much in love with the beautiful Sundarika. As a result he mourned her loss.

Buddha sent for Nanda, and gently talked with him while they walked through the forest paths alone. As always, Buddha's heart was filled with compassion, and he understood the turmoil within his younger brother. More than this, he understood that the reason for the turmoil was that the young man had not grasped the most elementary principle of the Karma taught by Buddha: release from suffering comes from release from the acquisitive impulse, from the desire to possess property, persons or sensate pleasures. Nanda was not able to disengage his emotions from Sundarika.

Consequently, the Buddha talked with him about the Fourfold Path: "Birth is suffering; old age is suffering; sickness is suffering; separation from loved ones is suffering; not to obtain what one desires is suffering. These are the fivefold branches of suffering to which one clings. This is the first of the great truths I have tried to teach you and all others. The release from suffering is found in the extinction of the causes of suffering. In your case it is separation from a loved one, and perhaps the desire for the comforts, luxuries and royal position of the court. You must not merely agree in your mind that you wish to release yourself, but you must in your total life become non-attached to such attractions. You must substitute other goals in their place. This you can do only by paying heed to the Eightfold Path. Take each step one at a time, and make each a part of your total life commitment. From joy and happiness comes sorrow, comes fear. Whosoever is free of sensate joy and happiness will know no sorrow, for why then should fear come to him? From love comes sorrow; from love comes fear. Whosoever is free from love, is free from sorrow, for why should fear or remorse come to him?"[2]

Nanda understood all this, he said, but it was not a simple matter to put such principles into practice. Buddha tried to explain to him that he could not have the whole until he first possessed the parts, that each of the fourfold steps must be studied and practiced, one by one. The Buddha then uttered this teaching:

> Make haste and do what is good; keep your mind away from evil. If a man is slow in doing good, his mind finds pleasure in evil.

> If a man does something wrong, let him not do it again and again. Let him not find pleasure in his sin. Painful is the accumulation of wrongdoings.

> If a man does something good, let him do it again and again. Let him find joy in his good work. Joyful is the accumulation of good work.

> A man may find pleasure in evil as long as his evil has not given fruit; but when the fruit of evil comes then that man finds evil indeed.

> A man may find pain in doing good as long as his good

has not given fruit; but when the fruit of good comes then that man finds good indeed.

Hold not a deed of little worth, thinking "this is little to me." The falling of drops of water will in time fill a water-jar. Even so the wise man becomes full of good, although he gather it little by little.

Let a man avoid the dangers of evil even as a merchant carrying much wealth, but with a small escort, avoids the dangers of the road, or as a man who loves his life avoids the drinking of poison.

As a man who has no wound on his hand cannot be hurt by the poison he may carry in his hand, since poison does not hurt where there is no wound, the man who has no evil cannot be hurt by evil.[3]

Nanda still had troubles with his deeper thoughts, and asked impulsively, "But how can we find satisfaction or peace of mind if we live without joy, without happiness?" Others had begun to gather about Buddha and Nanda where they had stopped, and Buddha motioned for all to sit. Then he said,

O let us live in joy, in love amongst those who hate! Among men who hate, let us live in love.

O let us live in joy, in health amongst those who are ill! Among men who are ill, let us live in health.

O let us live in joy, in peace amongst those who struggle! Among men who struggle, let us live in peace.

O let us live in joy, although having nothing! In joy let us live like spirits of light!

Victory brings hate, because the defeated man is unhappy. He who surrenders victory and defeat, this man finds joy.

There is no fire like lust. There is no evil like hate. There is no pain like disharmony. There is no joy like Nirvana.

The hunger of passions is the greatest disease. Disharmony is the greatest sorrow. When you know this well, then you know that Nirvana is the greatest joy.

Health is the greatest possession. Contentment is the greatest treasure. Confidence is the greatest friend. Nirvana is the greatest joy.

When a man knows the solitude of silence, and feels the joy of quietness, he is then free from fear and sin and he feels the joy of the Dharma.

It is a joy to see the noble and good, and to be with them makes one happy. If one were able never to see fools, then one could be for ever happy![4]

The Buddha stopped and then looked at Nanda, saying pointedly, "But pure joy is different from pleasure and passion." Then addressing the gathered bhikkhus, he said:

He who does what should not be done and fails to do what should be done, who forgets the true aim of life and sinks into transient pleasures—he will one day envy the man who lives in high contemplation.

Let a man be free from pleasure and let a man be free from pain; for not to have pleasure is sorrow and to have pain is also sorrow.

Be therefore not bound to pleasure for the loss of pleasure is pain. There are no fetters for the man who is beyond pleasure and pain.

From pleasure arises sorrow and from pleasure arises fear. If a man is free from pleasure, he is free from fear and sorrow.

From passion arises sorrow and from passion arises fear. If a man is free from passion, he is free from fear and sorrow.

From sensuousness arises sorrow and from sensuousness arises fear. If a man is free from sensuousness, he is free from fear and sorrow.

From lust arises sorrow and from lust arises fear. If a man is free from lust, he is free from fear and sorrow.

From craving arises sorrow and from craving arises fear. If a man is free from craving, he is free from fear and sorrow.

He who has virtue and vision, who follows Dharma, the Path of Perfection, whose words are truth, and does the work to be done—the world loves such a man.

And the man whose mind, filled with determination, is longing for the infinite Nirvana, and who is free from sensuous pleasures, is called *uddham-soto*, "he who goes upstream," for against the current of passions and worldly life he is bound for the joy of the Infinite.

Just as a man who has long been far away is welcomed with joy on his safe return by his relatives, well-wishers and friends; in the same way the good works of a man in his life welcome him in another life, with the joy of a friend meeting a friend on his return.[5]

On another occasion, as the Buddha was walking through the bamboo grove, he saw his Sakyan cousins, Updaka, Kimbala, Devadatta and Ananda. Behind them was another bhikkhu, whom he seemed to notice for the first time. "You there," he called out. "You are a Sakyan too, are you not?"

"Yes, honored Master, I am Upate, the barber, and I followed Anuruddham, Devadatta and Kimbala here."

"And why was that?" asked Buddha.

"Quite simply because I was afraid," the barber answered honestly.

"Afraid of what?"

"That I would be accused of stealing, and I did not know how to defend myself. You see, I met these Sakyans on their way out of town as they followed you. They gave me their jewels. At first I thought how fortunate I was. Here I had in my hands the rings of Ananda, the jewels of Udaka, the jeweled comb of Devadatta. But I knew once I entered the gate of the city people would say, 'You there, barber, how did you come by these fine jewels? Did you murder the princes to secure them?' And I was afraid, and remembered what you had said in the park that all suffering comes from possessing or coveting the wealth of others. I thought how contented I was with just my brush and razor, owning nothing, doing my work. Now that I had great wealth I knew that nobody would believe me, and I would be treated as a felon. So I thought, 'How right is the Buddha and how wise are the princes to follow him! Why don't I also go and follow them and become a bhikkhu?' So I hung the gems in a tree beside the road and turned to follow them. I have listened intently to Mogallana and Sariputta. I have aided Devadatta, and have tried hard to become a bhikkhu," explained Upate.

"You have already learned well the first lesson," said the Buddha. "Persevere and you may yet become the first of all the Sakyan bhikkhus."

This was distressing to Devadatta, who with the others had heard it all. Devadatta considered himself the leader of the Sakyans who became monks. He tried in various ways to have them follow him, to recognize him as their leader. When he was unsuccessful with them, he would try to persuade others that he, as a cousin of the Buddha, knew what was in his mind, and what it was they should do. Thus he gradually was building a small clique of his own followers, monks who did not like the pure interpretations of the Buddha's thought that they were expected to follow. Devadatta was able to gather about him a group who thought that Sariputta, Mogallana, Kassapa and the other senior disciples held too literally to the principles of Buddha.

According to Devadatta, their interpretations were too lax, not sufficiently strict. Devadatta disagreed with Buddha in his expectations that all people be their own guides, make their own decisions on many matters. No man was to be the master of another, but this assumption of responsibility was difficult for some bhikkhus, who were used to following the directions of others. The Sangha however was a great brotherhood of free men, and, as we have already seen, in a few years to be of women as well. Devadatta apparently became the spokesman for those who preferred a more military type of life, in keeping with traditional concepts of a religious order. But nothing was really traditional about the movement headed by Buddha.

It was not that Devadatta attained spiritual insight or power; quite the contrary. He lacked depth in spiritual perception and in addition was a poor student of matters religious. While he could comprehend the outer forms he had no feeling for what it meant to detach himself from the external trappings of life. Mediocre in matters requiring either intellectual or physical excellence, he had apparently chosen to enter the religious life rather than be surpassed by others at court and in the city of Kapilavastu. In addition, it was the fashionable thing to do when Buddha was in the capital. Perhaps the high degree of jealousy he felt when his cousins were extolled may have led him to join when they did, so that he would receive the same praise for his devotion and sacrifice.

Quite a different type was Ananda, also a cousin, whose eager willingness to achieve, whose desire for religious enlightenment, and whose sense of service made him one of the most agreeable young men. He comprehended what the Buddha was speaking about, and he earnestly desired to throw in his lot with him; he had an internal sympathy which far outstripped that of most of the newer recruits. Indeed he was so devoted to performing good deeds and being of assistance that perhaps he did not advance as rapidly as he could toward the state of liberation. Though it was to be many years before he was recognized as an arahant, his virtues were highly regarded by all except Devadatta, whose jealousy continued.

The Buddha usually walked along the roads with one or another of his disciples who offered to carry his bowl for him as they traveled. This left Buddha free to discourse and, as he so often did, to gesture with his hands as he expounded the various points under discussion.

Once, as they walked they came to a division in the highway. The Buddha thought he should go in one direction, but his companion decided to go the other way, and so laid down the Buddha's bowl and departed. The Buddha, looking after him, thought he should have a more reliable companion to travel with him now that the bloom of youth was past.

One day he mentioned this to the inner circle of bhikkhus who were his more personal friends. Thereupon they made it a point to take turns carrying his bowl and whatever else he needed, but for many years the Buddha had no permanent attendant.

The Buddha in his travels conversed with one Upali, a distinguished follower of the founder of the Jains, Mahavira, who was the most important rival to Buddha at that time. The Jains were very strict ascetics, with strong dogmatic tenets by which their members were bound. Buddha and Upali discussed their positions and beliefs at length. In time the Buddha convinced Upali, who announced that he, too, wished to renounce asceticism and become a follower of Buddha. The prospect of winning such a well-known adherent of the Jains to their cause must have excited the bhikkhus who were present, but imagine their dismay when they heard Buddha warn Upali, "Approach with caution, Upali; think it over carefully so that you do not make a hasty decision. A person of your distinction and fame should not act without considering the effects."

Upali was amazed. "If I had asked to join any other religious group, they would instantly have welcomed me, marching through the streets in a procession, announcing that they had persuaded a rival leader to join their cause, but you say, 'Approach with caution, Upali, think it over carefully so that you do not make a hasty decision.' You are indeed a most unusual religious leader!"

But Buddha did have to contend with rival leaders. After he had left the Jetavana Park, the swamis of six rival groups entered Savatti, and each sent word to the king that they had come to correct the errors and false testimony of the monk Gautama who called himself the Buddha.

King Prasenajit sent word to the Buddha that he hoped he would be able to return to defend his name and faith from these gurus who were defaming him. Buddha responded that he would meet them in the great hall which Prasenajit was building, and there the Buddha defended himself admirably to the disgrace of his defamers.

Thus did the Buddha meet challenges of many kinds. His following grew and his faith was spread far and wide, not only by his own bhikkhus, but by the many others who saw and marveled at the loyalty of his following, and the exemplary way of life he lived and taught.

13

SUPPORTERS AND DETRACTORS

The Master was greatly honored by his own followers, and as a result made many converts to the faith. Without question the power of his example contributed much to the rapid growth of his movement. However, this is not the whole story. There is the example and devotion of those close to him, who having become his followers persevered to the utmost in the extension of the faith. We cannot forget these apostles of the leader.

But was there another side to the Buddha? Was he too harsh? Too lenient? Too self-centered? Too audacious? Too much of a zealot for spreading his faith? We have already noted how he disrupted the palace families of his native city, Kapilavastu, leading off, somewhat like a pied piper, his son, his half-brother, and several nephews and cousins. Later we observed the chagrin and austerity he forced upon his devoted foster-mother before he would admit her and her followers into the Sangha.

We have seen him search out those who followed him when he was the ascetic Gautama before the enlightenment, in order that they might share with him the truths gained by his travail and enlightenment; we have seen how he had been humble when followers of other leaders turned to him, and we admire him for such loyalty, integrity and humility.

Yet there remains a disquieting question: why did he have enemies? Was it simply envy and competition for followers by the swamis of lesser cults? Was it just family jealousy in the case of Devadatta?

Let us begin by looking at the contributions of friends and the challenges of detractors. Was the attraction and the objection purely the result of external forces, or was there some inner response to persons, some magnetic, charismatic power of the Buddha which attracted some and repelled others? What was his personal psychological involvement in these responses?

Consider the visit of a wealthy merchant coming to India from the island of Paranta in the Indian Ocean. The merchant, Punna, first heard the Master as he was speaking at the Jeta-vana Park. Finding most of the populace spending the afternoon in the Park he went to see what attracted them, and there fell under the Buddha's spell. He listened, and returned each day, leaving business transactions to his brother-in-law. Eventually converted to the Buddha's way of thinking, he gave his business, the caravan and goods, to his brother-in-law, who left the city on the previously arranged trade route. Punna remained behind becoming a member of the Sangha.

Later, with only his alms bowl and spare robe, Punna went out with other monks to carry the message of enlightenment. This life was more fulfilling than his life as a rich caravan merchant had been, for he found great solace in such endeavors. But the few times in which he met persons who connected him with the rich caravan master, there were obstacles to his success as a missioner. Slowly it dawned upon him that he should return to his homeland, where he was known, and there test his ability. He knew he needed to prove his mettle as a disciple undeterred by hardship, suspicion and doubting listeners.

Accordingly he approached the Buddha asking approval for his return to his island home to establish the Dharma there. The wise leader did not immediately agree. He saw hardships which he was not sure Punna was prepared to meet.

"Your island is inhabited by barbarians and fierce natives who do not take kindly to outside ways or teachings. They are known to be suspicious of strangers from other lands. When you return as a bhikku, lacking in wealth, as a beggar, bringing a new doctrine, it will be as though you are a stranger in their midst. You will not be the lordly Punna, merchant prince and caravan owner, but the monk Punna, who has no wealth on earth. No doubt some will say you are a foolish man who surrendered all in a preposterous quest. They have abused and threatened other swamis, rishis, mendicants and bhikkhus who visited their island. If they threatened you, what would you, who believe yourself one of them, feel?"

"I would remember that these people are the same ones who were my neighbors in former days, I would know that in their hearts they are good, but have the misfortune to have lived in spiritual darkness and that I may now enlighten them," responded Punna.

"But if they did not merely jeer at you, but attacked you physically, throwing sticks and refuse, what would you feel?" asked the Buddha.

"I would feel that these are my neighbors, and I would remember that they are good and gentle people who are not beating me with clubs and weapons," he replied.

"But supposing they did beat you with clubs and weapons?" the Buddha persisted.

"I would recall that they were punishing me physically but were not taking my life," answered Punna.

"And if they killed you, what would you feel as you lay dying?"

"I would thank them with my last breath as good and gentle people who had released me from this rotten carcass of a body, loosening my fetters so that I was free at last."

"I bless you, Punna, and send you forth with my affectionate best wishes, for you are endowed not only with spiritual insight but with the necessary forbearance to live by example and explain the message of deliverance from suffering. I wish you well in this life, as well as when the wheel of life continues to turn. Live in Paranta teaching the inhabitants how to attain freedom even as you are now free."

Later the Buddha rejoiced to learn that by the end of the first dry season Punna had converted five hundred bhikkhus on the island, and in the next few years the message reached many thousands, making for the island a stronghold of the faith.

The controversy that Buddha discussed with Punna was not purely conjectural, for many people sought to discredit the Master himself. Following his defeat of the six antagonistic swamis at Savatti, some of his enemies combined together to attack him morally. They persuaded a beautiful actress to pretend to become a follower, attending his talks at the Jeta monastery, and seeking personal interviews with Buddha. After months of making herself conspicuous as a follower, she came forward before a large gathering, with padding beneath her dress which gave her the appearance of being pregnant.

Crying aloud, she wailed, "O great master, you whose body is so beautiful, whose lips are so warm, whose voice so soft, whose manner so alluring, behold what you have done to me! Why do you deny the child which will be born of your desires! You who call on others to serve justly and admit their deeds, have refused to acknowledge your responsibility. You know how to take advantage of the believing, but you do not know how to take your responsibility."

The Buddha listened meekly while she accused him, and then in a gentle voice said, "Sister, whether your words be true or false none can know except you and I." As she performed her accusing role, she tripped and her dress snagged on a projecting root. A gust of wind caught it like a sail and the padding fell to the ground—to the amazement of the watching throng, who seeing the deceit rose up angrily, shouting at her and driving her away.[1]

King Bimbisara, who had been the first regal patron of Buddha, was now growing old. Devadatta had become a close friend of his son, Prince Ajatasattu, and the two entered into a conspiracy. Ajatasattu would murder his father, the king, and rule the country while Devadatta would murder his uncle, the Buddha, and rule over the Sangha. Together they would be in total control of the people and their minds. Ajatasattu, the ungrateful son of the benevolent and wise King Bimbisara, accordingly plotted his death. But the king learned of his plans. Dearly loving his son, wishing him well and understanding the pressures of ambition, the difficulty for youth to practice patience, the king abdicated the throne, turning all power over to his headstrong son. Now Bimbisara was free to become a follower of the Buddha and through a total commitment a member of the Sangha. This was precisely what Devadatta did not want, for he viewed such a course of action as a threat to his intention to become the leader of the Sangha himself.

Accordingly the crafty Devadatta now planted false and disquieting thoughts in the mind of Ajatasattu, assuring him he could never easily wear the crown while his father lurked in the background, surrounded by his older advisors, who would plan a coup, and restore the aged king to the throne. "Only when he is dead will you truly be king," whispered Devadatta. The king, fearful for his newly achieved throne, insecure and headstrong, ordered his father imprisoned, and saw to it that he died of starvation in the dungeon.[2]

Ajatasattu as a young prince had been brought by King Bimbisara to Buddha and had been given a moral lesson about the greedy crane who sought to devour all the fish in a small pond, only to have justice right the balance. So it was to be with the headstrong, insecure king.

While his father lay dying of starvation, with the coup de grace administered at the last moment by the king's barber, the king himself was involved with happy events. His queen had just presented him his firstborn son, and Ajatasattu's heart was overflowing with love. The love in his heart for the tender young babe was indescribable, and his body thrilled with joy at the touch, or the sound, of this offspring of his. He never had known such joy as paternal love now brought to him. He hastened to his mother and said, "Mother, did father love me when I was a child?"

She responded, "I cannot begin to tell how deep was the love he held for you. All who knew him marveled at it, and it continued throughout all your life. You were the sunshine of his life and no deed was so generously offered as when he stepped aside and named you king. But let me try to tell how it was when you were a tender child. Only through his deeds can I explain the depth of his devotion to you.

"Before you were born, when I carried you in my womb, I became anemic and the doctors said in order to save my life they must sacrifice yours. But your father would not hear of it. He severed his right hand, forcing me to drink his blood that you could be nourished.

"Later, after you were born, you developed a high fever while your father sat at court administering justice. When word came to him of the fever he had you brought to him, and as he sat in the seat of justice he caressed and examined you. He found a festering abscess which he instantly lanced and while he sat in public he sucked the poison from your body into his own."

The prince, now realizing what he had meant to his father and how he was repaying him, summoned his courtiers and ordered them to rush to the dungeon to free his father. "Run and release my beloved father at once!" he shouted. But just then a letter from the barber was delivered into his hands, telling of the death of his father. Only now, after his father's death, did he realize what paternal love was. He shed bitter tears, blaming himself and suffering the pangs of guilt.[3]

Later he went to see Buddha to confess his weakness and shortcomings. At last he became the just man his father wished him to be.

In the meantime, Devadatta had hired bowmen to murder the Buddha. They attended some of the Sangha gatherings in the Deer Park to learn the routine of the Buddha so that they could carry out their deadly assignment. However, in mingling with the devout who came to hear the Buddha they were each impressed and, one by one, they became his followers. Thus Devadatta had to kill the Master alone.

The errant bhikkhu climbed the slopes of the Gijjhakuta mountain and waited for the Buddha to pass below. At the proper moment, Devadatta sent a large boulder hurtling down the cliff; but it struck a rocky ledge, and was splintered. Only a small portion fell on the Buddha's foot, causing a cut from which blood spurted. Fortunately, the physician Javaka was close by. He quickly attended the Master so that no permanent damage was done to the Buddha, who spent so many hours on his feet, walking, talking or alms gathering.

The evil nephew made still one more effort. He entered a village where there was a captive elephant. Infuriating it with liquor, so it was nearly crazed, he released it and drove it down the narrow street in which the Buddha stood. Ananda rushed forward to sacrifice his own life to save the Master's but the serene words of the Buddha immediately had a calming effect, and the usually docile and placid elephant quickly quieted down.

Many of the people in the village were aware of how Devadatta had intoxicated the elephant, tormented it, and driven it directly toward the Buddha. As a result, Devadatta became as unpopular outside the Sangha as within. King Ajatasattu no longer judged it prudent to befriend him, and broke off the alliance that previously existed.

Members of the Sangha now urged Buddha to renounce Devadatta, expelling him from the Sangha, but the Buddha serenely declined, pointing out that each bhikkhu determined whether he were a member of the order. It was not up to Buddha to pass judgment on his erring nephew; life itself would do that.

But Devadatta continued to brood and scheme how he might become important in the Sangha. He began again to talk about the leniency of the Master, saying that he was too tolerant, not severe enough to properly maintain the discipline of a religious order. Finally, at a gathering of the Sangha, he arose and publicly repeated this accusation, proposing that since the Buddha had not offered stringent enough regulations to guide the bhikkhus, the Sangha should adopt the following:

1. That all bhikkhus should live their entire lives in the forest.
2. They should live only on the alms each collected for himself.
3. That they should all desist in wearing robes made from fine cloth and henceforth wear only robes made from the rags collected at dustheaps and in cemeteries.
4. That each bhikkhu should choose a tree and live the rest of his life at its foot, departing only for *pindapāta.*
5. That henceforth they should be vegetarian, eating no flesh nor fish.

These were the rules of extreme asceticism, not those of the Sangha. It was obvious that Devadatta was seeking to change the nature of the order and of the Dharma offered by the Buddha. The followers of the Buddha were aghast at this proposal, but he was apparently not dismayed. He simply stated that all present had the opportunity to learn of the way of the Buddha, which leads to enlightenment. If any wished to live by the proposals of Devadatta they were free to do so.

Some newly ordained members of the Sangha held such beliefs, which were close to those of Mahavira and the Jains. These younger members joined with Devadatta, and he led his new found following to Gayasisa. After a fortnight, the venerable Sariputta and Mogallana traveled there to talk with the dissident bhikkhus. They found that after two weeks many were now ready to return to the Sangha. Thus the revolt of Devadatta collapsed. Left virtually alone, Devadatta fell upon evil days, and in the midst of his deepening depression, sickness overcame him. He sincerely repented and publicly stated that he wished to see Buddha once more; but he died a miserable death before this was possible. His last words were that he sought refuge in the Buddha.

When messengers came to tell Buddha, he showed great

compassion for his headstrong errant nephew, and reminded the Sangha not to think badly of him. Rather he urged them to recall his earlier years in the order when he sought to live a holy life, before greed and ambition captured him. Buddha then reminded his followers that one's good deeds are never fully lost, and that what good Devadatta had done in earlier days had gone before him, preparing the way for his future existence. Thus, he said, there was hope even for Devadatta, who in a future life might yet attain Nirvana.[4]

The swamis who had been bested by Buddha at Savatti made other attempts to discredit him. They entered into a pact with a band of assassins to murder a beautiful young lady named Sundari who had recently become a follower of the Master. She was waylaid one evening leaving the Jetavana grove, murdered, and her body thrown on the refuse heap. The swamis thereupon set up an outcry about what had happened to her. They claimed that she had been held captive by Buddha and had asked them for help. When her body was found, they instantly accused Buddha of murdering her to protect his reputation as a saintly one.

When the Buddha was asked to explain himself, he responded, "Anyone who declares something has happened which has not must accept the sad consequences of his evil action." The king's men in their investigation came upon the assassins, holding a drunken orgy with their ill-gained profits, bragging about their deed. They were taken before the king and incriminated the six swamis who were forced to walk through the city confessing their crime before their sentencing as murderers.

The Buddha, gracious and serene, turning aside attacks with soft words, still was sometimes misunderstood. One such occasion which brought years of unhappiness was created when the parents of a proud Brahman beauty, Magandiya, thought he would be the perfect husband for their lovely and winsome child. After all, the Buddha was renowned for his beauty also, as well as for the purity of his deeds and the nobility of his thoughts. Indeed they had seen where his imprint in the earth remained as a shrine. By offering Magandiya as his wife, they hoped to win his favor.

Buddha, taken aback by the offer, responded:

"I have seen the three daughters of the evil temptress and found no pleasure in them nor long I for the joys of love. Why should I desire this body you bring, which excretes urine and dung? If I were as pure as I long to be, I would not touch such, even with a foot."

Hearing his Dharma, the Brahman and his wife understood, but the daughter did not. She felt not only rejected but insulted. "If this man has no need of me, it is his right to say so, but he should not declare me filled with urine and dung. I shall not forget this. By virtue of my birth, lineage, social position, wealth and the charm of youth, I shall yet obtain a noble husband, and then I shall find out how to repay this monk Gautama." Her hatred grew with the passing months.

She went through life resentful, obsessed by a sense of wrong which she wished to right. When she became a consort to the King of Udena, she took advantage of her position in court to revile and denounce the Buddha at every opportunity.

When he entered the city, she started a campaign to have him driven out, and was responsible for those who followed him and his monks shouting, "You are a thief, a simpleton, a liar, a fool, a camel, an ox, an ass, a denizen of hell, and a beast. You have no hope of salvation and mislead the people. A state of punishment will be your only reward. Leave us alone!"

Ananda, hearing these cries against his Master, felt ashamed for his having to put up with these insults, and came to him in the evening saying, "Lord, these citizens are reviling and insulting you. Let us go elsewhere."

"Where shall we go, Ananda?" the Buddha asked.

"To another city, Lord."

"And if men revile or abuse us there, where shall we then go?"

"To still another city," responded Ananda.

"You should not speak thus, Ananda. Where the difficulties arise, there they should be settled. Only under circumstances where you have settled the issue are you free to go elsewhere. We must stay and have forebearance in this city. But who are they reviling, Ananda? Is it you that you should take offense?" responded the Buddha.

"Lord, they are reviling not only you but the Sangha as well."

"Then all of us should stay and accept the abuse, and if we do so with good grace and gentle responses, they will come to know who we are and what we offer. But you, Ananda, must begin by learning the virtue of patience, and the practice of it. As an elephant in the battlefield withstands the arrows shot from a bow, so will I endure abuse. But the undisciplined cannot.

"Look at the tournaments and take note. The disciplined will lead the trained horses and elephants to the assembly, and the king will mount the trained elephant. But the undisciplined will not avail; they will not endure the abuse heaped upon them.

"We are exalted by excellent mules, and the thoroughbred horses of Sindh, and the noble tusked elephants, but the man of discipline surpasses all."

In closing, the Buddha added, "I will be surprised if the taunts you now hear will last a week, particularly if our people follow the Middle Path." If he knew the cause of the trouble, he ignored it, and made no attempt to soothe the festering sore of Magandiya.[5]

As he had stated, the people came to accept Buddha in spite of the enmity of Magandiya. The following year, however, the discipline in the Sangha seemingly broke down, and the bhikkhus divided into two quarrelsome groups, each attacking or blaming the other for petty differences between them. The Buddha found his conciliatory words were not listened to, and so the thought occurred to him, "Why do I live here in a community among blockheads? Would it not be better to withdraw and live a solitary life in the forest, free of the problems existing here?" And so he left the Sangha and went to live alone in the woods.

Only after he was gone some time did the elders of the Sangha convince the members that they could not go on together without the Buddha. So they sent for him to return, assuring him they would live together in peace henceforth.

Upon returning the Buddha was walking in the country with his bowl when he came upon a wealthy Brahman landowner named Kasibharadvajasaw. The Brahman seeing him standing at the side of the road with his alms bowl accosted him saying, "I, O ascetic, plough and sow, and having ploughed and sown, I eat. You also, Ascetic, should plough and sow, and having done so you too could eat."

"I, too, O Brahman, plough and sow, and having ploughed and sown, I eat," responded the Buddha.

"But we do not see the Venerable Gautama's yoke, or plough, or ploughshare, or goad or oxen so how is it that you can say, 'I, too, plough and sow, and having ploughed and sown, I eat,'" retorted the Brahman. "A farmer you claim to be, but we see none of your acreage. Answer and describe to us how you plough, and what and where. Tell us of your crops and what they are."

The Buddha answered:

"Confidence is the seed, discipline is the rain, wisdom my yoke and plough, modesty the handle of my plough, mind the rein, and mindfulness ploughshare and goad.

"I am controlled in body and in speech, temperate in food. With truthfulness I cut away weeds. Absorption in the highest is my oxen.

"Perseverance is my beast of burden that carries me toward the bond-free state of Nirvana. Without turning I am carried, and having gone I do not grieve.

"Thus is the tilling done: it bears the fruit of Deathlessness. Having done this tilling, one is freed from all sorrow."[6]

The Buddha may have dismayed members of the Brahman caste by his alms seeking, his apparently non-productive life of living off the toilers of the earth, and he may have upset the merchants by draining off the youth who became his followers; but he distressed them for another reason. He accepted the untouchables as worthy converts, those who were without status in society, beneath the contempt of all other castes, who considered them fit only for the necessary duties of a society which did not want to soil its own hands. There are several accounts of how Buddha's universalism reached out to them.

On one occasion, as he and his followers were passing through the streets of the city, an untouchable was cleaning the sewers. Beholding the advancing ashram of a religious leader, this man slunk back into the shadows against the building, but he did not escape the Buddha's eye. Approaching him, the Buddha asked his name. Being told it was Sunita, he invited Sunita to come with them and leave his dirty work. Sunita replied joyfully, "Master, I would gladly follow you for you are the first one who has even spoken to me in a civil tongue, and with kindness."

The Buddha responded, "You are now my follower and henceforth of no caste, but are a member of the Sangha."

Such testimony against the caste system did far more than many sermons, and the members of the Sangha now found it necessary to accept an outcaste as one of them. This message was not lost on the Buddha's followers.

In Savatti one day, Ananda was returning to the Jetavana Park from alms begging when he saw a girl at a well. Being thirsty he approached her, and asked for a drink of water. The girl declined, saying she was an outcast, not worthy to serve water to one of higher caste.

Ananda replied, "Sister, I did not ask about your family or birth, but for water. Please give me some to drink." He then explained in conversation with her that all people were welcome to come to the Jetavana Park. She should come and there she would learn that rank meant nothing, only what one did with one's life. She became a devout follower of the Buddha and enamored of Ananda, to his own embarrassment. This was solved when Buddha summoned her to him, and in discoursing upon the golden mean, the Fourfold Path and the Eightfold Way, led her to be ordained.

To his followers such actions were seen as marks of his courage, but to others, such as the Brahman landowner, Kasisharadvajasaw, they were regarded as signs that this swami, or Buddha if one wished, was undermining the old ways and therefore dangerous to society.

But Buddha's universalism extended not merely to the rebels and the havenots. As we have seen, his message brought great solace to the wealthy and powerful. They could continue in the activities by which they flourished, so long as they purified their intentions, learned the meaning of the Four Noble Truths, and sought to practice the Eightfold Path leading to Nirvana. Of course, they could not follow paths the Buddha's way prohibited: murder, stealing, promiscuity, deceitfulness and intoxication. King Bimbisara and Anathapindika were two such wealthy followers.

What better example is there than the great merchant, Anathapindika? We already know much of what he did for Buddha, but what did the Buddha do for him?

Named at birth Sudatta, he became known by this more familiar name due to his great kindness toward the poor and helpless. In this he may have been moved by a discourse on generosity by the Buddha in which he stated that giving alms to the Sangha and the Buddha is very meritorious, but that giving alms for the building of a monastary for the use of the Order was more so, but that still more meritorious is seeking refuge in the Buddha, the Dharma and the Sangha, but still more is the observance of the five precepts. More so than that is meditation on loving kindness, but more so is the practice of loving kindness, but the most meritorious of all is insight into the fleeting nature of things, the doctrine of impermanence, of how all things change.

Thus Buddha pointed out that beginning with generous deeds, one must progress to spiritual insight, as one sought Nirvana. This was a course Sudatta desired.

In talks with Buddha, he was told of the four kinds of bliss a layman may enjoy apart from a monk. These are the bliss of ownership, the bliss of wealth, the bliss of debtlessness, and the bliss of blamelessness. Sudatta asked, "What is the bliss of ownership?"

The Buddha answered, "The householder whose wealth is acquired lawfully, by energetic striving may have bliss in reflecting that all this he has won."

"What is the bliss of wealth?"

"The clansman who, upon reflecting upon what he owns and has acquired lawfully, by his own efforts, uses that wealth to do meritorious deeds, thus comes to know the bliss of wealth."

"What is the bliss of debtlessness?"

"The clansman who owes no debt, great or small, who knows that he is free of obligation to any man, knows bliss, the bliss of debtlessness."

"What then is the bliss of blamelessness?"

"Here the ancient principle of Dharma enters, for one who is free of blame, blameless in body actions, blameless in speech and blameless in thought, will know the bliss of blamelessness, the satisfaction that brings repose:

> Winning the bliss of debtlessness a man
> May then recall the bliss of really having.
> When he enjoys the bliss of wealth, he sees
> It is such by wisdom. When he sees he knows.
> Thus is he wise indeed in both respects.
> But these have not one fraction of the bliss
> That comes to one of blamelessness."[7]

Such messages were an inspiration to Sudatta.

On another occasion, when the Buddha visited his house, he heard a great commotion, and inquired what was going on. Anathapindika responded, "Lord, it is my daughter-in-law, Sujata, who lives here with us. She is very rich in her own right, coming from a wealthy family. She pays no heed to her mother-in-law, nor to her father-in-law, nor to her husband. Further, she does not reverence or respect you as the Exalted One."

The Buddha asked if he might see her. He then discoursed with her on the seven types of wives he had noted in this world. They were:

"Those wicked in mind, ill-disposed, pitiless, fond of other men, neglecting their husbands, often prostitutes, and bent on harassing their families; these are called 'troublesome wives.'

"Those who squander whatever profits, though little, a husband has, or has gained by his craft, trade or plough; these are called 'thievish wives.'

"Those not inclined to action, lazy, gluttonous, harsh, cruel, users of foul language, domineering; these are called 'bossy wives.'

"Those who are kind, compassionate, protective of their husbands, family and household; these are called 'motherly wives.'

"Those who are respectful toward their husbands are like 'sisterly wives.'

"Those who rejoice in the husbands' presence and companionship are called 'friendly wives.'

"Those who endure all things, including harm and punishment, calmly, without anger, free from hatred, are called 'subservient wives.'

"Which, Sujata, of the seven kinds are you? The first three are undesirable wives, while the last four are good and praiseworthy because the husband can live with them. Which, Sujata, are you?"

"Lord, think of me who will be subservient from this day forward, a handmaiden to my husband," she responded.[8]

Fitting in, as this discourse did, with the commonly held attitudes of the subservient role of the women in the homes of that day, the Buddha's disciples often quoted it as showing the true relationship which should exist between men and women.

Anathapindika used to have daily visits with the Buddha when he was in Savatti, but all people were not so fortunate. So Anathapindika one day asked if it were not possible for devout followers, too humble to seek a meeting with the Buddha, or those who came when he was absent, to pay their respects in some concrete way that would bring them relief. Hearing this request, Ananda asked the Master if he might not plant a Bodhi Tree under which people could leave their offerings for the Buddha, particularly when he was absent on his preaching missions. The Buddha granted the request, and as a result the Ananda-Bodhi Tree was planted at the entrance to the monastery, becoming a longstanding shrine to the Buddha's ministry and memory in later days.

As the aged Anathapindika lay dying, Sariputta came to

him since the Buddha was on a distant preaching mission. When Sariputta entered, he asked the aged benefactor about his health, and was told it was not good, that he had a severe pain that was not improving. Sariputta preached a profound discourse on the entrance to Nirvana. It was so moving that tears came to Anathapindika's eyes. When asked if he were sinking, the merchant responded, "Not at all, Venerable Sir. Though I have long attended the Master's discourses, never did I hear such a one as this. It was magnificent."

"Such profound discourses are not taught to the white-robed laymen, but are reserved for the advanced disciples who can comprehend them," responded Sariputta. Thereupon Anathapindika, with practically his last breath, requested that such discourses not be reserved for the advanced student, but shared with all including the lay persons, who would gain by their insights.[9]

Later, in the Buddha's memorial oration to Anathapindika, one of his closest friends, the Master quoted words of the gods he had once heard:

> Goodwill and wisdom, mind by method trained,
> The highest conduct on good morals based,
> This maketh mortals pure, not rank nor wealth.[10]

Another great benefactor of Buddha was Visakha, a devout and generous daughter of Dhananjaya. She was an heiress of great fortunes in the kingdom of Anga. When she was seven years old, Buddha visited Bhaddiya, the capital city, and Visakha's grandfather took her, along with an entourage of five hundred handmaidens, to see the Buddha. She sat respectfully at the side while Buddha discoursed. After hearing the exposition of the Dharma, she was moved to deeper understanding, and from that time on took an interest in spiritual matters. She not only possessed all feminine charms but had great physical strength and ability. She had long hair reaching to her waistline, was beautiful in complexion, with sparkling eyes, and as she grew to womanhood, her figure was striking, her wisdom worldly and her insight spiritual.[11]

When she was fifteen or sixteen, she was on a picnic when

a rainstorm arose. All the others rushed for shelter, but Visakha, with self-possession, calmly followed the stampeding multitude to the shelter. She had been beheld by some Brahmans who had come to the park in search of a girl to recommend for courtship to a young master. The Brahmans criticized her for not rushing in out of the rain like the others, but she made a spirited defense of her actions, stressing the values of femininity, and proper decorum. She assured them that she could probably run as fast as any man if she chose to compete as an athlete. However, just as it was not becoming for a king dressed in his regal garments to go running through the courtyard, nor for an elephant to run in the crowded court, nor a monk to run through the streets of a city, so it was not fitting for a young lady to run helter skelter in from the rain.

The Brahmans were pleased with her answers, and reported back to Migara, the millionaire, that she was the most suitable maiden they had seen to become the wife of his son, Punnavaddhana. In time an elaborate marriage took place. She then moved to Savatti, the city of her husband, where she was close to the Buddha, although her husband and his family were not among his followers. Her generosity is attested by the fact that she returned gifts to all those who gave her wedding gifts, and distributed many of the gifts received to the poor.

Her father was a staunch follower of an ascetic leader named Nigantha Nstaputta. He and his followers were nudists, as part of their asceticism. When they came to visit Migara, he summoned Visakha in the middle of the night to come down to meet the Arahants who had honored their house. She was delighted with the news, thinking that by Arahants he meant members of Buddha's Sangha, and she hastily dressed and came down. She was unprepared for the presence of the naked ascetics, and showed her dismay, reproaching her father-in-law and immediately retired again. This created the first of a series of religious dissensions in the household. These were resolved only after she stood up to her father-in-law when he ordered her out of the house. However, she graciously absolved herself of any wrongdoing, displaying nothing but good intentions in her actions. Consequently, he forgave her. Then she told him she desired to leave of her own free will, but he had such a change of heart that he could not bear the thought of her departure. So she granted him pardon for the wrong he had done her previously, and he in turn agreed that she could follow her own religious desires.

Visakha now invited the Buddha to her home, and after dinner he offered her a sermon, as was his usual custom. Migara sat behind a curtain and listened to all he said. Thus he was converted to the Buddha's faith, wanting to assist Visakha in furthering the work of the Buddha.

Anathapindika had already built a monastery for the Sangha, but Visakha felt a separate one was needed for the women, and so decided to build a magnificent structure for the use of the female followers of the Buddha by the East Gate. She tried auctioning off a valuable garment. But no one could purchase it, so she bought it herself to make the money available. Then she was asked by Buddha to adjudicate disputes among the women, and help settle questions between the bhikkhus and bhikkhunis. The Buddha spoke many discourses to her concerning the role of women both in the Sangha (the Sasana) and as lay followers. When these were repeated they became the basis for his teachings especially meant for women.

In time she was recognized to be as important to the Sasana as Anathapindika was to the Sangha, and the chief benefactress and greatest female supporter of the Buddha. She lived a long life, raising ten boys and ten girls to maturity, and is described as one who was always graceful in deportment, courteous in speech, hospitable, and of a remarkable spiritual nature.

People such as King Bimbisara, Anathapindika and Visakha had much to do with the success of the Buddha's mission.

King Ajatasattu was seated with members of the royal court in the moonlight of the Lotus-Night[12] when the king sighed and uttered this plaintive call, "Fair indeed is this moonlight night, forsooth the night is fair, grand is the moonlight. What swami, what guru, what Brahman shall I go to hear tonight? Who is the teacher, the bhikkhu, who can cheer my soul?"

One counseler named this one, and another that, and when most had made a suggestion, the King of Magadha turned to his physician and said, "Javaka, why art thou silent, my friend?"

And the physician answered, "Sire, in my mango grove he resteth, the exalted one, the holy supreme Buddha, with a great group of his disciples. He is wise, the learned one, who knoweth the universe, who tameth man like the ox, the teacher of gods and of men. Sire, go to hear him, and perchance if thou seest him, the exalted one, thy soul may be refreshed."[13]

The king accordingly ordered his elephants and through the high moon of the Lotus-Night they rode to Javaka's mango grove to see the Buddha. Here it was that the Buddha again met King Ajatasattu after many years. It was their first encounter following the death of the Buddha's royal protector at the hands of this man. Buddha preached to him a sermon on the fruits of asceticism, so that Ajatasattu was uplifted and converted, and became a follower of the Buddha, who accepted him.

Who was Javaka, the physician who brought this about? Born of a prostitute, he had been thrown on the dung heap, and surrounded by crows. But he attracted the attention of a passing prince, half-brother to the young Ajatasattu. Prince Abhaya rescued the baby and named him Javaka Komarabhacca. As he grew he became a physician and skilled surgeon. It is related that he twice performed brain operations to relieve headaches, but he became most famous for being a follower of the Buddha, frequently traveling with him, and ministering to his needs. Thus when Devadatta's rock splintered and damaged the Buddha's feet, Javaka was nearby, ready to attend the injury. He had also built on his own property a monastery where the Buddha could stay.[14]

We have noted how the Buddha had strong attractions for

people of different classes, befriending the lowly and high caste, the poor and the wealthy, both men and women. We have seen him forgive wrongdoing and overlook evil. We have seen him speak strongly at times so that he hurt people, and yet we have seen the overpowering serenity of his basic nature. Should he be faulted for those whose waywardness he seemingly permitted, and on occasion prompted—as in his impatient rejection of the hand of a highborn gracious Brahman maiden who went through life stung by his insulting rejection? The world has tended to overlook such actions, placing them in the balance against all the good he performed and the countless lives he influenced for spiritual and ethical advancement.

TOWARD PERFECT UNDERSTANDING

As time passed, the nature of the Tathagata's progress, the fame and knowledge of his success spread not only through all India but in surrounding countries. Many came under the spell of his teachings. For the most part, however, his teaching was to the Sangha, to the monks who gathered about him. These were his special followers, and during the rainy season they would remain together in a great encampment, where they would discourse and instruct one another.

The Buddha paid attention also to the special needs of individual followers. Thus it was reported that on an occasion when the Blessed One was living near Rajagaha in the bamboo grove in the squirrels' feeding ground he heard that the Venerable Master Kassapa, staying in the Pipphali Cave, was gravely ill.

The Blessed One arose from his meditation at eventide and visited his old friend, Kassapa. Seating himself, the Master spoke to the Venerable bhikkhu, saying:

"Well, Kassapa, how is it with you? How are you bearing up and enduring your suffering? Do your pains increase or decrease? What are the indications: do you think you are improving or not?"

"No, Venerable Master, I am not bearing up. I am not improving; the pain is very great. There is no indication that the pain is decreasing, rather it gets worse."

"Kassapa, there are Seven Factors of Enlightenment which you need to set your mind upon. These are conducive to perfect understanding, to the attainment of Nirvana. You need to reflect upon the Four Noble Truths and upon the Seven Factors of Enlightenment. Now, what are the seven?

"First, there is mindfulness.

"Secondly, there is the investigation of the Dharma, Kassapa. To reflect upon the way of achieving Nirvana is conducive to perfect understanding and full realization.

"Thirdly, persevering effort, Kassapa, is required of anyone who would achieve enlightenment. This you have heard expressed by me; you have said it many times to others. Now you must practice it yourself if your condition is to improve and you are to overcome your pain, the manifestation of your suffering.

"Fourthly, enkindle your rapture, Kassapa. You know the need for delight and excitement in the daily experiences of life. Without rapture it will be hard to develop perfect understanding and find Nirvana. Keep up your spirit.

"Fifthly, you must maintain calm, Kassapa. Now is the time to use the fruits of your meditation and spiritual calmness if you are to overcome what must be.

"Sixthly, Kassapa, you need to maintain your concentration upon right values and right things, so that you can be fully enlightened.

"These six factors lead to the final one, which is the equanimity to accept with good grace what life has in store. Being at peace with life and with your lot will be a great help to you."

Then did Kassapa answer Buddha, "Most assuredly, Oh Blessed One, these are factors of enlightenment, factors which you do right in reminding me to follow."

Thus did the Blessed One instruct one of his eldest and dearest friends, comforting him in his illness and reminding him of the path to recovery from pain and suffering. He saw the need to set his mind back on the spiritual quest for serenity, which is Nirvana. He saw Kassapa's need for that right mindfulness by which he could set the priorities of life, of that rapture which maintains the spirit to live, of concentration which enkindles the will to live, and of that calm and equanimity which brings one into accord with the greater purposes of life so one does not fight against them. This is the way which leads to inner peace.

In similar manner did Buddha call upon the Venerable Mogallana when he too was ill, and on another occasion upon Cunada, the younger brother of the Venerable Sariputta, who as a long-time member of the Sangha fell ill. To all these monks, he gave personal attention, comfort and instruction in the seven factors leading to enlightenment.[1]

In a somewhat different way did the Buddha converse on the intricacies of the faith with Girimananda.[2] It was reported that on one occasion the Blessed One was living near Savatthi in the monastery of Anathapindika. At that time the Venerable Girimananda was afflicted with a disease and suffering grievously. Ananda, having visited him, came to the Buddha and said to him:

"Master, the Venerable Girimananda is afflicted with a disease, and suffers terribly therefrom. It were well, Master, if you out of compassion would visit him."

But the Buddha countered this suggestion by saying, "You, Ananda, should visit the monk Girimananda and recite to him the Ten Contemplations. If he takes them to heart and perfectly understands them, with full realization, then he will be able to cure himself of his disease."

"What are the Ten Contemplations?"

"Contemplation of impermanence.

"Contemplation of absence of a permanent self or soul, the doctrine of *anatta.*

"Contemplation of the profane nature of the physical world.

"Contemplation of danger, or of disadvantage.

"Contemplation of abandonment.
"Contemplation of detachment.
"Contemplation of cessation.
"Contemplation of distaste for the external world.
"Contemplation of impermanence of all component things.
"Mindfulness of in-breathing and out-breathing."

Ananda listened to the Master and sat locked in contemplation over his words. "And what is contemplation of impermanence?" he thought. As though Buddha read his mind, the Buddha spoke again:

"And what, Ananda, is contemplation of impermanence?

"Herein, Ananda, a monk having gone to a lonely place, contemplates this way: all matter which is made up of invisible objects is impermanent; feelings or sensations are impermanent; perception is impermanent; formations are impermanent; consciousness is impermanent. Reflect on this, Ananda."

Ananda considered the teachings of Buddha difficult for him to grasp. Matter, the Master taught, is not solid but is composed of many invisible objects clustered together to become visible. That visibility is seen only through the sensation of the eye, just as touch, smell, sound and feeling are all impermanent sensations, known to each individual, and perhaps perceived differently by each. Hence, the Master taught, all knowledge and all awareness are subjectively experienced; there is no way to be assured of their objective reality. Indeed, it is probable that there is no such thing as objective reality. Poor Ananda simply could not grasp this concept; it was too abstract for him. But he knew that for the Master and his chief disciples it was the most fundamental principle. All is impermanent, comprehended anew each moment in its changing flux and flow.

Then the Master continued: "And what, Ananda, is contemplation of *anatta,* of the principle that there is no permanent self, no soul?

"One must comprehend: the eye is not the self; visible objects are not the self; the ear is not the self; sounds are not the self; the nose is not the self; odors are not the self; the tongue is not the self; taste is not the self; the body is not the self; bodily contacts are not the self; the mind is not the self; mental agents are not the self; ideas and thoughts are not the self. Then where is the self? One must see that there is no self, that all is constantly changing as the sensations change, and hence one will contemplate that the self itself is impermanent. Consequently, one dwells contemplating 'not-self' in internal and external situations. This is what is meant by contemplation of anatta."

This was a thought with which Ananda, most loyal and faithful companion of the Buddha, had struggled for years. If there were no permanent self, then what was the self, this experience which he knew, this soul, this concern with birth and re-birth? Until now it had not yet made sense; only now was he beginning to understand it, as the Master instructed him on how he should instruct poor Girimananda.

After a pause, while Ananda reflected upon the Master's words, Buddha went on: "And what, Ananda, is contemplation of the profane?

"Herein, Ananda, a monk contemplates his body, upward from the soles of the feet, downward from the top of the hair, enclosed in skin, as being composed of many types of impurities—a composition of many profane particles, organs and parts. There are, for instance, in this body many component parts: head hairs, body hairs, nails, teeth, skin, flesh, sinews, bones, marrow, kidneys, heart, liver, pleura, spleen, lungs, intestines, intestinal tract, stomach, fecus, bile, phlegm, pus, blood, sweat, fat, tears, grease, saliva, nasal mucus, the oil lubricating the joints, and urine. Thus when he contemplates the body, he must contemplate all these component parts, many of which he cannot call sacred and holy, and all of which have elements repugnant to the sensitivities. In doing so he may come to understand that this body is not that desirable a possession, worthy of maintaining, and thus he should be free to let it go."

To Ananda this was the most blunt description of the body that he had ever heard. For the first time he began to understand what the Buddha meant when he spoke of the body as an unworthy vessel for the fire of life, a foulness from which life in time must be liberated. Now he was beginning to understand. He sat deep in thought until the Master broke the silence.

"What, Ananda, is contemplation of the dangers of life, of its disadvantages?

"Many are the sufferings, many are the disadvantages, many the dangers of this body, such as: eye disease, ear disease, nose disease, tongue disease, body disease, headache, mumps, mouth disease, toothache, cough, asthma, catarrh, heart-burn, fever, stomach ailment, fainting, dysentery, swelling, grips, leprosy, boils, scrofula, consumption, epilepsy, ringworm, itch, and many, many others; shall I go on? I have barely begun to list all the diseases that come to mind, and when I finish you no doubt could add still more. Sufficient is it not to say that the body, this life, is composed of many dangers for which each person born into this world must be prepared? It is as we have said in the Four Noble Truths: the existence of suffering abounds all about us, is always potentially within us, none can escape it. Thus one does well to contemplate the disadvantages of this life, fraught with many lurking internal dangers."

Again Ananda came closer to understanding than previously. He sat lost in contemplation as though for the first time he caught a glimmer of the internal dangers that made of life a path of misery.

Then Buddha continued, calling him back from his reverie to the moment. "And what, Ananda, is the contemplation of abandonment?

"Here it is that a monk does not tolerate the desire that has arisen in him, but expels it. He must make an end to such sensual desires that arise in his mind, annihilate them, eradicate them.

"He cannot tolerate a thought of ill will that arises within him, but must abandon it, annihilate it, eradicate it.

"He does not tolerate a thought of cruelty that arises in the mind, but must expel it, abandon it, annihilate it, eradicate it.

"He does not tolerate evil, those unprofitable states that arise in him from time to time, but abandons them, dispels them, annihilates them and eradicates them.

"All these unworthy or unprofitable desires that arise in the mind, the wise monk will abandon immediately, lest they corrupt him, turn backward the wheel of life. This, Ananda, is called the contemplation of abandonment."

Ananda thought of his own shortcomings, when he had not abandoned such sensual desires that arose, but succumbed to them, as with Pchiti, the beautiful young daughter of the prostitute Maudenka, with whom he became sexually involved.[3] He knew that sexual attraction was indeed impermanent, a delusion of a passing moment, not worthy of imperiling his eternal journey from the world of the present to the goal of Nirvana. He could not forget this moral lapse, this failure. Yes, indeed, such abandonment of unworthy desires is the course of wisdom.

The Buddha continued, "And what, Ananda, is the contemplation of detachment?"

"It is found when a monk goes to meditate at the foot of a tree, or in the forest, or at some lonely place. Finding here the fruits of solitude, his spirit uplifted, he says to himself, 'This is peaceful; this is sublime; herein with the stilling of all conditioned things, the giving up of all the substratum of becoming, the extinction of craving, and the cessation of striving, I have come to truly know myself.' This, Ananda, is what I mean by the contemplation of detachment."

Again, Ananda came closer to grasping the truth of nonattachment than previously. Buddha went on:

"What, Ananda, is the contemplation then of cessation?

"It is when the monk goes to the forest, sits at the foot of a tree, or in some other lonely place, and having detached himself from all sensations, from all material possessions, from wishes and desires, lets go, and says, 'This is peaceful, this is sublime, this stilling of all component parts, this giving up of all substratum of becoming, this extinction of all craving and sensation, this is truly to know Nirvana!' This, Ananda, is called contemplation of cessation."

"The one leads to the other," thought Ananda. But before he fell into deep meditation upon the Master's words, Buddha continued:

"Ananda, what is the contemplation of distaste for the whole world?

"It is simply, Ananda, the abandonment of any desire to cling to this world. It is the abandonment of mental prejudice, wrong beliefs, and latent tendencies concerning this world. It is to surrender that which binds one to this world, which stops one's forward progress from existence to existence. By not grasping that which can hold one too tightly to this world, one is free for a greater liberation. This, Ananda, is what I mean by the contemplation of the distaste for the whole world."

The Buddha, speaking so long, now cleared his throat. He reached for a dipper of water and continued:

"What now, Ananda, is meant by contemplation of the impermanence of all component objects? You should now be able to tell me, but let me put it simply:

"It is to understand all that I have now said about the first eight areas of contemplation. It is to be wearied and disgusted by all conditioned things. It is to see the transitoriness of all sensations, to long for the release that is offered, to seek liberation from the chains that bind one to the temporal and material and personal relationships of this life. This, Ananda, is what is meant by contemplation of the impermanence of all component parts. To understand this is to know freedom."

The Buddha now looked intently at his follower, and asked: "Finally, Ananda, what is mindfulness of in-breathing and out-breathing? It is the yoga practice of contemplation. There is no mystery to it. It is simply clearing one's being of all component parts, and the reducing of one's physical activity to one single exercise, always mindful of what is involved. Here it is that the monk, whether at the foot of a tree, in the forest or grove, or elsewhere, in either a lonely place or a central gathering, is able to sit in solitude, cross-legged, back erect, his mindfulness alive, all external sensations barred from his thought, knowingly breathing in and knowingly breathing out.

"When breathing in a long breath he knows, 'I am breathing in a long breath'; when breathing in a short breath he knows, 'I am breathing in a short breath'; and when breathing out a short breath he knows, 'I am breathing out a short breath.' He is conscious of the entire process, saying to himself, 'I shall breath in, and I shall breath out.' In this way he trains himself.

"He brings calm to his entire being as he says, 'I shall breath in, or out. Experiencing rapture, I shall breath in or out.' The same goes for bliss, for the experience of mental formations, for the calming of mental formations, for the mind in its activity, for gladdening the mind, for concentrating the mind and for liberating the mind. In such circumstances the man of contemplation is able to separate himself from all external considerations, from all internal sensations, and simply concentrates upon his breathing in or out, long or short. Thus he has freed himself from all temporal considerations and petty concerns.

"This, Ananda, is called mindfulness of in-breathing and out-breathing. If you, Ananda, visit the monk Girimananda and recite to him these ten contemplations, he can be cured immediately from his anxieties and freed from his afflictions."

After having learned these Ten Contemplations from the Buddha, the Venerable Ananda visited Girimananda and recited them to him. When the monk heard them, he was cured of his afflictions, seeing how inconsequential were the ailments that had troubled him, and how easy it was to learn to free oneself therefrom. Likewise, Ananda, always the most shy and subservient of the inner circle of Buddha's followers, found new confidence, deeper insight and better awareness regarding the path of Nirvana. By sending him, the Blessed One helped two, not one.

In order that they might understand the true nature of life, Buddha tried to impart to his followers in various ways the transitoriness of all manifestations of reality. At Isigili, for instance, he stood in the foothills of the Isigili Mountain near Rajagaha, and pointing to the peak said, "Do you, monks, see this Isigili Mountain?"

And they replied, "Yes, Master."

"There is another name for this mountain, monks. It is also known as the Vebhara Mountain. Do you recognize it as the Vebhara Mountain?"

And they nodded in agreement. Then said the Buddha:

"Do you monks know that this Vebhara Mountain is also called the Pandava Mountain?"

"Yes, Master."

"There is yet another name for this Pandava Mountain. It is called the Vepulla Mountain. Do you recognize it as the Vepulla Mountain?"

"Yes, Master."

"There is still another name for this Vepulla Mountain. It is called the Gijjhakuta Mountain. Do you see it as the Gijjhakuta Mountain?"

They agreed they saw it as the Gijjhakuta Mountain.

"There is another name for this Gijjhakuta Mountain. It is the Isigili Mountain. Do you see this Isigili Mountain?" again asked the Buddha, and they responded, "Yes."

"This has been the very name, the very name, monks, for this mountain, but in the past it has been called by many names. As I have mentioned, it still can be called by any of these names. Over five hundred holy men have lived on this mountain, and to some people it is called by the one name, and by others by a different name. All of these holy men were visible when they entered the mountain, but in time they became invisible. It has been named for one or another, but in time since none of the holy men remained, the people said, 'This mountain has swallowed the holy men who came to it, hence because it makes invisible the seers who sought it out (*isigilati*) it shall be called the Isigili Mountain.'

"So you may call it by one name or by another, but regardless of the designation, is it not the same mountain? So it is with the sensation of reality. It comes according to one's own experience of it, but does that make it the same or different to each one? What matters if one says it is the Vebhara Mountain, or the Pandava, or the Vepulla, or the Gijjhakuta, or the Isigili Mountain? Does the mountain change with the appellation, or merely the name change? Is it not in truth always the same mountain, which like the seers it swallowed up, can be both visible and invisible, named for one, named for another, or named for the manifestation observed here? It is always the same, yet different to each according to his own history of the mountain."

Thus he sought to teach that the stability observed in life is but a transitory illusion, different for each regardless of the name applied.[4]

Again he spoke to the Sangha at Savatti concerning what he called the aggregates, the particles which make up the whole. He said:[5]

"Develop concentration, bhikkhus, for one who is concentrated understands according to actuality. And what does one understand according to actuality? He understands the extinction of the body, the origin and extinction of feeling, the origin and extinction of perception, the origin and extinction of mental activities, and the origin and extinction of consciousness.

"The body, bhikkhus, is transitory. Suffering is transitory. Suffering is not-self. What is not-self? It is what we mean when we say 'This is not myself'; 'This is not mine'; 'I am not this.' By understanding this one is on the path to perfect wisdom.

"Feeling is transitory. So is perception, mental activity, consciousness. All these lead to suffering. They are not-self.

"As I have said, the body is not permanent. That which is the cause, that which is the condition, for the appearance of the body is also impermanent. That which is produced by the impermanent cannot be permanent. Feeling, perception, mental activity and consciousness, all these are impermanent. Accordingly, monks, we should understand that one should be dispassionate toward the body, toward feelings, toward perceptions, toward mental activities and toward consciousness.

"Before my enlightenment, bhikkhus, when I was unenlightened, a striving monk and ascetic, I thought, 'What is the satisfaction and misery regarding the body and the release from it? What is the satisfaction and misery in regard to feeling, to perception, to mental activity, to consciousness, and the release from them?'

"And then, monks, this occurred to me: whatever happiness and pleasure arises from the body, this is the body's satisfaction. Whatever there is of impermanence, suffering and changeability in the body, this is the misery of the body. Whenever one can rid oneself of desire and attachment in regard to the body, this is the release from the body. The logic is clear-cut.

"Whatever consciousness and pleasure arises dependent upon feeling, perception, mental activity, consciousness, this is the satisfaction of consciousness. Whatever there is of impermanence, suffering and changeability in consciousness, this is the misery of consciousness. Whenever one can rid oneself of desire and attachment in regard to consciousness, this is the release from consciousness.

"You see, as long as I did not know satisfaction as satisfaction, misery as misery, and release from the five aggregates of grasping as release from them according to actuality, I remained unenlightened.

"But when I knew satisfaction as satisfaction, misery as misery, and release from grasping at the five aggregates as release according to actuality, I became enlightened. When one rises above all consciousness, all aggregates, all misery, all satisfaction, all cessation, then one becomes enlightened."

Again, at Savatti, he taught his followers saying, "What is not yours, renounce it. Renouncing it will be to your good, to your happiness. And what, I ask, is not yours? The body is not yours. Feeling is not yours. Perception is not yours. Mental activities are not yours. Consciousness is not yours. Therefore renounce all these attributes, my bhikkhus, for to renounce them will be to your own good, to your happiness, to your serenity.

"It is as if a person were to carry away and burn the grass, the twigs, branches, and foliage in this Jetavana grove. Would it occur to you to say, 'This person is carrying us away, is burning us, is doing as he pleases with us?'"

"Certainly not, Master."

"For what reason?"

"Because, Lord, this is not ourselves nor what belongs to us."

"So it is, bhikkhus, with the body; it is not yours. Renounce it, and in renouncing it you will act for your own good, to your happiness. In like manner feelings are not yours, nor is perception, nor mental activities, nor consciousness. Renounce them to your own good.

"A Tathagata is a fully enlightened person, and being perfect in his knowledge, develops a dispassion for the body, detachment from the body, cessation of craving for the body. Thus he becomes a fully liberated person. He may be said to be 'liberated without grasping,' because he is liberated by wisdom and has ceased to cling to the body and its sensation."

And the monks murmured, some saying, "For us, Sir, such things originate with you. We have only you for our guide since we have not achieved perfect wisdom. Explain to us the meaning of this teaching. Having heard the Lord expound it, perhaps we can remember it."

"Then listen, bhikkhus, attend carefully and I will speak."

They answered, "We listen." And the Master explained,

"The Tathagata is a perfected, a fully Enlightened One, who makes manifest a previously unmanifested path. He recognizes an unrecognized path. He proclaims an unproclaimed path. He is the knower of the path, the discoverer of the path, and is skilled in the way to walk the path. Later, bhikkhus, his followers will come after him, and walk in that path, now manifest, now recognized, now proclaimed, now known."

After he had finished the bhikkhus talked about it among themselves. When they assembled again, the Venerable Radha approached the Lord, prostrated himself before the Lord, and sat down on one side. Then sitting at the side of the

Lord, the Venerable Radha said, "How can we know, Lord, how can we see, that in this consciousness-endowed body and externally among all other objects there is no ego, no I-ness, no mine-ness, no underlying tendency to conceit and egotism?"

"Whatsoever feeling, perception, mental activity, consciousness, past, present or future, internal or external, gross or subtle, inferior or superior, far or near, Radha, all of these we should look upon as 'not-mine.' We should say, 'This is not mine. This is not myself. I am not this.' All we do is visualize, perceive, feel conscious of that which is not, of that which appears to be. But we have no method of verifying its existence. Since the nature of all that appears to be is transitory, we must comprehend that it exists only in our perception, a perception which passes in the instant of perceiving. Thus knowing, thus seeing, in this consciousness-endowed body, there is no I-ness, no mine-ness, no underlying tendency to ego or conceit, no proof of the existence of an external actuality."

"Then the Venerable Radha arose, and went into the grove to meditate alone, pondering and reflecting upon this message. Here he soon realized through his own direct knowledge the unique quest for the holy life, for which sons and daughters of good families rightly go forth from home to the homeless state, hoping to discover the path to Nirvana. Now he knew: finished is birth; finished is suffering; finished is illusion. He lived in the holy life, doing what had to be done, knowing there is no more of this or that state. And thus did the Venerable Radha become one of the Perfect Ones.

Yet the Buddha, realizing how difficult it was to grasp this principle, persisted in his teaching. One day, as he instructed the Sangha in the Noble Path, he said, "I am being consumed by the body now, just as in the past I was consumed by the body. If in the future I should have any expectation of pleasure from the body, so in the future I would be consumed by the body just as I am now in the present. Truly, I have no longing for the body of the past, and no expectation of pleasure from a body in the future. In the present I must cultivate dispassion, detachment, cessation. There is no other path to liberation from the bondage to life.

"What do you think, bhikkhus? Is the body permanent or impermanent?"

"Impermanent, Sir."

"Is that which is impermanent satisfying or dissatisfying?"

"Dissatisfying, Sir."

"Now, what is of a changeable nature is such a substance suitable to be regarded as 'This is mine, I am this, this is myself?'"

"No, Sir."

"Therefore I repeat what I have told you before; separate yourself from attachment to the body, delight of the sense, appetites and cravings for material and sensual things. Then you will find serenity."

Again the Master spoke with his followers, saying in answer to a question, "I do not dispute with the world, bhikkhus. The world disputes with me. A proclaimer of Dharma does not dispute with anyone in the world. What is not believed by the acknowledged wise of the world, of that I too say, 'it is not so.' What is believed by them, I am inclined to accept also.

"And what is it, bhikkhus, that is not believed by the wise of the world and of which I say, 'It is not so?' The philosophers and scientists say that the body, the feelings, perception, mental activities, consciousness are not permanent, stable, or eternal. They all agree that these things are but passing substance and shadows of an unseen actuality. With this I agree:

"There is, bhikkhus, a world condition to which the Tathagata has fully awakened. Just as the water lily or a blue lotus or even a white lotus, born in water, growing in water, having risen above the surface of the water stands unwetted by the water, similarly the Tathagata, brought into the world and conquering the world, lives unsullied by the world. So you, through perfect wisdom, may rise above it."

Then the Venerable Malunkyaputta, having been in seclusion for a long period of time, rejoined the Sangha, saying to himself,[6] "Certain theories which the Master has put aside and left unexplained trouble me. He has dealt with the present, but does not answer the question whether the world is eternal or not eternal, whether the world is either finite or infinite, whether the soul and the body are identical, whether the soul is one substance and the body another, whether one who has obtained perfection exists or does not exist after death, whether there is immortality. These questions the Blessed One does not explain to me. And the fact that the Master does not explain them to me, nor deal with them, displeases me. Therefore I will take myself to him, and ask for guidance." Thus the Venerable Malunkyaputta arose at eventide from his seclusion and joined those who gathered about the Blessed One. Having drawn near and greeted the Master, he sat down respectfully at one side, and so seated, the Venerable Malunkyaputta spoke to the Blessed One as follows:

"Reverend Sir, it appeared to me as I meditated in seclusion that there are theories which the Blessed One has left unexplained. It is as though he has set aside or rejected such questions as these: is the world eternal or not eternal; do these who obtain perfection either live or not live after death? I desire answers to such questions. If the Blessed One can explain them to me, then I will continue to lead a religious life, but if he cannot, I will abandon religious training and return to the lower life of a layman."

"Pray, Malunkyaputta, did I ever say to you, 'Come, lead the religious life under me, and I will explain to you either that the world is eternal or not eternal, or that the saintly exist after death or do not exist after death?"

"No, Reverend Sir."

"Or did you ever say to me, 'Reverend Sir, I will lead the religious life upon the condition that the Blessed One will explain to me either that the world is eternal or not eternal, or that the saintly exist after death or do not?"

"No, Reverend Sir."

"So you acknowledge that I have never spoken to you about such teachings. That being so, vain man, why are you angry that I have not given such teaching, and so accuse me?

"Malunkyaputta, anyone who can say 'I will not live the religious life under the Blessed One until the Blessed One shall explain such questions to me,' will die, Malunkyaputta, before the Tathagata has ever explained this to him.

"It is as if a man had been wounded by a poison arrow, and his friends, and kinsfolk were to procure for him the best physician available. But the sick man were to say, 'I will not have this arrow removed until I have learned whether the man who wounded me belonged to the warrior caste, the Brahman caste, the agricultural caste, or the menial caste.'

"Or again were to say, 'I will not have this arrow removed until I know the name of the archer.'

"Or to say such trivial things, one after another as, 'It shall not be removed until I know the size of the marksman, or what village he came from.'

"That man would die, Malunkyaputta, without ever having learned these answers. In exactly the same way, anyone who says, 'I shall not lead the religious life until I know the answer to all questions concerning the nature of the world, and of immortality,' that person would die, Malunkyaputta, before he could find the answers.

"The religious life does not depend upon any dogma, and whether any dogma is true or not, pertains or not, does not really matter. Whether the world is eternal or not, or whether immortality exists or not, is beside the point. For there still remain birth, old age, death, sorrow, lamentation, misery, grief, and despair. I can prescribe for the extinction of these things, and this makes for a religious life.

"Therefore, Malunkyaputta, bear always in mind what it is that I have explained and not explained. Now, what, Malunkyaputta, have I not explained? I have not explained whether the world is eternal or not eternal; I have not explained whether the world is finite or infinite; I have not explained whether the soul and the body are identical or not; I have not explained whether the soul is one thing and the body another; I have not explained whether the saintly exist after death, or not. And why have I not explained these things? Because these issues profit not, nor have they anything to do with the fundamentals of religion.

"And what have I explained? Misery, Malunkyaputta, have I explained; suffering; the origin of suffering have I explained; the cessation of suffering have I explained; and the path leading to the cessation of suffering have I explained. And why, Malunkyaputta, have I explained these? Because this does profit a person; it does have to do with the fundamentals of religion; it does tend to the absence of passion, calmness, knowledge, supreme wisdom and Nirvana; therefore have I explained the Fourfold Truth of suffering. Therefore, Malunkyaputta, bear always in mind what it is that I have explained, and what it is that I have not explained."

AS TIME GOES ON

The most important of the Buddha's teachings was the means of relief from suffering. To find this release one has to let go of the attractions that bind one to the physical world. But what is the world? Once this question was asked of Buddha by Ananda, and the Tathagata answered, making a play on the Sanscrit words.

"You ask me what the world (*loka*) is. You ask, 'In what sense, sir, is it called the world?' and I answer:

"Whatever is of a nature to dissolve (*paloka*), Ananda, this is called the world (*loka*) in the discipline of the Noble Truths. Now what is of a nature to dissolve? The eye, Ananda—visible objects, visual consciousness, visual contact. Or take the mind—whatever arises conditioned by contact with the mind; whatever is felt as pleasant, or painful, or neutral—All these are of the nature to dissolve."

Then Punna stood up and said, "It would be good, Sir, were the Lord to teach me the Dharma briefly. Then I might live in seclusion—diligent, ardent, resolute."

The Master responded, "There are, Punna, visible objects recognized by the eye; sounds recognized by the ear; mind-objects recognized by the mind; things pleasing, agreeable, charming, endearing, desirable, arousing to passion. If a bhikkhu delights in them, welcomes them, cleaves to them, enjoyment of them arises. This origin of enjoyment is also the origin of suffering.

"But if a bhikkhu does not delight in them, does not seek them out, does not desire their pleasures, does not cleave to them, then that enjoyment ceases and that bhikkhu is liberated from their allurements, freed of the danger of the misery they bring."

The Buddha further taught his followers saying, "Bhikkhus, whatever there is of desire and attachment to the body, that is a corruption of the mind.

"Whatever there is of desire and attachment to feeling, that is a corruption of the mind.

"Whatever there is of desire and attachment to perception, that is a corruption of the mind.

"Whatever there is of desire and attachment to mental activities, that is a corruption of the mind.

"But, bhikkhus, when a bhikkhu has abandoned mental corruption with regard to these five, his mind is inclined toward renunciation. A mind filled with the thought of renunciation is fit to receive those things realized by direct knowledge, and find liberation from all inferior, all interior, all exterior snares."

Then one day at the Jeta grove in Savatti, a man stood up and questioned the Buddha:

"Those living in the forest,
Peaceful and calm of pure life,
Eating but one meal a day:
How is it they appear so radiant?"

And the Lord answered:

"They sorrow not for what is past,
They have no longing for the future,
The present is sufficient for them:

Hence it is they appear so radiant.
By having longing for the future,
By sorrowing over what is past,
By this fools are withered up,
As a cut down tender reed."

Another stood up and responded, "But those whom you extoll know no bliss." And then one of the bhikkhus responded,

"Fool, you know not the Arahant's saying:
Impermanent are all conditioned things,
Of a nature to arise and then decay.
Having arisen, they soon cease;
To be relieved of them is bliss."

But another tempter responded,

"Possessing children one finds pleasure in them,
A herdsman is pleased with his cattle;
Man's possessions bring pleasure to him,
Without possessions he finds no pleasure."

Then the Buddha answered:

"Possessing children one grieves for them,
A herdsman worries for his cattle;
Man's possessions bring grief to him,
Without possessions he has no grief."

But these who were challenging him were not ready to stop, and one continued, asking,

"Who is a good companion?
What is it that instructs him?
And what does a mortal enjoy
When released from all suffering?"

The Master responded,

"Faith is a good companion;
It is wisdom that instructs him,
And enjoying Nirvana a mortal
Is released from all suffering."

And the first tempter challenged again:

> "By what is the world led?
> By what is it defiled?
> And what is that one thing
> Controlled by which all follow?"

The Buddha answered:

> "The world is led by craving;
> By craving is it defiled,
> And craving is that one thing
> Controlled by which all follow."

Standing on one side, Kamada whispered in a harsh voice, meant only for himself, "It is difficult to do, Lord, very difficult to do!" But the Buddha heard him and responded,

> "Yet what is difficult to do they do—
> These disciples virtuous with collected minds.
> For those who enter into the homeless state
> There is contentment bringing bliss."

Then Kamada spoke loudly, "It is difficult to attain, Lord, this contentment!" And Buddha,

> "Yet what is difficult to attain they attain,
> Those devoted to stilling the mind.
> For them both day and night
> The mind delights in meditation."

"It is difficult, Lord, to concentrate the mind!" replied Kamada, and the Lord answered:

> "Yet what is difficult to concentrate they concentrate,
> Those devoted to controlling the sense,
> Breaking through death's net those
> Noble Ones walk freely, Kamada."

"It is difficult, Lord, going on an uneven path!" Kamada continued to insist, but the Buddha responded again:

> "Yet along this uneven path they walk,
> Those Noble Ones, Kamada.

On the uneven the ignoble fall headlong,
But the way becomes even for the Noble,
For over the uneven they walk evenly."[1]

It will be recalled that the Sangha and those interested in hearing the Buddha followed an annual, predictable cycle. In India the rainy season extends from July to November, and during this period it was impossible for the bhikkhus to travel throughout the villages and cities. Accordingly, they usually stayed at Savatti in the Jetavana Park, Benares in the Deer Park, or in Rajagaha at the bamboo grove. It was at such an encampment in the Jetavana Park that the above exchanges took place.

This prompted the senior bhikkhu, the Venerable Sariputta, to implore the Buddha to prepare a manual of discipline and teachings, so that the answers he gave would not be forgotten. Some of the older members had already died and others were aging and sickly.

"Patience, Sariputta, have patience," murmured the Buddha. "I will know when the time has come for such action. The Tathagata alone is aware of the time for it. Until certain defiling conditions arise in the Sangha, the Tathagata does not promulgate a manual of discipline for the disciples, nor does he lay down the Fundamental Precepts. When such defiling conditions come to exist in the Sangha, then it will be time to promulgate such rules and orders in order to eradicate such defilements. Happy are we that we now live in freedom.

"Until, Sariputta, the Sangha attains long standing, full development, worldly increase, argumentative contentiousness, and pompousness in erudition, defiling conditions will not have arisen in the Sangha. When they do, the Tathagata shall act, eradicating the defilements.

"Sariputta, the Sangha is now free from troubles, devoid of evil tendencies, free from stain, pure and well-established in virtue. Even Ananda, the last of my five hundred 'stream winners,'[2] is not liable to fall. Steadfast, and destined for enlightenment, we move ahead in concord."

The Buddha accepted a well-known criminal and fighter

into his order after a conversation with him in the woods. This man, Angulimala, was a distraught person. Though he strove for acceptance, he did so through violent actions, having a misconception of the right path to follow. The peace and serenity of the Buddha walking through the woods calmed him, so that his good Karma emerged. He threw away his armor and weapons, becoming a convert. When news spread that this fierce criminal was now a quiet monk, relief swept the countryside, and the King of Kosala, whose land he had terrorized, was greatly pleased.

Later, referring to his conversion, Angulimala recited these lines, as he taught others:

> "Some creatures are subdued by force,
> Some by hooks, and some by whips,
> But I by such a One was tamed
> Who needed neither staff nor sword."

It was observed by close followers that while the Buddha went forth to tame and convert the robber and murderer, Angulimala, and the wicked Alavaka, he was sought out by pious young Visajja, generous millionaire, Anathapindika, and intellectuals such as Sariputta and Mogallana. In fact, he was available for all manner of persons seeking relief and help.

Kings came to him for aid or counsel, and were among his most loyal supporters. King Bimbisara, his repentant son, King Ajatasattu, King Pasenadi of Kosala and his son, King Maha Kosala, not to mention his own father, the wise and just King Suddhodana, all are among those who sought his advice.[3]

Later in the Buddha's life, King Ajatasattu contemplated a war with the prosperous Vajjian Republic, but not certain of the wisdom of the assault, sent his Prime Minister to seek the counsel of Buddha, who responded:

"As long as the Vajjians meet frequently and hold many meetings;

"As long as they meet together in unity;

"As long as they enact nothing not already enacted; abrogate nothing that has already been enacted, and act in accordance with the already established Vajjian principles;

"As long as they support, respect, venerate and honor the Vajjian elders, and pay regard to their counsel and words;

"As long as children and women are not enslaved by them;

"As long as they respect, honor, venerate these objects of worship—internal and external—and do not neglect the customary ceremonies held traditionally;

"As long as the country continues to give customary protection and freedom to the bhikkhus and swamis who traverse its roads and instruct its people;

"So long may the Vajjians be expected not to decline but to prosper." The Prime Minister, after hearing this declaration of Vajjian strength from the Buddha, returned to Rajagaha and counseled the king against an invasion.

Then the Buddha discussed the situation and his counsel with the Sangha, noting that there were similar lessons for them, reminding them that the Sangha had similarities to the Vajjian Republic. He thereupon stated:

"As long, O disciples, as the bhikkhus assemble frequently and hold regular meetings;

"As long as the bhikkhus meet together in unity, rise in unity, and perform the duties of the Sangha in unity;

"As long as the Sangha shall promulgate nothing that has not already been promulgated by them; abrogate nothing which has been in effect; and act in accordance with the already recognized rules;

"As long as the bhikkhus support, respect, venerate and honor the long ordained and understood rules growing out of experience and consensus, following the senior members of the Sangha and respect the words and guidance of the senior disciples;

"As long as the bhikkhus remain unattached to worldly ways and sensations that destroy their independence of achievement of Nirvana;

"As long as the bhikkhus delight in forest dwelling;

"As long as the bhikkhus develop mindfulness within themselves so that they may continue to live in peace with one another;

"So long may the Sangha not be expected to decline but to prosper."

The Buddha now seemed intent on enlightening the Sangha regarding the future. Sariputta was delighted. Their ranks were rapidly being depleted of the original disciples, the "first five" whom Buddha knew before his enlightenment, and to whom he preached in the Deer Park in Benares. The close associate of Sariputta and his lifelong friend, Mogallana, had recently died. The Buddha's son, Rahula, who had been seen a perfect example of his father's teaching—meek, soft-spoken, and devout—had died quietly in his sleep. They were all worried about the Venerable Kassapa, who had been sick for a long time, and there were others whose health was failing, including Sariputta himself, the acknowledged leader of the Sangha.

Accordingly he was pleased that the Buddha was not addressing himself to guidelines for the future of the Sangha. On a number of occasions Buddha had said that the Sangha and the rule they promulgated of the Four Noble Truths, the Middle Way and the Eightfold Path might last for five hundred years. Sariputta, the thoughtful, knew that it required a discipline and rule of order to insure that this would happen.[4]

The Buddha discussed again the rules he had recently enunciated, and then added these thoughts concerning the future:

"As long as the bhikkhus shall not be fond of, or delight in, or engage in business;

"So long as the bhikkhus shall not be fond of, or delight in, or engage in gossiping or bearing false witness against one another;

"So long as the bhikkhus shall not be fond of, or delight in, or engage in daytime sleeping, becoming slothful, lazy and indigent;

"So long as the bhikkhus shall not be fond of, or delight in, or engage in the life of high society, over-socialization with the outside world to the neglect of their responsibility to expound the law;

"So long as the bhikkhus shall not be fond of, delight in, or fall under the influence of base desires;

"So long as the bhikkhus shall not be fond of, or delight in, or engage in cultivating evil friends whom they flatter and follow, so that they become prone to evil themselves;

"So long as the bhikkhus shall not stop at the halfway stations on the path to Nirvana, not be content to stop short of achieving Arahantship:

"So long shall the Sangha continue."

Afterward, the Buddha added that as long as the bhikkhus remained devout, modest, conscientious, mindful and full of wisdom, so long could they expect the order not to decline but to prosper.

So pleased was Sariputta that as he walked with Buddha and Ananda while traveling from Rajagaha to Nalanda, Sariputta extolled the wisdom of the Buddha, singing out, "Lord, so pleased am I with the Exalted One that I think there never was, nor will there ever be, nor is there anywhere else in the world, a Buddha as enlightened as you; surely you are the greatest of all time!"

The Buddha turned on him, exclaiming, "Sariputta, I presume you have known all the Buddhas of the past since time began, so that you are qualified to proclaim which is the greatest?"

"No, Lord."

"Then you know all the Buddhas of the present, not only in our own countries, but beyond the seas, in distant realms? Accordingly you are able to say from knowledge who is the greatest today?"

"No, Lord."

"Then perhaps you know all the Buddhas of the future and are able to pass judgment proclaiming which is the greatest of all time?"

"No, Lord."

"Then, Sariputta, you are not qualified to compare the Buddhas and pass judgment on which is the greatest. It behooves you, Sariputta, to think carefully of your words, and not make extravagant claims that you cannot defend or justify. It is not fitting that my chief exponent be so extravagant. It is wise that at all times we make no vain claims, but rather perform our duties, allowing the people and time to be the judge, and for the fruits of our work to prove themselves."[5]

Once when the Buddha was staying in the neighborhood of Bhaggas at the crocodile haunt in the Bhesakala Grove, an aged householder, Nakulapita, came to the Buddha and spoke these words to him: "Lord, I am a decrepit old man, aged, far gone in years. I have reached the last stage of my life, and am sick in body and always ailing. It is rare that I get an opportunity to see the Exalted One, and the monks traveling with him. Will the Exalted One instruct me so that it will be conducive to my well-being and happiness for a long time to come?"

The Buddha responded, "True it is, true indeed, householder, that your body is sickly and encumbered by age. For who, householder, would claim even a moment's health carrying about such a body, except through sheer foolishness? Therefore, householder, you should train yourself to think, 'Though my body is sick, my mind shall not be sick.'"

Then Nakulapita rejoiced in those words of wisdom, and arose and went about proclaiming the extreme wisdom of the Buddha. In doing so, he finally approached Sariputta, who invited the elderly gentleman to be seated. Then Sariputta said to the householder, "Clear are your faculties and jubilant your spirit today, Nakulapita. Your complexion is radiant. Have you had the opportunity today to discuss the Dharma with the Exalted One?"

"Indeed I have. How could it be otherwise, venerable sir? I have indeed been sprinkled with the holy nectar of talk on the Dharma by the Exalted One! I asked him questions that trouble me about my advancing age and growing poor health, and the Exalted One spoke words of wisdom to me, saying, 'Train yourself, householder, to think that though your body is sick, your mind shall not be sick.' It is the most marvelous of teachings and I rejoice that the Buddha gave it to me."

"But did it not occur to you, householder, to question the Exalted One further? Did it not occur to you to ask, 'Pray, how far, Lord, is body sick and mind not sick?'"

Nakulapita replied, "I would travel far to learn the meaning of these questions from the Venerable Sariputta. It would be well if you would explain such questions to me."

"Listen well then, householder, and I shall discuss with you. How is it, friend, that body is sick and mind not sick?

"Herein the untaught average person, unconcerned by the teaching of the wise ones, will take no account of forms. The complexities of such thoughts are too great for him. 'I am form,' he says, 'form is mine.' He is obsessed with this idea, but even while he is obsessed and concentrates upon it, form changes, becoming otherwise. Owing to his awareness of the changing nature of form, sentiments arise in him of sorrow, pain, grief, and despair.

"He regards self as having feeling, or feeling as belonging to self. 'I am the feeling' he says, and adds 'feeling is mine.' Even as he is so obsessed again that feeling changes, becoming otherwise.

"In like manner he regards perception as self and self as perception. But the perception alters with each passing moment, and so he is reduced to feelings of despair. The same with consciousness and so he is bound to suffer.

"That, householder, is how both body and mind are sick together. But how, householder, is body sick but mind well?

"Here you see how the well-taught, disciplined and trained follower of the Noble Path, skilled in the doctrines of the noble ones, deals with the problem of sickness of the body. He makes no claim that 'I am form' or 'form is mine.' He knows that he and form are different, and that form will change with each passing moment. There need be no sorrow or suffering as form changes.

"He does not regard feeling as self, nor self as having feeling; neither does he regard feeling as being in self nor self as being in feeling. He does not say, 'I am the feeling, feeling is mine,' nor is he obsessed with that idea.

"He does not regard perception as the possession of his self, and makes no such claim, so that in the same manner he is separate from the perception which the self participates in. When perception changes, as it will from moment to moment, there is no sorrow in the loss of perception by the self, for what is perceived is separate from him and without his being.

"The consciousness of self is not the self, but is a manifestation by which the self becomes aware of its nature. As consciousness changes from one moment to the next, it does not raise sorrow, lamentations, fears, pain and despair in the self. Thus it is, householder, that the body may be sick, but the mind observing and aware of this sickness is not ill."

"Now of a truth I understand," exclaimed Nakulapita, "and through the graciousness of the Venerable Sariputta the wisdom of the Blessed One has been clarified for me. I now understand how truly the body may be sick, but the mind remain whole!"

"It is well, householder, that in the future, when you hear what appear to be words of wisdom, you not only listen, but question. For it is in the asking of questions and seeking explanations that the Noble Path of Enlightenment can be comprehended," explained Sariputta as he arose from the earth, adjusted his robe, and continued on his way. The aged householder, Nakulapita, rejoiced in his words.[6]

The Master was resting beside a river when he saw a shepherd coming toward him. "Now there is a contented man," the Buddha mused aloud, as he noted the freedom of movement and relaxed ways of the herdsman. The shepherd observed the resting members of an ashram as he approached, but otherwise did not identify the bhikkhus or their leader. The Buddha called out to him, "Friend, by what name shall I call you? I see that you are indeed serene and happy and I would like to talk with you."

"My name is Dhaniya, and I am indeed happy and contented. And why should I not be? I am on my way home to my wife and children; the flocks are well cared for; and my good wife will have rice on the fire so I shall be well cared for as well. Behold my house yonder by the banks of the river: its walls are firm; its roof is sound. So fall if you will rains from the sky, I shall not fear!"

"Fortunate indeed are you, Dhaniya. But I, too, am fortunate. I am rid of anger; I am rid of stubbornness. I know no fear. I spend the night on the banks of the river in my house which has no roof nor walls to decay. So I, too, say, 'Fall if you will rains from the sky, I shall not fear.'"

"The insects never torment my herd; my cows roam on the grassy meadows; they can withstand the falling rain. So fall if you will rains from the sky, I shall not fear!" responded the shepherd.

"I build a sturdy raft to sail to Nirvana," said the Master. "I cross the torrents of passions and I reach the saintly shores. I need the raft no longer. So fall if you will rains from the sky, I know no fear!"

"But my wife is obedient, chaste and good," said the shepherd. "She has lived with me many years and is kind and pleasant. So fall if you will rains from the sky, I shall not fear!"

"My mind is loosed from its bonds," replied the Master. "I have trained it for many years, so that it is an obedient servant of my needs, and my body an obedient servant of the mind. So fall if you will rains from the sky, I know no fear!"

Thus they continued to converse. Finally Dhaniya exclaimed, "Indeed you, too, have wealth and have escaped life's fears. But I must labor and work. Tell me, what is your secret?"

"Mine is the joy that comes from the path of liberation, and my secret I share with all, for in giving it I do not lose it. Since I have freed myself from births and rebirths there is nothing that can happen that will bring me fear. Thus I live contented and serene in the knowledge of the good life, which is now," responded the Master. "Because of this freedom from fear of the crushing wheel of life, I am truly liberated. You, too, may find that release, O Dhaniya."[7]

The Buddha and his followers now approached Savatti. Here the Venerable Bhumija, arising at eventide from his solitary meditation, came into the presence of the Buddha's company. Seeing the Venerable Sariputta sitting alone on the side, Bhumija approached him, offered complimentary greetings, spoke of their past friendship, and sat down beside him. So seated, the Venerable Bhumija spoke thus to the Venerable Sariputta:

"There are, friend Sariputta, certain recluses and Brahmans, believers also in Karma, who declare that happiness and ill have been wrought by others. There are likewise, friend Sariputta, yet other recluses and Brahmans who declare that happiness and ill have been wrought in part by oneself and in part by others. Still others there are, friend Sariputta, both recluses and Brahmans, believers in Karma, who declare that happiness and ill are wrought neither by oneself nor by others, but that they arise by chance.

"Herein is the question which I have long pondered. Tell me, dear friend, which view is held by the Exalted One? What has he declared? And how, if he were answering, would he tell us, in words that bear repeating? I ask that you correctly interpret his view, without misrepresentation, in accordance with the Dharma, so that no blame can with justification come upon us for saying, 'This is the Master's view.'"

"The Exalted One has been clear on this point, friend. He has explicitly stated that happiness and ill have arisen through a cause. And because of what? Because of contact; because of the relationship between things. Thus speaking, one will be representing and repeating the view of the Exalted One correctly.

"Happiness and ill come not from oneself, nor from others, nor from chance, but from the contact between self and form, self and feeling, self and perception, and self and consciousness. These relationships create the harmony you call happiness, or the friction which is called ill.

"Therefore when believers in Karma declare that happiness and ill are caused by oneself they are correct, because happiness and ill are caused by the dependence arising from contact between the self and the other. Whatever believers declare they are created by others, are correct because they come from the contact between the self and the other. Even those who declare happiness and ill are not caused by the self and another but by chance are correct, because that chance is the result of contact between the self and the other.

"However, any believer in Karma who declares that happiness and ill are wrought by oneself without benefit of contact speaks the impossible; and indeed even if they state that happiness and ill arise through chance without contact, they state the impossible."

The Venerable Ananda had listened to this conversation between Sariputta and Bhumija, and shortly thereafter he went into the presence of the Buddha. When seated, the Venerable Ananda repeated the conversation he had heard insofar as he could recall it. Whereupon the Buddha responded:

"Well said! Well said, Ananda! Well might Sariputta explain as he has done. Indeed, Ananda, I have said that happiness and ill arise through a cause. And because of what? Because of contact. Thus speaking, one will be repeating my views correctly without misrepresenting me, and be explaining in accordance with the Dharma, and no blame can with justification come to him.

"When body is there, Ananda, due to bodily intention, there arises internally pleasure and pain. When speech is there, Ananda, due to verbal intention, there arises internally pleasure and pain. When mind is there, Ananda, due to mental intention, there arises internally pleasure and pain.

"Conditioned by ignorance, Ananda, either one by oneself concocts a bodily formation, from which there arises pleasure or pain; or others concoct for him that bodily formation owing to which there arises internal pleasure and pain. And, Ananda, either he deliberately concocts that bodily formation or he does it unwittingly.

"Likewise one concocts the verbal formation, or the mental formation, as I have already indicated.

"These items, Ananda, are affected with ignorance. But with the cessation of ignorance, that body is not—nor is speech—nor is mind. That field is not, that ground is not, that sphere is not, that occasion is not, from which there arise for him internal pleasure and pain."[8]

DIFFICULT QUESTIONS

The Buddha, while staying at the Jetavana Hall in Savatti, delivered a discourse to twelve hundred of the great disciples. These were all Arahants, perfectly emancipated from sensual attachment and defilements, free of the use of intoxicants, and deemed worthy of the message he offered. They might be said to be the group who were the true heirs of the Buddha, ready to share the Blessed One's role with him. All the great names were present, with the exception of Ananda.

King Prasenjit desired to honor the anniversary of his father's death and, aware of the great company present at the Meditation Hall, invited the group to a festive meal. Owing to a previous commitment in a distant district Ananda had not yet returned when the assembled throng departed for the king's banquet hall. Shortly thereafter he came into the Meditation Hall and was surprised to find it empty, knowing not why. But he took his alms bowl and walked into the city to seek food.

He went as was his custom on such occasions from door to door, and submissive, taking whatever was offered, without awareness whether the alms were great or small, generous, attractive, repulsive, or whether given by a high or low caste person. What was important to him was to practice compassion and kindness to all, without discrimination, and to be humbly grateful.

He had heard the Lord chastise on some occasions those bhikkhus who showed discrimination and so he dutifully treated all persons alike, as he sought to emulate the Lord's liberal mind. He was neatly attired; his dignity was such as to give the impression that he might be on a mission to receive a ceremonial offering of great merit.

So begging without regard to whose house he approached, Ananda came to the home of the prostitute Maudenka. She was renowned for her beauty but had an even more beautiful daughter, Pchiti. The young maiden was attracted to Ananda, whereupon her mother determined to entice and involve Ananda with her. So alluring and so cunning were her ways, that before the innocent Ananda was aware of what was happening, he came under her spell. Ananda, in spite of his utter devotion and personal loyalty to Buddha, had more trouble than most in grasping the concepts of the Master. He had struggled for years to comprehend how it was possible to divorce the emotions, sensations, and relationships from the self. The desires and sensate feelings of the body always had seemed to him to belong to the self, and it was for this reason that he did not attain Arahantship up until the very end of the Buddha's life. Now he faced his greatest temptation, and being so fully human, he succumbed. He entered not only Maudenka's house, but the room of the lovely Pchiti, and there forgot his holy vows.

The Buddha, as the party ended, felt deep concern and uneasiness for Ananda, and intuitively knew that his hour of temptation had led him astray, that he was in need of help. He called Manjusri and sent him into the city to chant aloud the Great Dhammarani. Hearing the chanting of the Buddha's Dharma as Manjusri approached Maudenka's house, Ananda was quickly brought back to his senses, recalling his monkly vocation and vows. Hastily he arose, excused himself and returned to the Meditation Hall in the Jetavana Park.[1]

Coming into the presence of the Buddha, Ananda bowed down to the ground in great humility, blaming himself for his failure to have fully achieved his potential toward enlightenment. He pleaded with the Buddha for support so that he might achieve it in spite of his failure.[2]

Then the Lord Buddha spoke to Ananda, saying, "Ananda, you and I come from the same ancestral blood, and we have always cherished a close family affection for one another. Let me ask you a few questions to which you give a spontaneous answer. What most influenced you to the study of the Dharma?"

Ananda replied, "It was you. I beheld in your presence and countenance all the thirty-two marks of excellence. In you, they appeared so fine, so tender, so brilliant and transparent like crystal.

"I have thought of these marks I have seen in you from time to time, and reflected that they would be impossible in anyone not free from all sexual passion. Why? Because when anyone becomes inflamed with sexual passion his mind becomes confused, he loses self-control and becomes reckless and crude. Besides, in sexual intercourse the blood becomes adulterated with impure secretions. From such a source there could never originate the radiance of such transcendency as emanates from the person of the Lord. It was this which influenced me to become one of your true followers."

"Very good, Ananda! All those listening here in this great assembly should appreciate the importance of your observation. The very reason why sentient beings from beginningless time to the present have formed a succession of deaths and rebirths, life after life, is because they have never realized the true essence of the mind and its self-purifying brightness. Instead they too often spend their time deluding themselves in transient thoughts that are false and vain. They have prepared for themselves the conditions of this ever returning, meaningless cycle of deaths and rebirths.

"Ananda, you now more perfectly understand the factor of Supreme Enlightenment than you have ever done in the past. You are now on the road to comprehending the true nature of mind-essence, and so I wish to have you give answers to still other questions.

"Tell me, Ananda, you have just said that at the time your faith in me was awakened, you saw the thirty-two marks of excellence. What was it that gave you the sensation of seeing? What was it that experienced the sensation? And who was it that experienced the feeling of being pleased?"

Ananda answered, "My Lord, at the time I experienced the sensation of being pleased, it was through both my eyes and my mind. When my eyes saw the marks of excellence, my mind immediately experienced a feeling of pleasure. It was then that I made up my mind to become a disciple so that I might be delivered from the cycle of deaths and rebirths."

"From what you have said, Ananda, your feeling of being pleased originated in your eyes and mind. But if you do not know truly where the perception lies, you will never be able to subjugate your worldly attachments and contaminations. You are like a king whose city is invaded by thieves, creating turmoil in the night and then fleeing, only to return another night. The king cannot put an end to the terror because he and his men cannot locate the secret hiding place of the robbers. So it is in our worldly lives, troubled indeed with attachments and contaminations. Your perception of sight is perverted and unreliable. It seduces your thoughts, so that you lack mental control. Ananda, do you know the secret hiding place of these perceptions?"

"Noble Lord, in all the ten different orders of life, the eyes are in the front of the face. The other sense organs are likewise on the surface of the body, but the mind is hidden within the body."

Buddha interrupted him. "Ananda, you are now sitting in

the lecture hall, are you not? And when you look out the window you behold the Jetavana Grove. Can you tell me where the lecture hall and grove are located?"

"Certainly, Lord. They are located in Anathapindika's beautiful park here in the city of Savatti."

"Now, Ananda, what do you see first: the people inside or the park outside?"

"First I see the Master, then I see the noble audience, and then I see other objects within the lecture hall. Only afterward as I raise my eyes do I see the lovely park outside."

"True, Ananda, now tell me: while you are looking outside at the grove, what is it that enables you to distinguish the different views that your eyes see?"

"Lord, it is because the windows and doors are wide open. That is why I can see the distant views from my seat here."

Then the Blessed One, before the whole assembly, stroked the head of Ananda, and said, speaking not only to him, but to the entire company, "It is through concentration, the last step of the Eightfold Path, that we bring to consciousness the various manifestations which we perceive. The Eightfold Path opens the doors and windows to the mind. It is this right concentration of which I wish to speak, so listen carefully." And the Tathagata then proceeded to give instruction to the assembled multitude, saying,

"Ananda, you have said that from the inside of the hall you can see beyond, so that you look out upon the distant park. Do you think it possible that some inside this hall can see only the grove and not see the objects or people inside, including the Tathagata?"

Ananda hastily responded, "But, my Lord, how could it be that anyone in this hall could see the grove without seeing the Lord within?"

"It does seem absurd, Ananda, but it is just that way with you. You say that your mind exists in your body, and is quite clear of all obstructions. But it sees only the external objects, not the inside of the body. Now, if your mind exists within the body, shouldn't it be able to perceive internal objects as well as external? We know there are no sentient beings who can see such organs as the heart, kidney, lungs and stomach, although they do see the fingers, nails, hair and even the pulse. If the mind is an entity within the body why does it not see these other internal organs as well? Can it be that what you say about the perceiving mind is untrue?"

With a respectful bow, Ananda replied, "Listening to the words of my Lord, I begin to realize that my mind, after all, may be outside my body. It may be like a lamp; if the lamp is inside a room it will illuminate the interior of the room first, then shine through the open doors and windows. Perhaps the mind is exterior to the body. If a bhikkhu clearly understood this he would no longer be puzzled but would be enlightened."

The Master then discussed mind and body, the nature of perceiving and of the mutual correspondence that exists among the various senses.[3] He concluded finally by pointing out to Ananda, and to all in the audience, that it is not a question of existence but of non-grasping, liberation from the sensate perceptions, which is the reality.

Thereupon, Ananda arose from his place, adjusted his robe, and knelt before the Master, palms together, saying:

"My Noble Lord, I have the honor of being the youngest relative and you have always treated me with affectionate kindness. Although I am now only one of your many converts, you still continue to show affection toward me. But in spite of my much study and your many kindnesses I have not yet become liberated from attachments and contaminations. Consequently I succumbed to the spell of a harlot. My mind was confused and I was at the point of drowning in its defilement. I can see now that it was due to my ignorance of what is true and essential mind. I pray you to have pity and mercy upon me in my weakness and ignorance, and continue to show me the right path so that I may attain self-mastery, become emancipated from the lure of evil, develop true concentration, and be able to free the unenlightened from the bondage which imprisons them."

Despite the excitement with which the entire assembly watched this admission and plea of Ananda to the Master, the

Enlightened One did not dismiss him. He said, "Ananda, from beginningless time, from life to life, all sentient beings have had their disturbing illusions that have been manifested in their natural development each under the conditioning power of his own particular Karma. The reason that devoted disciples do not at once achieve supreme enlightenment is that they do not understand the two primary elements.

"What are these two elements, Ananda? The first is ignorance and individualization. It leads to transformation, to succession. The second element is the primary cause of unity, of enlightenment and Nirvana. Having existed since the beginning, it leads to compassion and purity.

"The reason why this unifying spirit is so often lost among the conditions of life is because one fails to comprehend one's own essential nature." The Buddha thereupon rebuked Ananda sharply for thinking that his being was his mind, that thinking and reasoning were his mind. He stressed to him how important it is to keep the mind free from all discriminating thoughts of self and not-self. Then the Buddha cried aloud, "Ananda and all my Disciples, I have always taught you that phenomena and their developments are simply manifestations of the mind! All cause and effects, from the great universes to the fine dust seen only in sunbeams, come into apparent existence only by means of the discriminating mind. If we examine the origin of anything in all the universe we find it to be but the manifestation of some primal essence.

"You are now listening to my teaching and your minds are making discriminations by means of the sounds arising from my speaking, but when the sound ceases and all the perceptions arising from the sounds come to an end, still the mind goes on discriminating the memory of those sounds.

"When I became enlightened I went to the Deer Park in Benares, where Kaundinya and the other four disciples heard my first teaching. And that teaching was this: The reason why all sentient creatures fail to attain enlightenment is that they have been led astray by false conceptions, which defiled their minds regarding phenomena and objects. Since that time they have understood the importance of that teaching and become enlightened."

Difficult Questions

Then His Highness King Prasenajit, having accompanied the Blessed One and his followers back to the Jetavana Grove from the royal banquet hall, arose and addressed the Lord Buddha, saying, "Honorable Teacher, before I came under your instruction I had been instructed by learned swamis and reputed great religious leaders such as Katyayana and Vairotiputra. They all taught that after one's death the destruction of one's body and mind meant Nirvana. Afterwards, through conversations with my Lord, I have had doubts within me as to the truth of this concept. How can I clearly understand non-death and non-rebirth? I think that all those disciples present who have not yet attained Arahantship are equally desirous of more perfectly understanding this profound teaching from my Lord Buddha."

The Buddha responded, addressing the king: "Your Majesty, may I have the honor of asking you some questions about your present body? Is your body as durable as gold and iron or is it impermanent and destructible?"

"My Lord, it is true that this body has not yet come to total destruction, but as I have watched it and cared for it, I know it is in need of constant renewal. It seems as though it is slowly being changed into ashes, gradually decreasing and fading away. From this I am well aware that its destruction is but a matter of time."

"Yes, Your Majesty, that is all too true. You are growing older and your health is less perfect than in former days. Tell me a little about your present appearance as compared with your youth."

"Your Lordship, when I was a boy my skin was tender and smooth; in young manhood my blood and energy were in full supply; now as I am getting old, my strength is failing; my appearance is languid and dull; my brain is slower and uncertain; my hair has become grey and white; and my face wrinkled. All these changes certainly show that I cannot live much longer. How can I compare my present with my youth?"

The Buddha replied kindly, "Your Majesty, do not be discouraged. Your appearance will not become decrepit as quickly as that." Then through questions and answers, the Buddha led the king into an exploration of the various stages of life, appearances and manifestations. Finally the Buddha asked King Prasenajit, "Your Majesty, do you remember when you first saw the River Ganges? How old were you?"

"It was when I was three years old and was carried there in my mother's arms. I saw it again when I was thirteen, and at intervals ever since."

"Your Majesty, you were three years old, then ten years older, and down to the age of sixty the process of change has been going on. Tell me, when you saw the river after ten years, was it different in appearance from the first time?"

The discussion then proceeded to show that the river waters changed, but the river always appeared the same, regardless of the passing of time. Then the Master pointed out that in similar manner though his outward appearance might have changed, his sense of self had not. His perception through most of his life remained unchanged, and only now, as he became aware of the nature of reality, did he begin to perceive the transitory nature of all sensate aggregates.[4]

Then various disciples, including Ananda, questioned the Buddha about the essential mind and the true nature of transitory perceptions.

The Buddha explained again, "When one becomes weary, he lies down to sleep; when his sleep is satisfied, he wakes up; when he opens his eyes he sees objects and begins to think about them; when he loses his memory he becomes worried. These are to be considered as reverse conceptions of death and re-birth, of transformations and continuities. The mind-sense in contact with the other senses receives notions of ideas, thoughts and recollections in reverse order because they are always moving toward diversity or uniqueness rather than harmony. This is a characteristic of all conscious and discriminative thinking. It leads to dualism almost impossible to separate from the phenomena of deaths and re-births."

In this manner did the Buddha labor to show the false dualism between objects and subjects, between sensations and realities, between mind and matter, between perceiving and that perceived, and between death and re-birth. He sought to show that rebirth is no problem to him who has found the perfection and peace of Nirvana, for which all bhikkhus strive.

But this was the most difficult question to answer. Finally one of the elders, named Vaccha, asked him, "It is as though a newborn infant, lying on its back, were to grow up and become a strong man. Would not the life be unified, and the tiny embryo and the grown man be one and the same?"

"It is as if a man were to light a torch at the first watch of the night. Tell me, would it burn all night?" asked the Buddha.

"It could, Lord," replied Vaccha.

"Now, is the flame in the middle watch the same as in the first, or the last?"

"No, Blessed One."

"Pray tell me then, was there one light in the first watch and another in the second and another in the third?" asked the Buddha.

"No, Blante, there was one light all night."

"In exactly the same way the elements are joined in continuous succession, one element perishing as another is created for each passing moment. Therefore neither as the same nor as a different person do you arrive at your latest aggregation of consciousness."[5]

The Master then summarized again, "Strictly speaking the duration of the life of a living being is exceedingly brief, lasting only while a thought lasts. Just as a chariot-wheel touches only at one point of the rim, in exactly the same way the life of a living person lasts only for the duration of a fleeting momentary thought. As soon as that thought has ceased, that being has ceased. As has been said, 'The being of a past moment of thought has lived, but does not live, nor will it live.

"'The being of a future moment of thought will live, but has not lived, nor does it live.

"'The being of a present moment of thought does live, but has not lived, nor does it live.'"[6]

The elder asked, "Then do you hold that the world is finite? Or do you hold that the body and soul are one and identical? Or that the saint exists or does not exist after death? Answer me these questions for I hear that the Lord does not hold any such theory, and I am desirous to know what theories you teach."

"The Tathagata, O Vaccha, is free from all theories; but this the Tathagata knows: the nature of form, and how form arises, and how form perishes; the nature of sensation, and how sensation arises and perishes; the nature of perception and how it arises and perishes; the nature of predisposition, and consciousness. Therefore I say that the Tathagata has attained deliverance and is free from attachment, because all imaginings, or agitations, or false notions concerning the ego, or anything pertaining to the ego, have perished, have faded away, have ceased, have been given up and relinquished."

"But Gautama, where is the reborn priest who has attained to this deliverance?"

"Vaccha, to say that he is reborn would not fit the case."

"Then you are saying that he is not reborn?"

"To say that he is not reborn would not fit the case."

"Then what does fit the case? Is he reborn or not reborn, or neither reborn or not reborn? I am greatly confused, Gautama, as to what your teaching is."

"Enough, Vaccha. Profound is this doctrine; it is recondite and difficult of comprehension, not to be reached by mere reasoning. It is subtle, and intelligible only to the wise; indeed, it is a hard doctrine, not easily learned. You who belong to another sect, another faith, and sit at the feet of another teacher, cannot expect to understand the subtleties of our faith and our reasoning without futher thought. Let me ask you some questions. If a fire were to burn in front of you, would you be aware it was burning?"

"Of course I would."

"But suppose, Vaccha, someone were to ask you on what this fire burning in front of you depended. How would you answer?"

"I would answer it depends for fuel on grass and wood."

"But if the fire in front of you became extinct, would you be able to say where the fire had gone? Had it gone to the east, west, north or south?"

"The question would not fit the case, Gautama, because the fire that depended on fuel had now burned out. Since it was without nourishment it became extinct."

"In precisely the same manner, Vaccha, all form by which one could predicate the existence of the saint, all that form had been uprooted, destroyed, abandoned and become non-existent and not liable to spring up again in the future. The saint has been released from form, sensation, perception, pre-dispositions and consciousness, and so has become extinct. To say that he is neither born nor reborn would not fit the case anymore than with your fire."[7]

In the end, after further discussion, Vaccha saw the light and exclaimed, "O wonderful it is, Gautama! It is as if one were to set up that which has been overturned; or to disclose that which was hidden; or to point out the way to a lost traveler; or to carry a lamp into a dark place. Even so has Gautama expounded the doctrine in many different ways. I betake myself to Gautama for refuge; I betake myself to the Dharma for refuge; I betake myself to the brotherhood of the Master for refuge. I now know that you are the Buddha. Let the Blessed One receive me as a disciple from this day forth as long as life shall last."

The story is told that King Milinda, approaching one of the Buddha's followers, asked him to describe how the Blessed One would explain the ego to him. In various ways the disciple tried. At last, after many arguments and illustrations, which the king could not understand, the Master said, "Sire, you are a delicate prince, an exceedingly delicate prince. Pray, did you come on foot or by riding?"

"Teacher, I do not go by foot; I came by chariot."

"Majesty, if you came by chariot, explain to me the chariot. Is the pole the chariot?"

"No, Master."

"Is the axle the chariot?"

"No, Blante."

"Is the chariot body the chariot?"

"No, Master."

"Is the banner staff the chariot?"

"No, Master."

"Is the yoke the chariot?"

"No, Master."

"Pray, your Majesty, if pole, axle, wheels, chariot body, banner staff and yoke are not the chariot, are all united together a chariot?"

"No, Blante."

"Is it then something else which is the chariot?"

"No, it is not something else than these which constitute the chariot."

"Your Majesty, although I have questioned you very closely, I fail to see what is the chariot. Your Majesty, it is as though you speak a falsehood. You tell me you came in a chariot, and yet when I describe its component parts, you tell me they are not a chariot. You cannot declare to me what a chariot is. How do you explain this to me?"

"Master, I speak no lie. The word 'chariot' is but a term, a convenient designation, a name for the pole, axle, wheels, chariot body, banner staff and yoke."

"Well do you understand a chariot, Majesty. Having evaluated its component parts, you see their relationship to the whole. In exactly the same way are we to understand body, mind, form, sensation, consciousness and all the other aggregates that make up the ego. In an absolute sense you see that there is no ego to be found, but it is a convenient designation, a way of accounting, an appellation, a mere name. This is the Buddha's teaching."[8]

The Buddha's compassion and concern for all people knew no bounds. Once the sorrowing mother, Kisa Gotami, approached him, carrying with her the corpse of her infant son, whom she refused to take to the funerary tier.[9] She carried it like a child on her breast, alternately wailing and sobbing, as overcome with grief she finally sought out Buddha in Savatti. The Buddha saw her approaching with the uncontrollable suffering and misery that marked her features. It was for such as she who suffered that he had dedicated a long life of service.

Kneeling before him she said, "O Merciful One, I have sought you out for none with whom I spoke have been able to help me. My baby is dead, and I cannot endure his loss. I plead with you to restore him to life, for others have said that only the Buddha could solve my problem."

With eyes filled with compassion, and deep sorrow for her suffering, the Buddha said to her in a comforting voice, "I will give what help I can, but first I will need some mustard seed from a house that has known no suffering, no death, no grief. Go to such a house and bring me some mustard seeds. Then I will breathe life into your baby's body."

With the first stirrings of hope in her mind in many days, she went eagerly from door to door seeking such a house. But everywhere she went, she found the same answer: "We will give you a mustard seed, but this house has known death, and we have mourned our loss."

After much seeking, traveling from house to house, from town to town, she finally returned to the Jetavana Grove, and the Master saw that she was approaching without her child. "Have you done as I asked, and have you found the mustard seed from such a house?" he asked her.

"Master, everywhere I went the answer was the same: 'We can give you seed, but we have mourned, known death, felt grief.' I have learned that all life shares this common sorrow, and none may escape. So I took my child to the funerary pyre, and placed him with the others."

The Buddha then said to Kisa Gotami, "Come sit with me, and my words shall remove the curtain of illusion that beclouds your wisdom. I shall teach you the Fourfold Noble Truth of suffering, and of the law by which we may overcome it and find release. I shall teach you the law by which you can be freed from birth and death and their attendant sorrows. Only then will you be liberated."

The Buddha began his final journey as the rainy season ceased, and as the dry season ran its course he soon found himself near Vesali. This mango grove was the gift of the beautiful dancing girl and courtesan, Ambapali. Years ago, when the Buddha was in his prime, he had first stopped at Ambapali's mango grove, and had met her there. Although she was a courtesan, which is to say a prostitute, of great wealth and influence, and generally considered outside of the circle of persons concerned about religious teachings, she had heard of Buddha. Now that he was staying at her mango grove, she decided she would go to meet him and listen to his instruction. In the meantime the inhabitants of Vesali, pleased that the Buddha had arrived, were eager to see him, and so the princes determined to invite him into the city.

Ambapali approached the Master's encampment, and was met by a monk who, knowing her profession, turned her back, saying the Buddha could not see her. Fortunately another monk heard him, and rushed up just as Ambapali, hurt and humiliated, was turning her carriage around, he told the first monk, "Take her to the Lord, brother, for all are welcomed by him. We have no right to turn away those whom he would not. The Master makes no distinctions between the rich and poor, the low caste or the high caste, the good and the bad."

The two monks then led the beautiful courtesan to the Buddha, and she stood spellbound in his presence. She prided herself on her own beauty which had humbled many a king, the princes of the realm, and the wealthy who sought her services. But she saw in him a more lovely person than any she had ever imagined and, dropping to her knees at his feet, worshipped him.

He raised her to her feet and asked her to sit with him while he discussed the law and the meaning of life and the nature of suffering. It was as though she were a new initiate whom he desired to instruct; her appearance and reputation mattered not at all.

In the meantime the princes of Vesali were coming to invite the Buddha to eat with them at the palace. But when they arrived, he told them he had already accepted an invitation to eat with Ambapali. They were annoyed and jealous to think he would prefer to eat with a prostitute than with them. Some who frequented her house for their own convenience, exclaimed, "How can he accept an invitation from such a woman?" But the Buddha in his serene way was undisturbed by their mumblings, and soon both she and the princes were pleased to have him visit Vesali. She indeed had offered him the use of the Mango Grove, hoping he would come annually to visit their city and state.

So it was that now in his eightieth year, and as the time for the forty-fifth annual retreat approached, he found himself near Vesali as the rainy season came. Accordingly, he sent the bhikkhus to the Mango Grove for the season, while he decided to tarry a while at the nearby village of Beluva. It was too far to return to Savatti, Rajagaha or Benares this time.

AT THE GATE
OF NIRVANA

When the Buddha had been enlightened forty-five years earlier, he had set out to Benares to begin spreading the message by which all people could find liberation. He was stopped on the way by Mara, the voice of evil temptation, which suggested that having found liberation for himself, he could enter immediately into the state of Nirvana, leaving it to others to find their own release. His response, true to his nature, was that he would not enter Nirvana while others were without, and while it lay within his power to guide them toward liberation. He had held to that resolve, but now the years lay heavily upon him. His recent trip had found him slowed down and he had not covered the distance he hoped. Now he was far from his familiar winter quarters at the great monasteries built for his teaching and comfort by grateful followers. Yet, as always, he accepted serenely the reality of the situation, and, having arranged for the comfort of the members of the Sangha who were with him, he prepared for his own approaching winter.

He had not complained to others, but those close to him saw that he was ill. Ananda and others knew that sharp pains made his daily routine difficult. Only his iron will, his mindfulness and reflective powers by which he could separate himself from the imprisonment of the body, kept him going. They were now aware that he was conscious of his approaching end. Yet there was little they could do. He had outlived most of his strongest leaders already—Sariputta, Mogallana, Kaundinya, Rahula and many others. Of his personal family, only Ananda remained. Of his first great benefactors, Anatha-pindika, Visakha, and kings Bimbisara, Pasenadi and Pasena-jit, all had preceded him to the final rest.

But the Buddha recovered, and the delighted Ananda, on seeing the Buddha up and about again, expressed his relief, stating that he knew the Buddha would not depart this life without final instructions to the Sangha. To this Buddha rebuked Ananda in sharp tones: "What, Ananda, does the order expect of me? I have taught the Dharma, making no distinction between esoteric and exotic truths. In respect to the doctrines, the Tathagata has no closed fist. It may occur to some to say, 'It is I who should lead the Sangha,' or 'The bhikkhus are dependent upon me,' or 'I should instruct the many concerning the order.' But the Tathagata does not think that it is he who should instruct the order of bhikkhus, or that the order is dependent upon him. Why then should they expect me to leave instructions to the Sangha?"[1]

"I too, Ananda, am now decrepit, and approaching my end. Now in my eightieth year, I am like a worn-out cart that is made to move with thongs. I think the Tathagata is moved by the aid of such thongs. Only when the Tathagata, living by the concentrated power of his mind, repels all thoughts of pain and rejects all sensations, then only is the body of the Tathagata free of pain.

"Therefore, Ananda, be you islands unto yourselves. Find your refuges within yourselves. Seek no external refuge. Live with the Dharma as your island.

"How, Ananda, can a bhikkhu live as an island unto himself, as a refuge unto himself, seeking no external refuge, living by the Dharma as he understands it?

"Herein, Ananda, must a bhikkhu live a strenuous, reflective, watchful, non-grasping life, constantly developing his own mind control over his body, feelings, consciousness and the Dharma.

"Whosoever should live now or after my death as an island unto himself, as a refuge unto himself, seeking no external refuge, shall be foremost among those who are intent on upholding the Sangha."

The Buddha then went on to stress the importance of each individual striving for purification from the ills of life, for deliverance and liberation from the limitations of life, and for freedom in achieving this goal. He taught Ananda at this time that there is no efficacy in praying to others or in depending on others. He now pointed out that the Triple Gem of seeking refuge in the Buddha, in the Dharma and in the Sangha is only a guide. In the future there would be not only the words he had spoken but others who would follow, Buddhas equal to him. So long as they were judged by their ability to show the path of deliverance, instruct wisely in the meaning of the Dharma and encourage the brotherhood of seekers through the Sangha, they would be examples worthy of emulation. Merely to seek refuge in them, as in external sources, would not lead to deliverance, however.

The Buddha now wished to talk with any of the bhikkhus who desired to converse with him, and in spite of the fact that he was now old and feeble, he invited their visits. Also, in spite of his infirim condition, bowl in hand, he insisted upon going on his regular round of alms seeking. He was, however, grateful when he received invitations to dinner so that this was not necessary on a daily basis.

One day when he entered Vesali, he went with Ananda to the Capala Cetiya, where he spoke of how delightful this city was with its many shrines. Here he expressed a last fleeting wish that he might remain alive. But shortly thereafter all indications were that he was now prepared for death. He made clear that he felt his life was over, and that his eighty years on earth were sufficient. He stated he had given all necessary instruction, done all within his power, to his followers, both in the Sangha and to lay members in their own homes. Now it was up to them to keep his teachings alive by expounding them to others. It was now their responsibility. He confided in Ananda that he did not expect to live more than three months.

"Please don't say that. Remember your words that you wished to live forever!" exclaimed the distraught disciple.

"Enough of that, Ananda! Do not make such a request of the Tathagata. The time for such is past." He then led the Venerable Ananda to the Pinnacled Hall at Mahavana and requested him to assemble there all the disciples who were in the vicinity of Vesali. When they had come, the Buddha addressed them as follows:

"Whatever truths have been expounded to you by me, study them well, practice them, cultivate them and develop them so that this holy life may last long and be perpetuated out of compassion for a suffering world. The good and happiness of many depends upon it.

"What are those truths which I have expounded to you? Think of them, beginning with the Four Noble Truths which are the foundation, through the various rules and guides, including the seven factors of enlightenment and the Noble Eightfold Path."

He thereupon concluded his last public sermon, stating:

"Behold, O bhikkhus, I speak to you now. Transient are all conditioned things. Strive on with diligence. The passing away of the Tathagata will take place before long. You may expect it in three months.

"Ripe is my age. Short is my life. Leaving you, I shall depart. I have made myself my refuge. O bhikkhus, be diligent, mindful and virtuous. With well-directed thoughts guard your minds. He who lives a life which heeds the message given, following the Dharma, in the dispensation of this life will escape life's wanderings and put an end to suffering."

Looking at Vesali for the last time, the Buddha now went with Ananda and some of the bhikkhus to Bhandagama, and on the way summed up:

> "Morality, concentration, wisdom and deliverance supreme,
> These things were realized by the renowned Gautama.
> Comprehending them, the Buddha taught the doctrine to his disciples,
> The Teacher with sight has put an end to suffering and extinguished all passions."

In this final pilgrimage in the Vesali district, Buddha went from town to town with Ananda. In Bhoganagara, he taught the Four Great Citations or references by which the word of the Buddha could be tested and clarified:

"A bhikkhu may say, 'From the mouth of the Buddha have I heard this,' or 'This is the Doctrine, this is the Teaching, this is the Discipline, this is the teaching of the Master.' But his words should be neither accepted nor rejected. Without either accepting or rejecting such words, they should first be studied thoroughly, every word and every syllable, and then put beside the Discourses[2] and compared with the Disciplinary Rules.[3] If, when so compared, they do not harmonize with the Discourses or agree with the Disciplinary Rules, then you may come to the conclusion, 'Certainly this is not the word of the Exalted One; this has been wrongly grasped by the bhikkhu.' Therefore you should reject it.

"If when compared and contrasted, they harmonize with the Discourses and agree with the Disciplinary Rules, you may come to the conclusion, 'Certainly this is the word of the Exalted One; this has been correctly grasped by the bhikkhu.'

"Let this be regarded as the First Great Reference.

"Again, a bhikkhu may speak, saying, 'In such a monastery lives the Sangha together with leading teachers.[4] From the mouth of that Sangha have I heard, have I received thus,

'This is the Doctrine, this is the Discipline, this is the Master's teaching.' His words should neither be accepted nor rejected. Without either accepting or rejecting such words, study thoroughly every word and syllable and then put them beside the Discourses and compare them with the Disciplinary Rules. If when so compared they do not harmonize, reject them; if when so compared they do harmonize, accept them.

"Let this be regarded as the Second Great Reference."

The same tests were applied for the third and fourth great references. The third pertained to able teachers and bhikkhus who proclaimed to speak the Buddha's words, and the fourth referred to a venerable and aged bhikkhu who might proclaim he had heard a principle from the Master's lips. In each case comparison must be made with the Discourses and the Disciplinary Rules. These four teachings are said to have been given by Buddha at the village of Bhoganagara. However, at this time the Discourses and Disciplinary Rules were not set forth in writing, but were still an oral tradition.[5]

The Buddha continued with his followers to the village of Pava, where they were entertained by Cunda, the smith. Cunda prepared a meal composed mainly of wild boar and mushrooms. Upon viewing the dish, Buddha is reported to have told the smith, "This is a very special dish, which can be served only to the Tathagata. Serve him, and then bury the rest in the ground, serving my bhikkhus and yourself only such fruits and vegetables as you have on hand today."

Thus it was that only the Buddha ate from the dish that hastened his death, and which is believed by many to have poisoned him. After the meal, the Buddha suffered from a severe attack of dysentery, with sharp cramps in the abdomen. Calmly he bore the suffering without complaint. Without controversy, he had pleased his host and prevented his bhikkhus from partaking of the apparently rancid pork. Always in the past, mind had surmounted bodily functions. But this time the body was too weak to endure, mindfulness was not enough. All nature in time runs its course, and as he had already indicated, both privately and publicly, the body was giving out. As he had taught his followers, reality occurs at the point of contact. His contact with the spoiled pork was beyond his mindful power of control. Ultimately time itself becomes the enemy.

Yet so strong was the will of Buddha that, after the meal, he tarried with those in the household. Following his custom when he ate at a home, he gave instruction and gladdened the heart of Cunda, the smith, with a religious discourse. Only then did he withdraw with the ever faithful Ananda, to face his illness. After he had rested, he said to Ananda, "Come, we will go to Kusinara."

But as they traveled, Buddha was forced to stop along the way, and handing his extra robe to Ananda, said, "Fold, I pray you, this robe into four parts, and spread it beneath yonder tree so that I may rest again, since I am weary." While he rested, Ananda brought him clear water from a neighboring stream.

Then a young man by the name of Pukkusa passed by, and seeing the Buddha came over and saluted him. Thereupon Buddha gave him some religious instruction, and in return Pukkusa offered the Buddha two robes. One he accepted and the other he gave to Ananda. As Pukkusa continued on his way the ailing Buddha confided to Ananda that he doubted he would last through the third watch of the approaching night.

Buddha now desired to bathe in the waters of the nearby Kakuttha River and after resting, he prepared to go on, as he insisted he wished to do, to the Sala Grove of the Mallas. He said to Ananda, "Now it may happen, Ananda, that some one will stir up resentment against Cunda, the smith. Or Cunda may feel remorse. Any such remorse should be checked by saying, 'How fortunate it is, Cunda, that the Tathagata ate his last meal with you. From the very mouth of the Exalted One have I heard him say that two meals surpass in value all others: that meal which one eats when he attains supreme enlightenment, and that which is his final meal when he passes away and attains perfect insight.' Thus will be laid up to Cunda a Karma assuring him long life, good fortune, good birth, good health and an inheritance of blessedness. Let

Cunda feel no remorse, or others any resentment against him."

Thereupon they entered the Sala Grove of the Mallas. He now instructed Ananda to prepare a couch for him between the twin Sala Trees. The trees were in bloom out of season, and the Buddha with a wry smile said, "See how all nature respects me. Let all those who reverence or honor me live in accordance with the teaching, conduct themselves dutifully and act righteously. Therefore, Ananda, should you train yourselves, saying 'Let us live in accordance with the teaching, dutifully conducting ourselves, and acting righteously.'"

Then the Buddha mused that after he was gone followers would wish to come and remember him at those places important in his career. He said he could think of four: Where he was born, the place of his enlightenment under the Bo Tree, the place where he established the wheel of truth in his first sermon at Benares, and the place where he would die.

Another wanderer, this time an ascetic by the name of Subhadda, who lived in Kusinara, having heard of the prescence of the Buddha came out and asked to see him. He told Ananda, "A doubt has arisen in my mind. I wish to secure the view of the ascetic Gautama."

"Enough, friend," replied Ananda, "The Master is too sick, too weary to be disturbed."

The Buddha however overhead the conversation and called out, "No, Ananda, do not prevent Subhadda. Let him ask what he will and I shall attempt to answer." Whereupon Subhadda expressed the doubts from his former teachers. The Buddha discussed with him the Four Noble Truths and the Noble Eightfold Path and the stages of development for spiritual growth.

Subhadda then responded, "Excellent, Lord, excellent! It is as if a man were to hold a lamp amidst the darkness so that whoever has eyes may see. I now seek refuge in the Buddha, the Doctrine and the Order." He was the last to become a follower of the Blessed One.

The Buddha after he had rested a short while motioned to Ananda, and said, "Go into the village of Kusinara and in-form the Mallas that the Tathagata is about to die, in case they wish to come to him. Do this so that later they shall not hear of my passing and reproach themselves by saying, 'In our own village the Tathagata died, but we took not the occasion to visit him in his last hours.'" The elders of the Mallas, the young men and women, came out to the Sala Grove, where the Buddha was lying. Ananda presented them to the Master, family by family, in the first watch of the night.

Members of the Sangha, hearing that the Master was surely dying, came hurriedly to the Sala Grove. After the Mallas and townsfolk withdrew, the Buddha raised himself to greet his faithful followers. He saw Ananda leaning on the lintel of a door, sobbing and crying, "Alas! I must still be a learner, one who has yet to work out his own perfection. And the Master is about to pass away; he who was so kind!"

The Buddha asked a nearby bhikkhu to bring Ananda to him. Then the Exalted One said, "Enough, Ananda, do not weep! Have I not on former occasions told you that it is the very nature of all things most near and dear to us that they must be separated from us, and we must be prepared for their loss. Impermanence is the law of all that is. How then, Ananda, can grief be possible since whatever is born, brought into being, created, organized, contains within itself the inherent necessity for its dissolution? How can it be possible that any such being should not dissolve?

"For a very long time, Ananda, you have been very close to me by acts of love that never varied. You have done well, Ananda. You are on the true path of enlightenment, about to become an Arahant."

The Master then added, "It may be, Ananda, that you will say, 'The Sublime teaching is left without the Teacher. There is no Teacher for us.' No, Ananda, you should not think this. Whatever doctrine and discipline I have taught you, that will be your Teacher when I am gone.

"Let the Sangha, if it is necessary, abrogate the lesser and minor rules after my death; but let them hold fast to the teachings and the doctrines expounded by He-Who-Has-Thus-Attained."

The Buddha now addressed all the disciples and said, "If, O Disciples, there be any doubt as to the Buddha, or the Teaching, or the Order, or the Path, or the Method, question me now while I am still with you. Repent not afterward saying, 'We were face to face with the Teacher, yet we were not able to question the Exalted One in his presence.'" The disciples remained silent. For the second and third time, the Buddha called upon them for any final questions, but none were asked. Thereupon the Venerable Ananda, exclaimed,

"Excellent! Lord, wonderful! Thus am I pleased with the whole company of the followers. There is not a single doubt among them regarding the Buddha, the Doctrine, the Order, the Path or the Method."

"You speak out of faith, Ananda, regarding their silence." Then the Buddha again said, "Decay is inherent in all component parts! Strive on with diligence."

Looking at Ananda again he repeated his earlier words: "Therefore, O Ananda, be you lamps unto yourselves. Rely on yourselves, and not on any external help. Hold fast to the truth as a lamp. Seek salvation alone in the truth. Look not for assistance to any beside yourselves. Such, Ananda, among all my bhikkhus shall reach the topmost height!

"And how, Ananda, can a brother be a lamp unto himself, rely on himself only and not on any external help, holding fast the truth as his lamp and seeking salvation in the truth alone, looking for no assistance from anyone besides himself? They must be anxious to learn. . . ." His voice trailed away, and then he aroused himself to repeat, "Decay is inherent in all component substances. Work out your salvation with diligence."

Thus did the Buddha die in 483 B.C.[6] on a Vesak full moon night in the third watch. Serene and thoughtful until the end, he now passed through his third great transition. The first had come through the observance of the serenity of the monk in the frenzy of the Kapilavastu marketplace, leading to his withdrawal from secular life and his entry into the religious way. The second had come through the compassion of the maiden Sujata, who fed him as he lay on the verge of death from his fasting as an ascetic before his enlightenment. This third time it was not due to the example of others but of himself, in his own fortitude and solitude, in his compassion for those about him, and in the serenity which came through his sublime faith in his teachings. His death was a perfect passing, giving reassurance and final wisdom to his followers.[7]

EPILOGUE

The Buddha's death left the loosely organized Sangha in disarray. Kassapa, who had been in Rajagaha, was the acknowledged leading monk following the deaths of Mogallana and Sariputta, but he too was old, and encumbered with too many personal concerns to give strong leadership. As the word spread throughout all the regions of India where the Buddha's followers lived or were traveling, a deep concern set in. Some of the bhikkhus thought the proper course of action, now that the Teacher was dead, was to find a different, a new Teacher to whom they could attach themselves. Others felt the time had come to choose a new leader of the Sangha. A third group thought Buddha's last teachings implied each should go his own way. At least one was reported to say, "Enough, friends, do not mourn, do not be sorrowful; we are well rid of the ancient Buddha. He had become too set in his ways, and did not accept new ideas easily. Let us do as we like and adopt new rules for the order."

In addition, there was an immediate need among the senior bhikkhus to agree upon the final form of his teachings. They wanted to clarify his thought in accordance with the Four Great Citations by which his words were to be authenticated, as they either harmonized or failed to harmonize with his teachings. They wished to reach a consensus.

He had been given the funeral rites as befitted a person of royal blood, and his body cremated. Much as he had stressed the impermanence of all material things, that the true life was not the life of the body, almost immediately some tried to secure a remmant of his body for a sacred shrine; a desecration of his ideas seemingly appeared almost at once. The Mallas laid claim to his bones since he had died in their land, desiring to build a mound above them and create a great memorial, but representatives of King Ajatasattu, and of the kings of Vesali, the Sakyas, the Bulis of Allakappa, the Koliyas and the Brahman of Vethapida, all announced their right to a sacred relic of the Buddha. A compromise was proposed whereby the skeleton was divided into eight parts. Thus eight shrines were shortly to arise each with a portion of the Buddha's body. Dona, the Brahman who arbitrated among the assembled chieftains, retained the vessel which had contained the ashes of the body, and the Moriyas of Pippalivana, who arrived too late to be included in the settlement, took the ashes of the fire as the basis of their memorial to the Exalted One.

With this immediate emphasis on his physical remains, it was clear to the more sensitive followers of the Buddha that his ideas, teachings, principles and doctrines were in danger of distortion. Kassapa, Ananda and the other senior disciples were greatly concerned. Kassapa returned to Rajagaha to find the monasteries virtually deserted, refuse and garbage everywhere, and the buildings in need of repair. The Sangha discipline was not standing up well following the death of the Master. In the meantime, King Ajatasattu was erecting an imposing memorial to Buddha over the relics he had secured. Such was the incongruity of the situation: honoring his physical remains while his teaching centers were falling into decay and neglect. Would his words also be neglected, misinterpreted or confused?

Kassapa set his mind to restoring the monasteries and reorganizing the Sangha so that it would be an orderly and disciplined body of the faithful. In a short time the repairs to the monasteries were completed. Then Kassapa and his closest associates petitioned King Ajatasattu to give his royal support to a convocation of the Buddha's followers to summarize his teachings and set them forth in clear words so that none could confuse or doubt what it was that he taught. The king agreed, and ordered a great hall be carved out of the cliff in the Webhara Mountain. This was prepared in two months. It was an amazing structure, supervised by the architect, Visvakarma. Built on various levels, with great pillars carved, or left standing in the stone, there was a terraced amphitheater with five hundred carpeted seats for the bhikkhus who were to be invited. A preaching dais facing the cast was prepared for speakers, with an ivory fan upon it. Five hundred Arahant bhikkhus, including Ananda, were invited. It is reported that Ananda achieved his final status of an Arahant only on the night before the opening session.

Kassapa opened the session, calling upon the learned Upali to detail Buddha's injunctions on discipline. Holding the mystic ivory fan, he recited, or recalled, the various Disciplinary Rules, and these were repeated, in a chant, by the gathered bhikkhus. Thus were the rules memorized.

Ananda was asked to come forward and recall all the utterances of the Buddha as they were given. He would begin, "Thus have I heard, upon a certain occasion while the Lord Buddha was staying at Anathapindika's meditation hall in the Jetavana Grove in the city of Savatti, the Master deliver a discourse. . . ." Others would rise and add their versions, make corrections, or alterations, and then the entire assembly would chant the discourse as it was agreed upon. Such were the suttas of the Buddha as they became known to many.

After Ananda went through all the discourses he could recall, whether given in Savatti, at the Bamboo Grove in

Rajagaha, or the Deer Park in Benares, or elsewhere, other bhikkhus arose and repeated the discourses, or instructions given to them by the Buddha. These were all chanted and memorized by the assembled members. In this way the first agreed upon collection of the true teachings of Buddha was established. Since at this time in India with its long rainy seasons there was no assured method of permanent preservation of written materials, this oral tradition was the best method for maintaining the doctrine and teachings of the Master.

The assembly lasted seven months.[1]

A second convocation was held approximately a century later, followed by a third convocation, 235 years after the Buddha's death. Out of these three convocations came the written accounts. They were revised in various traditions, sometimes harmonizing, sometimes in conflict with one another.

The third convocation is particularly important because it was held in the reign of King Asoka, the greatest of all Buddhist kings. He unified all India and became its emperor. A firm convert to Buddha's teachings, he spread his faith wherever he went so that it became virtually the universal religion of India. He was diligent in building monuments to Buddha, tracing his footsteps, and erecting markers that visually established the earthly journeys and events in the Buddha's life. A Buddhist civilization now flourished.

However, what is established virtually as a state religion from the top is not apt to survive the regime which has sponsored it. So with the steady refining of the Brahmin religion, the writing and updating of the Upanishads, and the codifying of the philosophic concepts of the evolving Brahminic religion (drawing from the reforms of both the religions of Buddha and of the Jains) modern Hinduism evolved. The old caste system which Buddha opposed remained, but new insight into Karma, Dharma and Nirvana broadened the earlier primitive views. Hinduism replaced Buddhism as the religion of India. Later, Buddhism was to find the more militant, highly organized religion of Islam in the north and northwest would make heavy inroads into its following. However, Buddhism also moved easterly into Indochina, southerly into the islands of the Indian Ocean, and northerly across the Himalayan Mountains into both Tibet and China. It spread to Japan, and was established in the islands of the South Pacific and throughout Southeast Asia. In these regions it was not so seriously threatened by the Hindu or Islamic faiths, and it has remained a continuous influence down to the present day.

Buddhism, the religion of Buddha, was spread by two great vehicles: Mahayana and Hinayana Buddhism. These have been called the two major schools of Buddhist thought, and might be likened to the denominations of other faiths. Mahayana was the religion of the "greater vehicle of salvation," more mystical and metaphysical than Hinayana Buddhism, which is called the "lesser vehicle of salvation." The Hinayana, in general, spread southerly and easterly: into Ceylon (Sri Lanka), Burma, Thailand, and throughout Indochina. Mahayana crossed the Himalayas into Tibet and China, and great scribes came from these lands to write and report on what they saw. The Mahayana religion became reinterpreted still more in China, where the major principle, Ch'an meditation, developed. In Japan it became Zen. (In addition to Zen there are other modern lay Buddhist movements evolving today in Japan.)

In the background remains Theravada Buddhism—"The Teaching of the Elders." Some believe that it contains the original Buddhist teachings going back to the Sangha.

Considerable interest in the teachings of the Buddha is now growing in the Western world; their impact is reaching far beyond any of the traditional schools or sects of Buddhism. It may be that a new orientation of his thought will develop. Whether or not this happens, the life and teachings of Buddha remain the possession of the human race.

END NOTES

Foreword

1. E. A. Burtt, *The Teachings of the Compassionate Buddha* (New York: American Library, Mentor Classics, 1955), p. 27.
2. Arthur Lillie, *The Life of Buddha* (Delhi: Seema Publications, 1974), p. 127.
3. Huston Smith, *The Religions of Man* (New York: Harper and Row, 1958), p. 86ff.

Chapter 6   The Quest for Serenity Begins

1. *Arupa Jhane*, Book 3.
2. *Arupa Jhane*, Book 4.

Chapter 7   Enlightenment

1. Mucalinda Tree. Generally referred to as the Bo Tree or Bodhi Tree. See *Maha-Vagga* for accounts of opening episodes of the enlightenment.

End Notes

2. See the *Majjhima Nikaya, Ariya-Pariyesana Sutta* for descriptions of the inner turmoil of the Buddha's Enlightenment on which this account is based.

Chapter 8   Five Disciples

1. Arthur Lillie, *The Life of Buddha* (Delhi: Seema Publications, 1974), p. 127. A "tank pilgrimage" is an Indian colloquialism for a pilgrimage to a shrine.
2. E. A. Burtt, *The Teachings of the Compassionate Buddha* (New York: New American Library, Mentor Classics, 1955), p. 27.
3. Rhys Davids, *Buddhism* (London: Society for Promoting Christian Knowledge, 1877, 1910), pp. 42–43.
4. Ibid., p. 44.
5. The account of this sermon is drawn from Rhys Davids' translation of the *Maha-Vagga* in Max Müller, *Sacred Books of the East*, (Oxford: The Clarendon Press, 1879) Vol. XI, pp. 146–154. See Henry Clark Warren, *Buddhism in Translation* (Cambridge: Harvard University Press, Oriental Series, 1909), Vol. III, p. 33ff.
6. The usual formulation is as follows: *Wisdom:* 1. Right Views, 2. Right Intention; *Morality:* 3. Right Speech, 4. Right Action, 5. Right Livelihood; *Meditation:* 6. Right Effort, 7. Right Mindfulness, 8. Right Concentration.

Chapter 9   Into the Towns and Cities

1. Rishi (Sanscrit), risi (Pali) a holy man, hermit, recluse, prophet or seer; having acquired wisdom, he has retired from the world except for *pindapāta* (begging).
2. Arnold, Edwin, *The Light of Asia*, as quoted in *The Wheel*, The Buddhist Publication Society, No. 73 (Kandy, Sri Lanka: 1964), p. 1. (This epic poem written and published in the 19th century has been through many editions. See Edwin Arnold's *Poetical Works*, Vol. I, Boston: Roberts Brothers (Little, Brown & Co.), 1880, 1899, p. 246ff. (renumbered pp. 1–238) for the epic poem in its entirety.)
3. *Dhammapada*, No. 308. Many translations are available. We use Penguin Classics, trans. Juan Mascaro (1973) through-out text.
4. Arnold, op. cit., pp. 196–197.
5. *Dhammapada*, Nos. 266–267.

6. Ibid., Nos. 100–105.
7. Ibid., Nos. 110–115.
8. Ibid., No. 19.
9. Ibid., No. 6.
10. Ibid., Nos. 37, 39, 40.
11. Now the Buddha Gaya.
12. Kashyapa in Sanscrit accounts.

Chapter 10   The Victorious Return

1. Rhys Davids, *Dialogues of the Buddha* (Oxford: The Clarendon Press, 1881), Vol. I, p. 84.
2. *Dhammapada*, Nos. 197–200.
3. Ibid., No. 28.

Chapter 11   Conversion of the Sakyans

1. Maha Thera Narada, *The Buddha and His Teachings* (Kandy, Sri Lanka: The Buddhist Publication Society, 1973), pp. 128–138.
2. Ibid., pp. 158–163.
3. Ananda Coomaraswamy, *Buddha and the Gospel of Buddhism* (New York: Harper & Row Torchbooks, 1964), pp. 52–53.
4. Narada, op. cit., pp. 150–158.

Chapter 12   Jetavana Park

1. Narada, op. cit., p. 164ff.
2. *Dhammapada*, Nos. 197–208, 209–216.
3. Ibid., Nos. 116–124.
4. Ibid., Nos. 197–206.
5. Ibid., Nos. 209–220.

Chapter 13   Supporters and Detractors

1. Coomaraswamy, op cit., p. 58.
2. Narada, op cit., p. 159ff.
3. Ibid., pp. 194–197.
4. Ibid., pp. 160–163.
5. Ibid., p. 209ff.

End Notes

6. Ibid., pp. 213-214.
7. Ibid., p. 169.
8. Ibid., pp. 170-172.
9. Ibid., p. 173.
10. Ibid., p. 174.
11. Ibid., pp. 175-188.
12. The October full moon.
13. Coomaraswamy, op. cit., p. 64.
14. Narada, op. cit., pp. 188-189.

Chapter 14   Toward Perfect Understanding

1. *Maha Kassapa Thera Bejjhanga* (S.v.p. 79); *Maha Mogallana Thera Bejjhanga* (S.v.p. 80); *Maha Cunda Thera Bejjhanga* (S.v.p. 81); or see Thera Piyadassi, *The Book of Protection* (Kandy, Sri Lanka: The Buddhist Publication Society, 1975), pp. 48-53.
2. *Girimananda Sutta* (A. V. 108), see Piyadassi, *The Book of Protection*, pp. 53-60.
3. See the "Surangama Sutra" in Dwight Goddard, ed., *A Buddhist Bible* (Boston: Beacon Press, 1970), pp. 108-111ff.
4. *Isigili Sutta*, M., 116.
5. These passages which follow will be found in the *Samyutta Nikaya,* one of the five divisions of the *Sutta Pitaka* of the Pali Canon (the Ti-Pitaka or "Three Baskets" of the Theravada Buddhist Tradition, i.e., the tradition of the Elders.) See Epilogue to this volume. For easy English access see translations of Pali Text Society (London); or *The Wheel,* The Buddhist Publication Society, Nos. 107-109 (Kandy, Sri Lanka); and published separately by John D. Ireland, ed., *An Anthology from the Samyutta Nikaya* (Kandy, Sri Lanka: Buddhist Publication Society, 1967), Nos. 34-50, pp. 36-54, in slightly altered form from this abridged rendition.
6. From the *Majjhima-Nikaya*. Translations are found in E. A. Burtt, *The Teachings of the Compassionate Buddha* (New York: American Library, Mentor Classics, 1955), p. 32ff; and H. C. Warren, *Buddhism in Translation* (Cambridge: Harvard Oriental Series, 1909), Vol. III.

Chapter 15   As Time Goes On

1. Ireland, John D., ed., *An Anthology From the Samyutta Nikaya* (Kandy, Sri Lanka: Buddhist Publication Society, 1967), p. 1ff.

2. A "stream winner" is a medium level disciple on the road to attaining Nirvana. He has more to attain, but has made a beginning.
3. Narada, op. cit., p. 234.
4. Ibid., pp. 235–236.
5. Ibid., p. 237.
6. Part 3: *The Book of Aggregates* (*Khandha Vagga*), found in Bhikkhu Nanananda, *An Anthology from the Samyutta Nikaya*, Buddhist Publication Society, Kandy, Sri Lanka, 1972, Part 2, pp. 20-25.
7. *Samyutta Nikaya*, in the *Sutta Pitaka*.
8. Nanananda, op. cit., pp. 16–20.

Chapter 16   Difficult Questions

1. See the "Surangama Sutra" in Dwight Goddard, ed., *A Buddhist Bible* (Boston: Beacon Press, 1970), p. 108ff.
2. Ibid., p. 111ff.
3. See the *Surangama Sutra*, op cit., for the teaching given in this episode.
4. Aggregates *(Khandha)*—the "groups" of existence.
5. *Milindapanha* (40) (Warren, op. cit., p. 149).
6. Ibid. (70), p. 232.
7. Translated, condensed and adapted from the Majjhima-Nakaya Sutta 72, by Henry Clark Warren, *Buddhism in Translation* (Cambridge: Harvard University Press, Oriental Series, 1909), p. 123ff. This is known as the *Aggi-Vacchagotta Sermon.*
8. *Milindapanha* (25) (Warren, ibid., p. 139ff)
9. Funerary Tier (or pyre)—the areas set aside for dehydration or cremation of corpses.

Chapter 17   At the Gate of Nirvana

1. These episodes from the final days, including the final words and teachings of the Buddha, are taken from the *Mahaparinibbana Sutta*, the oldest and probably most authentic account of the Buddha's death.
2. *Sutta.*
3. *Vinaya.*
4. *Theras*—elders, hence teachers as we learn from the elders.
5. See Epilogue, above.

End Notes

6. 543 B.C. is the traditional date for Buddha's death. However, this is uncertain. E. J. Thomas in *History of Buddhist Thought*, page 10, gives the date as 483 B.C. Oldenberg in his volume *Buddha*, page 196, says 480 B.C. Rhys Davids discusses the possible dates in various places in his volumes.

7. All quotations in this chapter are from the ancient Pali sources, translated into English in 1893 by Rhys Davids and subsequently retranslated, substantially without change, many times. We have taken these words from Thera Narada of Sri Lanka in his volume previously quoted. See Narada, op cit., "The Buddha's Parinabbana," pp. 233-269.

Epilogue

1. Rhys Davids, op. cit.

GLOSSARY

Abhaya, Prince—brother of Ajatasattu.

Agni—God of Fire in early Brahmin tradition.

Aggregates—see Khandha.

Ajatasattu, Prince—young son of King Bimbisara, later King Ajatasattu.

Alavaka—criminal converted by Buddha, who entered the Sangha.

Ambapali—courtesan (prostitute) who gave Buddha the Mango Grove at Vesali.

Ananda—a cousin of Buddha who converted on his first mission in Kapilavastu; later became a chief disciple of Buddha; important in the codifying of his teachings following his death.

Anathapindika—wealthy merchant of Savatti; Buddha's most generous benefactor.

Anatta—the principle of concentration.

Anga—Kingdom, home of Visakha; capital was Bhaaddiya.

Angulimala—fierce criminal (murderer), turned into a bhikkhu, who entered the Sangha.

Anuruddham—a Sakyan cousin of Gautama who became a bhikkhu.

Arahant—one who has perfected his spiritual powers and stands at the gate of Nirvana—the goal of all bhikkhus.

Glossary

Arahatta—state of attainment of Nirvana.

Arata Kalama—teacher of Gautama; swami; philosopher; head of ashram.

Aryan—invaders from Iranian Plateau who settled in India, created caste systems, subjugated original black aboriginal natives.

Ashram(s)—commune.

Asita—an old sage (Brahman, guru, swami) who prosphesied holy career for infant Gautama.

Asoka, King—greatest of all Buddhist kings.

Asvajit—the bhikkhu (one of original five) who brought Sariputta to meet Buddha.

Aumi River—Indian river.

Bamboo Grove—park located in Rajagaha used by Buddha for Sangha gatherings and teaching.

Banares—see Benares.

Beluva—city near Vesali where Buddha stopped on final teaching mission.

Benares—holy city to which Gautama went as beggar and to which he returned as the Buddha.

Bhaddiya—city visited by Buddha.

Bhadrika—one of five original disciples.

Bhaggas—town visited by Buddha before his paranirvana.

Bhallika—a merchant, one of two brothers who fed Buddha under the Bo Tree.

Bhandagama—city near Vesali.

Bhesakala—a teaching grove used by Buddha, near Bhaggas.

Bhikkhu(s)—a monk (monks) who followed Buddha.

Bhikkhuni(s)—female monk; feminine of bhikkhu.

Bhikshu—Sanscrit spelling of bhikkhu—a monk.

Bhoganagara—village near Vesali.

Bhumija—a Brahman holy man, a monk who questioned Sariputta.

Bimbisara, King—king of Magadha, whose principal city was Rajagaha (Giribaja).

Blante—title meaning "Blessed One" or "Master."

Bodhisattva—in the wheel of life, one about to become a Buddha if proven perfect in this existence.

Bo Tree (Bodhi Tree)—tree of enlightenment; actually a mucalinda tree, shoots of which were preserved into the modern period.

Brahma—the ascendant God, superior to all lesser Indian deities.

Brahman—priest, caste; when spelt with "a" it refers to persons.

Buddha, The Quest for Serenity

Brahmin (ism)—the religion. Refers to the religion or religious system when spelt with "i."

Buddha—Gautama, Siddhartha (563–483 B.C.). Siddhartha was popular name; Gautama, family name; and Buddha is religious title meaning "The Enlightened One."

Bulis of Allakappa—king who claimed skeletal relics of Buddha.

Capala Cetiya—central shrine area of Vesali.

Ceylon—country which nourished Buddhism (now called Sri Lanka).

Ch'an—Chinese for meditation; see Zen or Dhyana.

Chanda (Chandaka)—Gautama's youthful companion.

Cunada—Sariputta's younger brother, and a member of the Sangha.

Cunda—the smith, served Buddha's last meal.

Deer Park—park in Benares, used by Buddha for Sangha gatherings and teaching.

Devadatta—cousin of Buddha, who sought to become successor and otherwise created problems for the Master; died in disgrace.

Dhamma—see Dharma.

Dhammarani, Great—recitation of Buddha's central teachings.

Dhananjaya—father of Visakha.

Dhaniya—shepherd, who was contented with lot.

Dharma—the law of existence, Sanscrit spelling; spiritual law or way. In Pali, *Dhamma*.

Dhyana—Sanscrit for Jhana (Pali), Ch'an (Chinese) or Zen (Japanese), meaning "meditation."

Dona—Brahman who arbitrated the disposition of Buddha's remains, and who retained the funerary vessel.

Euro-Asian—cultural and linguistic ethnic grouping.

Gautama—see Buddha.

Gavampati—friend of Yasa who joined the Sangha in Benares.

Gayasisa—encampment of Devadatta's dissident following.

Gijjhakuta Mountain—an Indian mountain; another name of Isigili Mountain, where Devadatta injured Buddha.

Giribaja—see Rajagaha.

Girimananda—a bhikkhu whose illness led to Buddha's teaching.

Gods of India—Brahmin and Hindu religions: Indra, Dyauth Pitar, Asura, Mithra, Altman, Vishnu.

Gotami, Kisi—griefstricken mother whose infant was dead.

Guru—a holy man.

Himalayas (Hindu Kush Mountains)—Indian mountains.

Hinayana—one of two major schools of Buddhism that developed in centuries following Buddha's death; Pali Buddhism; the system of salvation of the "lesser vehicle." Evolved from Theravada Buddhism.

Hindu(ism)—Indian religion which evolved from earlier Vedic and Brahminic religions. Maintains the caste system. Displaced Buddhism as major Indian religion.

Ieta, Prince—sold Jetavana Park to Anathapindika for Buddha's use.

India, Indian, Indostan—terms for the Indian nation, subcontinent, people and the cultural grouping.

Indo-China—Southeast Asia.

Isigili Mountain—Indian mountain used as illustration by Buddha; also called Gijjhakuta Mountain, Pandava Mountain or Vepulla Mountain—place where Devadatta injured Buddha.

Jainism—an ascetic sect founded by Mahavira (or Vardhamana) in century before Gautama's birth.

Janapada Kalyani—see Sundarika.

Jatila—the sect of which Kassapa was a leader before he converted to Buddha.

Javaka Komarabhacca—Buddha's doctor, a follower.

Jetavana Grove (Jeta, Jetavan Park)—Buddha's headquarters in Savatti, given by Anathapindika.

Jhana—see Dhyana.

Kakuttha River—Indian river in which Buddha took last bath.

Kamada—a tempter of the Master.

Kamma—see Karma.

Kantaka—Gautama's horse.

Kapilavastu (or Kapila)—capital city of Kingdom of the Sakyas, ruled by King Suddhodana; home city of Prince Gautama.

Karma—spiritual grace achieved by faith in Hindu and Buddhist thought. It is dependent upon right actions and right thoughts. Kamma in Pali and southern accounts.

Kasibharadvajasaw—Brahman landowner who challenged Buddha.

Kassapa—monk of Uriuila; converted by Buddha, became leader before and after his death.

Katyayana—rival religious leader.

Kaundinya—Buddha's first disciple. A leader until his death.

Khandha—aggregates; the five "groups" of existence or "clinging." These are the five aspects by which Buddha summed up physical and mental phenomena. What is called individual existence is nothing but a process of such mental and physical phenomena.

Kimbala—Sakyan cousin of Buddha, who converted.

Kisi Gotami—see Gotami, Kisi.

Buddha, The Quest for Serenity

Koliya—kingdom of Maya's parents; a Sakya kingdom across River Rohini.

Kosala—an Indian kingdom ruled by King Pasenadi; later by his son, King Maha.

Kshatriya—warrior caste (Gautama's).

Kusinara—vicinity of Sala Grove where Buddha died.

Lotus-Night—night of the October full moon.

Lumbini—grove where Gautama was born; identified by King Asoka.

Magadha—kingdom; neighboring Kingdom to Kapila; capital is Rajagaha (Giribaja).

Magandiya—proud Brahman beauty who carried a resentment against Buddha throughout her life.

Maha—king of Kosala, claimed skeletal relics of Buddha.

Mahanaman—one of the original five disciples of Buddha.

Mahaprajapati—see Prajapati.

Maharajah—See Rajah.

Maharani—see Rajah.

Mahavana—see Pinnacled Hall.

Mahavira, Verdhamana—Jain; founder of Jainism, an ascetic Indian sect.

Mahayana—one of two major schools of Buddhism. The "Great Vehicle"; the northern school of Buddhism; prominent in Sanscrit literature and northern countries such as Tibet and China. Opposite of Hinayana.

Mallas—residents of district in which Buddha died; city near Vesali; site of Pinnacled Hall.

Mango Grove—grove in Vesali used by Buddha for Sangha gatherings and teaching.

Manjusri—a bhikkhu sent to chant the Great Dhammarani.

Mara—the divine tempter; prominent deity in Indian culture.

Maudenka—a prostitute.

Maya—queen; mother of Gautama, died in his infancy; favorite wife (queen) of King Suddhodana.

Meditant—one who makes a vocation of meditation; one who meditates; a monk.

Mendicant—one who makes a vocation of alms seeking; a begger for holy reasons.

Migara—father-in-law of Visakha.

Milinda, King—questioned a Buddhist disciple.

Mogallana—friend and assistant to Sariputta; one of Buddha's chief disciples; pre-deceased him.

Mucalinda tree—see Bo Tree.

Glossary

Moriyas of Pippalivana—king who claimed skeletal relics of Buddha.

Najjian(s)—citizen of a republican state in India.

Nakulapita—householder who questioned Buddha.

Nanda—half-brother of Buddha, who converted, also renouncing the throne.

Nepal—country to northwest of India; in this land are found sites of Gautama's upbringing.

Neranjara River—river near the Jatila monastery (now the Buddha Gaya River).

Nigantha Nstaputta—nudist ascetic cult leader of an extremist sect.

Nirvana—state of perfect peace as expounded by the Bodhisattva and Buddhas.

Pali—language indigenous to Ceylon (now Sri Lanka) and used for many Buddhist books in the southern tradition.

Pamita (Dandapani)—Yasodhara's father.

Pandava Mountain—see Isigili Mountain.

Paranta Island—home of Punna the bhikkhu; island in Indian Ocean; converted by Punna, a native of it.

Parnajit—one of the original five disciples of Buddha.

Pasenadi, King—king of Kosala.

Pava—home of Cunda, the smith, who served Buddha his last meal.

Pchiti—daughter of Maudenka, the prostitute who seduced Ananda.

Pindapāta—the art of alms seeking.

Pinnacled Hall—at Mahavana, where Buddha preached his last sermon to the Sangha.

Pipphali Cave—monk's dwelling.

Prajapati (or Mahaprajapati)—foster mother of Gautama; wife of Suddhodana; sister of Maya, queen. Founder of the sasana, the female order of Buddhist monks.

Prasenajit, King—king of Savatti; supporter of Buddha.

Pukkusa—one of last visitors of Buddha.

Punna—maid of Sujata, who brought nourishment to Gautama.

Punna—merchant who converted to become a Buddhist monk.

Punnavaddhana—husband of Visakha.

Purnajit—friend of Yasa, joined Sangha in Benares.

Radha—a bhikkhu troubled for comprehension of Buddha's teaching.

Radhakrishnam, Sri—20th-century Indian sage who interpreted Indian culture and Buddhist religion.

Rahula—Gautama's son, later a monk and follower of Buddha; predeceased him.

Rajagaha—also called Rajagriha (Sanscrit) or Giribaja; capital of Magadha; site of the Bamboo Grove. Ruled by King Bimbisara and later his son Ajatasattu.

Rajagriha—Sanscrit spelling of Rajagaha

Rajah, Maharajah (m), Maharani (f)—kings and queens in India.

Reincarnation—Indian concept of the transmigration of souls. Under Buddha, it is this life continued, not the soul in a round of rebirths until Nirvana is achieved.

Rishi—a holy man.

Rohini River—border of Koliya and Kapilavastu; an Indian river.

Sakya—warrior race of Gautama's family; an Aryan race.

Sala Grove of the Mallas—where Buddha died.

Sangha—the order of monks established by Buddha.

Sanjaya—a noted ascetic leader in Magadha, early teacher of Sariputta.

Sanscrit—ancient Indian language brought in from the Iranian Plateau; considered to be the mother tongue of Euro-Asian languages. Sacred language of Vedas and Upanishads.

Sariputta—the chief disciple in the Sangha for many years.

Sasana—the female order of monks founded by Buddha.

Savampati—early disciple of Buddha.

Savatti—city of much of Buddha's teaching at the Jetavana Park where Anathapindika created a great teaching center for Buddha.

Siddhartha—see Buddha.

Sotāpanna—see "stream-winner."

Sravasti—see Savatti.

Stream-winner—tr. of sotāpanna. A sotapan, i.e., "stream-winner," is a member of the Sangha who has attained a medium level of advancement toward Arahantship.

Subahu—a friend of Yasa who joined the Sangha in Benares.

Subhadda—final person instructed by Buddha; an ascetic holy man from Kusinara.

Sudatta—familiar name of Anathapindika.

Suddhodana, King—king (Rajah) of Kapila, father of Gautama.

Sudra Caste—servant caste (the fourth and lowest).

Sujata—shepherdess who saved Gautama when overcome by fasting.

Sujātā—daughter-in-law of Anathapindika; converted by Buddha.

Sundari—maiden murdered at Jetavana Park.

Sundarika (Janapada Kalyani)—princess rejected before marriage by Nanda when he converted to Buddha.

Sunita—untouchable who became a bhikkhu.

Glossary

Suttas—discourses of the Buddha. Suttras, in Sanscrit

Swami(s)—Indian holy men; meditants who become teachers.

Tathagata—title for the Buddha meaning "The Perfected One."

Theravada—original early school of Buddhist teaching called "The Teaching of the Elders"; (see Mahayana, Hinayana Zen).

Tibet—Buddhist country in high Himalayas between India and China.

Trapusha—one of two merchant brothers who fed Buddha under the Bo Tree.

Udayin—childhood friend of Gautama; messenger King Suddhodana sent to the Buddha.

Uddaka—teacher of Gautama.

Udena—kingdom visited by Buddha.

Upaka—a Brahman who met Buddha on the road to Benares.

Udaka; cousin of Buddha who converted.

Upali—noted Jain who converted to Buddha, becoming a chief disciple.

Upanishads—Indian philosophic or religious literature written around 600 B.C.

Upate—a Sakyan barber who became a bhikkhu, converted after Buddha's first return to Kapilavastu.

Uruvila—monastery near Rajagaha which Kassapa once headed.

Vaccha—a wandering ascetic who finally converted to Buddha.

Vajjian Republic—an Indian state.

Vairotiputra—religious leader.

Vardhamana—see Mahavira.

Vashpa—one of original five disciples.

Vassakara—Ajatasattu's prime minister.

Vedas, Vedic, Vedism—early Indian literature of first Aryan invaders of India, nurtured through centuries.

Vepulla Mountain—see Isigili Mountain.

Vesak—a spring month; Buddha died in this month on a night of the full moon.

Vesali (Vaisali)—location of Ambapali's Mango Grove.

Vethapida—an early disciple of Buddha.

Vimala—friend of Yasa, joined Sangha in Benares.

Vinaya—disciplinary rules of the Sangha.

Visakha—greatest female benefactress of Buddha; concerned for the bhikkhunis.

Visvakarma—architect.

Buddha, The Quest for Serenity

Webhara Mountain—site of first convocation of Buddha's survivors.

Yasa—a wealthy, high bred youth of Benares who converted to Buddha, as did his parents and four friends.

Yasodhara (Gopa)—the beautiful bride and wife of Prince Gautama, whom he deserted in quest of the holy life; mother of Rahula, Gautama's son; also spelled Yashodhara in Sanscrit.

Yoga—a religious discipline of concentration, meditation and exercise carried on by yogis.

Yogi—a disciplined holy man, following yoga practices; a series of exercises called yoga, used for spiritual cleansing of the individual in Indian religions as well as in the Sangha.

Zen—a school of Buddhism which thrived in Japan and was from there introduced to Western countries. (See Dhyana, Jhana or Ch'an.)

BIBLIOGRAPHY

Arnold, Edwin, "The Light of Asia." In *Poetical Works*. Vol. I. Boston: 1880. Reprint (Little, Brown & Co.), 1899.

Ariya-Pariyesana Sutta. Ancient text.

Arupa Jhana. Ancient text.

Burtt, E. A., *The Teachings of the Compassionate Buddha*. New York: New American Library, Mentor Classics, 1955.

Carus, Paul, *Buddhism and Its Christian Critics*. Chicago: Open Court Publishing Co., 1897.

Carus, Paul, *The Gospel of Buddha*. Chicago: Open Court Publishing Co., 1904.

Coomaraswamy, Ananda K., *Buddha and the Gospel of Buddhism*. New York: 1916; Harper & Row Torchbooks, rev. ed. 1964.

Davids, Rhys, "Buddhist Suttas." In *Sacred Books of the East*. Ed., Max Müller, Vol. XI. Oxford: The Clarendon Press, 1900.

Davids, Rhys, *Buddhism: Being a Sketch of the Life and Teachings of Gautama, the Buddha*. London: Society for Promoting Christian Knowledge, 1910, rev. ed.

Davids, Rhys, *Dialogues of the Buddha*. Oxford: The Clarendon Press, Vol. I, 1881; Vol. II, 1882. Also included as Vols. XIII, XVII of Müller, *Sacred Books of the East*.

Buddha, The Quest for Serenity

Davids, Rhys, *Early Buddhism*. London: Constable & Co., 1910.
Davids, Rhys, *Origin and Growth of Religion as Illustrated by Some Points in Early Buddhism* (Hibbert Lectures); New York: Putnam, 1882.
Dhammapada. Numerous translations; see Mascaró, below.
Fussell, Ronald, *The Buddha and His Path to Self-Enlightenment*. London: The Buddhist Society, 1955.
Goddard, Dwight, ed., *A Buddhist Bible*. Boston: Beacon Press, 1970. (Includes selections from the Pali, Sanscrit, Chinese, Tibetan and modern sources.)
Ireland, John D., ed., *Anthology from the Samyutta Nikaya*. Kandy, Sri Lanka: The Buddhist Publication Society, 1967.
Lillie, Arthur, *The Life of Buddha*. Delhi: Seema Publications, 1974.
Maha Cunda Thera Bejjhanga. As found in Piyadassi (below), and elsewhere in ancient texts.
Maha Kassapa Thera Bejjhanga. Found in Piyadassi and as above.
Maha Mogallana Thera Bejjhanga. Found in Piyadassi and as above.
Mahaparinibbana Sutta. Ancient Buddhist Pali Text, available in Müller, Vol. XI (see below).
Maha Vagga. Ancient text.
Majjhima-Nikaya. Translations found in E. A. Burtt, and H. C. Warren, and elsewhere. Ancient text.
Mascaró, Juan, ed., *The Dhammapada*. Baltimore: Penguin Classics, 1973.
Milindapanha. Ancient text, see Warren (below).
Müller, F. Max, ed., *Sacred Books of the East*. 50 vols. Oxford: The Clarendon Press, 1879. Especially Vols. XIII, XI, XVII.
Nanananda, Bhikkhu, *An Anthology from the Samyutta Nikaya*. Part 2. Kandy, Sri Lanka: Buddhist Publication Society, 1972.
Narada, Maha Thera, *The Buddha and His Teachings*. 2nd ed. Kandy, Sri Lanka: Buddhist Publication Society, 1973 (2517); first edition, 1964 (2508).
Niwano, Nikkyo, *Buddhism for Today*. Tokyo: Kosei Publishing Co., 1976.
Nyanatiloka, *Buddhist Dictionary: (Manual of Buddhist Terms and Doctrines)*. 3rd ed. Colombo, Sri Lanka: Frewin & Co., Ltd., 1972.
Nyanatiloka, *The Word of the Buddha: An Outline of the Teachings of the Buddha in the Works of the Pali Canon*. Kandy, Sri Lanka: Buddhist Publication Society, 1971.
Oldenburg, Hermann, *Buddha, His Life, His Doctrine, His Community*. London: The Pali Text Society, 1889.
Piyadassi, Thera, *The Book of Protection (Paritta)*. Kandy, Sri Lanka: Buddhist Publication Society, 1975.
Piyadassi, Thera, *The Buddha's Ancient Path*. Kandy, Sri Lanka: The Buddhist Publication Society, 1974.

238

Bibliography

Radhakrishnan, S., 1938, "Gautama the Buddha." In *Proceedings of the British Academy*. Vol. XXIV. London: British Academy, 1938.

Smith, Huston, *The Religions of Man*. New York: Harper & Row, 1958.

Story, Francis, *Dimensions of Buddhist Thought*. Kandy, Sri Lanka: Buddhist Publication Society, 1976.

Surangama Sutta. As found in Goddard, above.

Sutta Pitaka (the Ti-Pitaka or "three baskets" of Pali). See Ireland, or Nanananda, above.

Thomas, E. J., *History of Buddhist Thought*. New York: Barnes & Noble, 1951.

Voss, Carl Hermann, *Living Religions of the World: Our Search for Meaning*. Cleveland: William Collins & World Publishing Co., 1977.

Warren, H. C., *Buddhism in Translation*. Vol. III, Cambridge: Harvard University Press, Oriental Series, 1909.

THE AUTHOR

George N. Marshall, Minister of the Church of the Larger Fellowship, an auxiliary of the Unitarian Universalist Association, has been a student of comparative religions and of Buddhism for the past three decades—and since 1964 a member of the Buddhist Publication Society in Sri Lanka. He is also a contributor to *Dharma World,* Tokyo.

One of Marshall's previous books, a biography of Albert Schweitzer, co-authored with David Poling, was praised by Norman Cousins: "[It] is an absorbing, deep-reaching, enormously rewarding study. It reads like a novel, but has the sobriety and savor of first-rank scholarship." Marshall has written also *Challenge of a Liberal Faith,* a best-selling story of Unitarian Universalist beliefs.

A native of Bozeman, Montana, Dr. Marshall studied at Tufts, Harvard, Columbia, and Walden universities. He currently resides in Boston, Massachusetts.